Haunts of the Black Masseur

Haunts of the Black Masseur

The Swimmer As Hero

Charles Sprawson

Pantheon Books   New York

Copyright © 1992 by Charles Sprawson

*All rights reserved under International and Pan-American Copyright
Conventions. Published in the United States by Pantheon Books, a
division of Random House, Inc., New York. Originally published in
Great Britain by Jonathan Cape, London, in 1992.*

Text illustrations by Clare Sprawson

LIBRARY OF CONGRESS CATALOGING-IN-PUBLICATION DATA

Sprawson, Charles.
Haunts of the Black Masseur: the swimmer as hero/Charles Sprawson.
ISBN: 0-679-42051-7
p. cm.
1. Swimming — Social aspects — History.   2. Swimming — Philosophy.
I. Title.
GV838.53.S63S68   1993   92-50471
797.2′1 — dc20   CIP

Manufactured in the United States of America
First American Edition
9   8   7   6   5   4   3   2   1

For Ann Fenton

When I see a swimmer, I paint a drowned man.

Jacques Prévert, 'Quai des Brumes'

Here you are gabbling Baudelaire or Donne,
Here you are mimicking that cuckoo clock,
Here you are serving a double fault for set,
Here you are diving naked from a Dalmatian rock,
Here you are barracking the sinking sun,
Here you are taking Proust aboard your doomed corvette . . .

Louis MacNeice, 'The Casualty' (In memoriam G.H.S.) on
the death of a friend drowned in mid-Atlantic during the War

Contents

Introduction

'The gods who left us hundreds of years ago in Naples are still in India, so it's like going home for me. In India I can feel what it was like in Italy many years ago.'

Francesco Clemente

I LEARNT TO SWIM in India, in a pool donated to the school by the Edwardian cricketer Ranjitsinhji. I was the only English boy in the school. My father was the headmaster, and Sir K. S. Ranjitsinhji, the Jam Saheb of Nawanagar, its most eminent old-boy, though he was only one prince among many there. Sometimes his successor allowed us to bathe in the flooded subterranean vaults of his palace nearby, among columns that disappeared mysteriously into black water. On the walls of the palace above there still hung Tuke's paintings of bathing boys that the Jam Saheb had collected during his cricketing years in England.

In this arid backwater on the western plains none of the other English seemed to swim at all. There were no pools in the gardens of the administrators, none in the cantonments for the soldiers. When they travelled to the hills for relief in the hot weather, it was principally to sail or row on the lake at Naini Tal. There hangs above me as I write a watercolour by Samuel Daniell, of Indian girls bathing and washing their hair in a jungle clearing, among the cataracts and pools of a river in southern India. In English paintings of India, Indians are shown diving from temple balconies or lounging in the shallows of the lakes. For the English themselves, however, it seemed that swimming was not quite acceptable. They felt they had to keep up appearances, in the manner of those portraits by Arthur Devis of Englishmen and their wives dressed formally just like his father's exquisite figures in English gardens, with merely a hint of the exotic in a bending palm or the ragged leaf of a banana tree, or an Indian servant standing deferentially in the background. It was as though the English had taken to heart George Borrow's precept that a 'gentleman' should avoid swimming, 'for to swim you must be naked, and how would many a genteel person look without his clothes'.

In the memoirs of soldiers and civil servants, swimming is hardly mentioned. Yet in the accounts of those English who travelled to India from motives of their own, as a means of self-discovery and fulfilment, to satisfy some mystical strain in their character, swimming seems an essential and enriching experience. Awoken one dawn in the middle of a forest by a panther's bark, the adventurer Eric Muspratt, who roamed the world to escape the contamination of civilisation, walks down to a 'lonely Hindu temple, a simple archway of stone with steps leading to a little lake of glass-smooth water. Palms fringed it and waterlilies floated on it. In bathing there at sunrise a spirit of worshipful thanksgiving came to me. The stillness lay on me like a benediction.' In his spirited attempt on K2, laden down with innumerable volumes of poetry, Aleister Crowley was confronted one morning, in the foothills of the Himalayas, by a brilliant white curtain spread over a hillside, formed by crystalline deposits from a hot spring like that at Pamukkale in Turkey, above which the Romans set up a temple and where I lingered once for an entire day reading Pindar's Olympian odes on a submerged column. Crowley climbed to the top of the curtain to the basin from which it proceeded, the largest of several similar formations, '31 feet in diameter, an almost perfect circle. It is a bath for Venus herself. I had to summon my consciousness of Godhead before venturing to invade it. The water streams delicately with sulphurous emanations, yet the odour is subtly delicious. I spent more than an hour reposing in its velvet warmth, in the intoxicatingly dry mountain air. I experienced all the ecstasy of the pilgrim who has come to the end of his hardships.' On his ascents of Everest, Mallory bathed in the Kashmiri streams. Swimming for Mallory, like mountaineering, was an 'emotional and spiritual necessity'. He would be filmed by Odell swimming decorously in a costume, then would strip it off, 'even finding a pool to dive into, and at length'.

My earliest recollection of India is staring in the early morning through the muslin of a mosquito net at my father practising yoga on a small towel at the foot of his bed, twisting his body into contortions and postures that seemed strange for a headmaster. He had been influenced by recently reading Yeats Brown's *Lives of a Bengal Lancer*, that ends with the author meditating in the Himalayas, awaiting the dawn after a night of prolonged discussion about the mysteries of love and devotion. Smoking charas from a hookah induced in Yeats Brown visions of crawling through keyholes, stepping over the Himalayas. The book that was made into a Hollywood film to celebrate the glamour of imperial India was in fact a description of a spiritual quest, an attempt to submerge himself in the sensuous and mysterious rituals of the East that held little appeal for the average colonial.

Shortly before I was dispatched to a school in England, my father took me on a three day train journey to the coast of southern India. We were given the use of a maharajah's personal carriage, with a metal balcony attached to the back where we sat throughout the day, longing to swim in the green rivers full of buffaloes and laughing boys as the train rattled over the bridges. Once we arrived in the South, our entire time there was devoted to bathing among the streams and waterfalls depicted in the Daniell engravings, sacred to the Hindoos and attended by innumerable devotees, though now rarely visited as their waters have been reduced by dams to a faint trickle that dribbles down the bare rock face.

It was to these southern rivers that Yeats Brown was drawn, where he found a 'glory and a grace' in surrendering his body to their sacred water, usually by moonlight. The bedroom window of our small rest-house on Cape Cormorin looked out to sea. My father pointed out the very rocks where Yeats Brown and the swami once talked and meditated – 'A hundred yards to the south of the Virgin's shrine, one of the oldest temples at the tip of the triangle of India, is a smaller shrine for the worship of ancestors. Here we undressed, and swam out, a few yards, to two domed rocks, against which the rollers of the Indian ocean surge lazily, decorating them now and then with a lovely lace-work of foam. It was here, on the farthest rock, with no land between him and the Antarctic, that Vivekananda sat meditating on that evening when he took his high resolve to go out and conquer the West with the teaching of the Vedanta.' Yeats Brown adds a footnote: 'In reading M. Romain Rolland's account of how the pilgrim swam back to India, as if it were the Channel or the Hellespont, instead of five yards of fact, we have an illustration of how myths grow.'

Though very young, I began to form a vague conception of the swimmer as someone rather remote and divorced from everyday life, devoted to a mode of exercise where most of the body remains submerged and self-absorbed. It seemed to me that it appealed to the introverted and eccentric, individualists involved in a mental world of their own. Last summer I was about to leave Portofino when I remembered that it contained the ancient home of the Yeats Browns. His father had bought a disused Moorish castello on the promontory for £40 in the 1860s, and when returning from India Yeats Brown would break his journey at Genoa to travel there. So I stayed another night, and early the next morning walked down through the cypresses and umbrella pines to a little sandy cove below the house. I swam round to a smooth white rock at the bottom of a path that runs down steeply through his garden. It was from here that, according to a cousin, Yeats Brown had indulged his 'passion for bathing – a wonderful diver – he would dive down and hold onto a rock below and grin up at us through the translucent water for so many minutes that he alarmed his young cousins thoroughly'.

From India my father moved to the other side of the Mediterranean from Portofino. For some years we lived in Benghazi, not far from the old Greek city of Cyrene. We spent every Christmas among its ruins, the only guests of a ghost of a hotel among fir trees. On Christmas Day we made a ritual of bathing in a natural rock pool, long and rectangular, its sides encrusted with molluscs and anemones, where once Cleopatra and the Romans reputedly swam. The waves broke against one end, and beyond them, beneath the surface, lay most of the remains of the classical city. The recent publication of books by Hans Hass and Jacques Cousteau had opened up another world. When we dipped our masked faces into the water there emerged on the corrugated sand mysterious traces of the outline of ancient streets and colonnades, their sanctity disturbed by the regular intrusion of giant rays that flapped their wings somnolently among the broken columns as they drifted in from out of the shadowy gloom of deeper water. Fragments of sculpture, bases of fountains became scattered around our flat, used as doorstops and bookends.

In the summer a swimming regatta took place in

Benghazi. My greatest friend, whom I thought couldn't swim as he never entered the water and spent all his time boating, rose up lazily from the rocks on which he was sunning himself and won every event by yards. He said it was easy as long as one used the Japanese crawl. I wondered what he meant. Not long ago I wrote to him after over thirty years, having procured his address from his old school, asking him to explain exactly what this entailed. Unlike myself he had obviously moved on, as in his reply from his African farm he related every detail of his career since we'd known each other, but made no mention of swimming at all.

In the antique rock pool of Cyrene an association of swimming with the Ancient Romans evolved obscurely in my imagination, but the seeds of this book were sown in the four years I worked lecturing on 'classical culture' in an Arab university. I had applied for the post after noticing an advertisement worded in Latin in the personal column of *The Times*, while working as a swimming pool attendant in some old Victorian baths in Paddington, so dismal and dirty that no one ever came. In Arabia, as in the Paddington baths, the only form of amusement was reading, so in the long afternoons, while the whole town was sleeping, I devoured book after book among the shadows of the courtyard of our mud house in the Arab quarter, then again late into the night among the stars on our crenellated rooftop. As there was nothing else to do I made extensive notes on everything I read. The heat, the parched atmosphere and the non-existence of pools made me acutely sensitive to the slightest trace of water, any passing reference to swimming. Looking through these tattered notes now I see that on page 180 of Hemingway's *The Sun also Rises* some character 'swam with his eyes open and it was green and dark', that Sinclair Lewis' Babbitt was 'one of the best swimmers in the class', and when he took a bath 'the shadows of the air bubbles clinging to the hairs were reproduced as strange jungle mosses'. I remember still the mesmeric effect of Coleridge's lines describing a rock pool below a waterfall, where the water regrouped continuously in 'obstinate resurrection' to form the shape of a rose. In the strange, unnatural climate in which I existed all such details struck me as extraordinarily significant. Paragraphs would be devoted to the relevance of fountains in Nathaniel Hawthorne, the varying depths of the sea in Melville, the fish in Thoreau's Walden pond, the shark in American literature. Novels and poetry seemed to revolve around water and swimming, in a way that was quite out of proportion to the author's intentions. I can sympathise now, in confessing to the crazed irrelevancy of these notes, with a certain nineteenth-century chronicler of early swimming, who devoted his whole life to a history of the subject and in his journeys through England and France in search of books always felt 'ashamed in asking librarians, with much hesitation, if they had any books on swimming'.

Among the odd variety of books in the university library was a French history of the Olympic games. In it I came across an impassioned account of the last few yards of the race between Crabbe and Jean Taris that decided the outcome of the 400 metres final in 1932.

I began to make lists, just as Scott Fitzgerald had done of his favourite quarter-backs and Napoleonic marshals during the lost years of his 'crack-up', of swimmers' names of the period, the Sixties, such as Zac Zorn and Donna de Varona, that like those of Southern generals in the American Civil War seemed redolent of dash and romance.

It was, though, in 1956, from a chance reading of a report in *The Times* when a very junior boy at school, that I first became aware of a Homeric dimension to swimming. It was the year of the Melbourne Games. At the time Australian men and women dominated every stroke, and every day news came through of some record broken. Their outstanding swimmer was Murray Rose. He had already won the 400 metres when they lined up for the start of the longest event, in a race that brought together in fierce rivalry representatives of the three leading swimming nations of this century, America, Australia, and Japan:

It was the mens' 1500 metres final that drew most attention under the arclights tonight and it proved the outstanding triumph of all the Australian swimmers. Two days ago Breen from America, immensely strong but with an ugly style, had depressed the supporters of the English-born Rose by the impressive way in which he beat the latter's world record by nearly 7 seconds in his heat. On that occasion Breen went out in front of his comparatively poor opposition after 50 metres and stayed ahead of the record schedule all the way. It was feared that tonight he would burn off the slender, seemingly less strong Rose in the first 800 metres but, as it happened, Breen could never break away from the close attentions of the young Australian and Yamanaka.

It was even more tense than usual at the start as the eight finalists crouched forward on their starting stands and then the gun, as shocking as ever in this great echoing hall, sent them swooping away in racing dives. Breen off best and touching for the first time half a length ahead of Yamanaka with Rose only inches behind in third place. After eight laps (400 metres) these three had broken away from the others and the time was 4 min. 36.6 sec., nearly 4 seconds ahead of Breen's world record schedule on Wednesday. Just after 800 metres, with the time now 1½ sec. behind the world record, Rose, who had been lying nicely poised, smoothly went into the lead and from then on was never led again. Breen kept thrashing along just behind in his ungainly way for another six laps and then Rose went away from him by a length. At 1200 metres Yamanaka had overtaken Breen for second place and then, as the American began to slip back, started to make ground on Rose. With two laps to go Rose was two lengths in front but Yamanaka was overhauling him rapidly and the last lap was swum to a great roar of encouragement, on one side from Australian spectators and wild cries from the other from feverishly excited Japanese supporters and journalists. It was Rose who had swum the most intelligent race, however, and it was he who eventually got home fairly comfortably, though another length would have given a different result.

As I searched through back numbers of *The Times* thirty-five years later and read again the account, I wondered why it had made such an impression at the time. I had never in my life so much as glanced at *The Times*, and it was the only newspaper to describe the race at length. In fact no other paper mentioned it at all. I knew no other boy in the school would have read the report, or if they had, reacted with any interest. Perhaps it was the air of distinction lent by *The Times*, the fact that it endorsed and reflected an arcane obsession on my part that was impossible to communicate, as it was to a large extent the product of a childhood and experiences that were essentially different. At an age when one looks out for heroes, I was drawn to the determined performance of Rose, poised and smooth, 'slender, seemingly less strong', flanked by two rugged and uncompromising competitors, a David among Goliaths. I admired too the softness of his name, his cool intelligence, the quiet control he seemed to exert from the start, his graceful, easy style. He was swimming, I was to learn later, in conditions that he favoured, by night in a floodlit pool.

Four years on I happened to switch on the television late one night during the Rome Olympics, and there on the speckled screen was the faintly discernible figure of Rose, gripping the rails in emerging modestly from the pool after having won another gold medal. He was not one to punch the air in triumph. Blond and classically built, he seemed to me, as a mawkish adolescent lately returned from my first visit to the museums of Greece, everything I was not. 'Don't worry,' I remember my mother remarking without much conviction, 'perhaps you have more brains.' Rose's mother was to write that his most prized possessions as a boy were his 'much worn' books by Ancient Greek writers. 'These he studied and thought about constantly', while she brought him up on a diet of seaweed, sesame, and sunflower seeds, to imbue him with the 'Greek reverence for a disciplined mind and a perfected physique'.

On a recent visit to Los Angeles I was amazed to hear from Richard Lamparski, a popular chronicler of the declining fortunes of Hollywood stars, that Rose was living there, in fact just down the road from him. Now married to an ex-principal dancer of the Joffrey Ballet, he had been awarded a scholarship by U.S.C. after his Olympic triumphs, where he had taken the part of Hamlet in a college production, then played some minor roles in the 'beach' films of the early Sixties. We arranged to meet for a game of squash and a swim in the venerable Los Angeles Athletic Club, among the office blocks and skyscrapers of the downtown area. After a frantic game I left him to swim for an hour, then proposed a four length race. He had eyed me swimming and realised I would present no challenge, so he just stood casually in the shallows and motioned me to start whenever I liked. He would follow. At the halfway mark I might almost have been ahead, but then he just glided in front with his graceful, effortless style and won easily. So he should have. American coaches described him as the greatest swimmer there has ever been, greater even than Weissmuller. Only recently he had been swimming faster times than he had in the Olympics. He still looked much as he did in his prime, and I noticed he had the long hands and feet that all the best swimmers seem to possess.

We went on for a meal to the garden of Butterfields, once the home of Errol Flynn, on the corner of Sunset and Olive. Rose no longer adhered to seaweed, sesame, and sunflower seeds. Among the orange trees he talked quietly about his early memories as a boy in Australia, when he swam in the Manly reservoir, the natural pool on Bondi Beach, where the waves came over the sides as he raced and propelled him to extraordinary fast times in one direction. The most intense experiences were early morning bathes in Sydney Harbour, where the water was smooth, its texture silky, when swimming seemed like an 'adventure into a different world', particularly during Christmas when the swollen 'King' tides rolled in from the Pacific. It was in these conditions that he felt he had swum his fastest times, with a sense of exhilaration that he never quite experienced in a manmade pool. For Rose swimming was an intensely sensuous involvement, a rhythmic succession of sounds as the hands cut through the water that passed under the body and formed a wave against the side of the face. Rhythm reduces effort. Before a race he would listen to particular music that was close to the rhythm of his stroke. Glenn Miller's 'In the Mood' coincided exactly.

The principal quality, he continued, demanded of a swimmer is a 'feel for water'. He should use his arms and legs as a fish its fins, and be able to feel the pressure of the water on his hands, to hold it in his palm as he pulls the stroke through without allowing it to slip through his fingers. Rose believed that like water-diviners, only those succeed who have a natural affinity for it. Sometimes water can become an obsession, as in the case of Rick de Mont, a beautiful stylist who won a gold medal in 1972, only for it to be taken away when traces of a drug were found in his system that had been prescribed by the team doctor for asthma. Now he lives in Tucson, on the edge of the Arizona desert, and devotes himself to a 'spiritual quest for water'. He can sense like a diviner where desert streams are likely to appear suddenly after rain, and records their momentary presence in watercolour. Large oil paintings, inspired by dreams, reveal dim shapes of prehistoric fish swimming through jungle rivers. He loves the sound of water, the feel of it on his hands and legs. For de Mont, the streams and dreams 'force' interpretation.

In order to intensify this feel for water, Australian swimmers of the Fifties started shaving down their legs before important races. The idea spread to America in 1960 when Rose moved to Los Angeles. American swimmers began to shave, as well as their legs, their arms, chests and heads. Minutes were knocked off times over the longer distances. It was not so much the elimination of the hundreds of minute air-bubbles which cling to hair and slow down movement that counted, as its psychological effect. Rose described the immediate sensual awareness of water as he dived in, the feeling that he was suspended, united with the element, the sudden surge of power like that experienced by ballet dancers who remove their hair to activate their nerve-endings. When a swimmer achieves a good time, the first question invariably asked is 'shaved or unshaved?' The problem then arises of how often shaving is possible. If one can delay it till after trials or preliminary heats, it then becomes a psychological advantage over one's rival. Shaving has become a complex science. The secret is not to overdo the shaving or the thrill is lost, to restrain the shaves so more hair comes off when required. Before a race some swimmers are observed rubbing their hands on the rough matting of diving-boards, in the way that a safe-cracker sands the tips of his fingers to increase their sensitivity. The East German women took shaving a stage further when they adopted the 'skin suit', made from a single layer of stretch nylon that appeared to be glued to the body. At first embarrassed television cameramen would only film them from the neck up, but now they are universally accepted. The Australian Dawn Fraser claimed she could have broken every record in the book if allowed to swim naked. Nudity originated in the Greek Olympics when Orsippus dropped his loin-cloth and was seen to gain a distinct advantage thereby.

Olympic swimmers are subject to conditions unique to them. They remain isolated in their lanes. There is no convergence or contact as with runners. Chance plays a considerable part even at the highest level. A swimmer can be far ahead at the finish, yet mistime his final stroke, or be drawn in a lane where he is forced to breathe on his 'wrong' side up the final length. A photograph from 1936 shows the Japanese Uto well ahead towards the finish, yet losing to the lunging American outside him. If a swimmer can remain on his rival's hip, he can be carried along in his surge, inherit the other's momentum, and also act as an anchor on the man in front. 'I just surfed in on his wake,' was Armstrong's answer to reporters who wondered how he had ever beaten Biondi.

Nor are the physiques of swimmers like those of other athletes. The best swimmers rarely excel at other sports, as their bodies are too finely tuned to adapt.

A swimmer's muscles are long and pliable. 'You can't do anything violently or suddenly in water,' observed Bachrach, the great Chicago coach of the Twenties, 'it even takes time for a stone to sink. Things must be done with relaxation and undulation like that of a snake.' From observing the superior speed of long slim fish like the sandpike and pickerel, he looked for 'snaky' swimmers and felt he had found the perfect streamlined form in the elastic Weissmuller.

Bachrach insisted that in swimming one must ignore rivals: 'In most sports they have a physical effect on your performance, in swimming only psychological. If you worry about what your rival is doing, you take your mind off what you are doing and so fail to concentrate on your performance.' Once the swimmer hits the water he is his own man and immune from outside influence, but before the race begins much can be done to disturb his state of mind. Even the way a swimmer acknowledges the crowd and removes his track suit by the starting blocks can be significant. 'I was scared,' remarked a fellow-finalist when confronted by Gross, 'this monster of a guy swings his arms in your face. I tried not to look at him before the race, he's such a dominating figure.' The changing room is a particularly emotional area. One Australian used to sit in front of her principal rival and just stare into her eyes. Schollander describes how before one Olympic semi-final he broke the nerve of the Frenchman Gottvalles, the world record-holder, by moving gradually closer to him on the bench as they changed, then when in desperation Gottvalles dashed to the urinal, Schollander followed and stood behind him waiting although there were others free.

Bachrach was aware of various 'mental hazards, psychology kinks' among his leading swimmers in Chicago, who held almost all the world records in the Twenties. There were many, he felt, who might be real champions, 'if only they could straighten out those kinks'. The swimmer's solitary training, the long hours spent semi-submerged, induce a lonely, meditative state of mind. Much of a swimmer's training takes place inside his head, immersed as he is in a continuous dream of a world under water. So intense and concentrated are his conditions that he becomes prey to delusions and neuroses beyond the experience of other athletes. The peculiar psychology of the swimmer, and his 'feel for water', form the basic themes of this book.

I

The English Ascendancy

'If I die, they will do something for my wife.'
Captain Webb, by the Niagara Falls

IN THE NINETEENTH CENTURY the English were acknowledged as the best swimmers in the world, at a time
when a passion for athleticism and for games became
their distinguishing feature, and made them an object of
fascination to the rest of Europe. 'They even taught us
Swiss how to climb our own mountains,' remarked Jung,
'and make a sport out of it.'

London was looked upon as the capital of world
swimming. There were six permanent pools, and in
the summer floating baths were moored at Waterloo
and Westminster bridges. Annual swimming galas took

place in most coastal towns, where the shape of the harbour provided a natural amphitheatre, accommodating thousands of spectators. Swimming contests were held in rivers throughout England, and people leapt off the tops of bridges for wagers. A few died. There were fatal leaps off Charing Cross and Tower bridges. The most daring was Samuel Scott. It was his custom to execute a number of acrobatic feats before plunging into the water, and to create a sensation he used to imitate, on a scaffold on Waterloo Bridge, a public execution by hanging. This was to prove his undoing, as in the summer of 1841 the noose slipped and strangled him.

The English never for a moment doubted their pre-eminence. 'None of the black people that I have ever known approach a first-class English swimmer,' stated Webb, the Channel swimmer, and in his view the fastest swimmer the world had seen was E.T. Jones, of Leeds. A Victorian treatise on swimming begins: 'There is no instance of any foreigner, civilised or uncivilised, whose achievements in the water surpass those of the British.' The champions of England sailed to America and returned unbeaten. The great Beckwith beat Deerfoot the Seneca Indian, despite his quarter minute start. The women too were exceptional in their way. The naturalist Richard Jefferies was once watching a 'wanton' young girl by the sea, lying stretched out at the edge of the foam, when suddenly a huge wave curled over and dropped on top of her – 'she was under the surge while it rushed up and while it rushed back; it carried her up to the steps of the bathing machine and back again to her original position. When it subsided she simply shook her head, raised herself on one arm, and adjusted herself parallel to the shore. An English lady could resist it,' Jefferies concludes, 'but could any other? – unless, indeed, an American of English descent.'

Nearly all the stars came from the North of England. The last, Jarvis, the champion of the 1900 Paris Olympics when the races were held in the Seine, was described as 'fat all over, which literally hangs in some parts. His breasts fall like a woman's, but he has powerful shoulders and tremendous thighs.' They swam in the cold lakes and reservoirs, and dark, dingy baths, many of which still survive. The pool at Salford was apparently 'one of the best places ever seen for suicidal purposes. Whoever swam there in a melancholy mood would be seriously inclined to drown himself.' It was in one of these morbid pools that Graham Greene was to make an attempt at suicide, when towards the end of one holiday he swallowed twenty aspirins before swimming in the empty school baths – 'I can still remember the curious sensation of swimming through cotton wool.'

Robert Watson, a journalist who specialised in criminals and swimmers, recorded the heroes of his time, names now forgotten – E.B. Mather, Peter Johnson, Dave Meaken, J. Aspinall, George Poulton. The Leaf Street Baths were the centre of the Manchester swimming fraternity. There he would take his stand among the celebrities 'as near to them as circumstances would permit without being considered rude, and listening with a greedy rapture to all they said. In my eyes just then they were more than men of mighty importance, they were colossally great. It was the proudest moment of my life when I received a reply from any one of them; indeed it was considered a great condescension for these celebrated people, whom I venerated, to speak and speak so nicely, to a strange, inquisitive reporter.'

Watson deplored the new overarm strokes that were becoming fashionable towards the end of the century, inspired by the natives of the Orinoco and the South Seas. He objected to their ugly gestures. He called it 'trick' swimming. His attitude was principally aesthetic. He preferred the graceful motions of a 'never to be forgotten period' of earlier swimmers, like Pamplin, the 'Scudding Seal', who always kept both arms underwater and whose style was like 'dancing, the poetry of motion'. Poulton could revolve on the surface of the water and lie motionless on his side for hours. And there was Charley Moore, the champion one-legged swimmer of the world. For many years he challenged any one-legged man on earth to race any distance from a hundred yards to a mile for £15 or £25 a-side. But it was as an 'ornamental' swimmer that he particularly excelled. A photograph illustrates his prize performance, which was floating and swimming with his one leg entwined around his head. This feat always commanded deafening and prolonged applause, though his subsequent career was melancholy: 'As you turn out of the Strand, on the right side of the road leading to Waterloo Bridge, a man may be seen seated on a chair, not begging, but offering for sale matches. He is much altered in appearance, but a close inspection reveals the once well-known features of Charley Moore. Swimmers might do very much worse than extend their pity and pecuniary assistance to a man whose name once upon a time was indeed a household word, and whose distress appeals very forcibly to their charity.'

For years swimmers had adopted as the model for style the actions of the frog, which had displaced the dog that had been the inspiration until the Elizabethan age. Webb swam breaststroke all the way across the English Channel. Their confidence in the stroke was confirmed when two Indians, 'Flying Gull' and 'Tobacco', were sent over by the Americans to challenge the English supremacy and, like the unfortunate black pugilist Molyneaux, lost easily to the English champion, although in the words of *The Times* they 'lashed the water violently with their arms like the sails of a windmill'. The cult of the breaststroke lasted until the end of the nineteenth century, where we find Corvo's Nicholas Crabbe enumerating the qualities he finds attractive in his new-found friend by the Serpentine: 'Then I admire your swimming. I do adore the breaststroke when the head is poised superbly.' 'So do I. I use no other. I'm sure that our friends the Greeks must have used it.' 'Because of their magnificent broad chests?' 'Precisely. But do finish the list of my charms.'

Frogs were kept in tubs by the sides of pools as a means of instruction. People admired the wonderful screwlike motions of their legs below the knees. When learning to swim, Richard Jefferies procured a frog from some ivy by a garden wall, and deposited it in a trough. On observing its actions, he was disappointed to find it hardly used its arms, and his instructor agreed, but advised him to follow two particular characteristics of its style: 'first in the way it kicked, and secondly in the way it leaned its chest on the water'. Benjamin Haydon, when on holiday with a fellow-painter David Wilkie, found him one hot afternoon sprawling on the drawing room carpet of their lodgings, in a desperate attempt to become a swimmer. Whereupon Haydon spread out a table for him, and Wilkie 'got upon it face downwards, moving his limbs like an awkward frog, little to the purpose'. This must have been a common sight in drawing rooms of the nineteenth century, as the *Boys Own Paper* of 1879 recommends the learner place a basin half-full of water on the floor, put a frog in it, lie face downwards over a stool, and try and imitate its movements. The advice though was hardly novel. As far back as Shadwell's *The Virtuoso* of 1676 Lady Gimcrack is describing her husband learning to swim thus: 'He has a frog in a bowl of water, tied with a pack-thread by the loins, which pack-thread Sir Nicholas holds in his teeth, lying upon his belly on a table; and as the frog strikes, he strikes, and his swimming master stands by, to tell him when he does well or ill.' When asked if he had ever tried out the stroke in the water, Sir Nicholas replies: 'No Sir, but I swim most exquisitely on land. I content myself with the Speculative part of swimming, I care not for the Practick. I seldom bring anything to use, 'tis not my way.'

Everyone swam naked, until the popularity of bathing gathered momentum in the Victorian age. By the mid nineteenth century naked men were only allowed to bathe off certain parts of the beach and at certain times. When mixed bathing became fashionable at Llandudno, it met with general disapproval. Families travelled to the continent in order to swim more freely, and Marie Lloyd was to sing: 'Belle, along with beau, went swimming in a throng,/ A terrible thing, but the regular thing, on the naughty Continong.' The Calecon was instituted for men, which stretched down to the knees, while women were encased in waisted, bloomered, skirted outfits. These costumes, before the introduction of wool after the Great War, were made of woven cotton, which when wet tended to become transparent and cling to the body, revealing more than they concealed. The bathing machines which towed the swimmers out to deeper water were now equipped with 'modesty hoods', the invention of a Quaker to save the embarrassment of those troubled by the sight of women emerging from the sea in soaking costumes. But whatever the restrictions, they failed to prevent women from becoming objects of the greatest curiosity. In the Victorian coastal resorts, when the sea was normally 'black with bathers', the females did not venture beyond the surf but lay on their backs, waiting for the approaching waves, with their bathing dresses in a 'most dégagée style. When the waves came,' commented one onlooker, 'they not only covered the bathers, but literally carried their dresses up to their necks, so that, as far as decency was concerned, they might as well have been without any dresses at all.' All this used to take place in the presence of thousands of spectators. Gentlemen used to come from miles around to watch the women bathing. Telescopes were trained on women descending into the sea, and in certain resorts men were prohibited from hanging around the bathing machines. It was not until 1901 that in swimming baths women were allowed to swim in the presence of men.

The imposition of any form of clothing was strongly resisted. When in 1860 the wearing of drawers of 'a large roomy pattern' was instituted at the Pimlico baths, it caused great annoyance and discomfort. People felt like Smollett's Jerry Melford who loved swimming as an exercise 'without the formality of an apparatus', while Smollett himself was known to have bathed naked off Nice, as early as May, which provoked a good deal of curiosity locally, and imitation. The reserved and curious Francis Kilvert, when a curate in Wiltshire, described in his diary while on holiday in Weston-super-Mare the people swimming naked off the shore, which encouraged him to do the same before breakfast the following morning: 'There was a delicious feeling of freedom in stripping in the open air and running down naked to the sea, where the waves were curling white with foam and the red morning sunshine glowing upon the naked limbs of the bathers.' Two years later however in the rather more respectable Shanklin on the Isle of Wight he discovered that he had to adopt the 'detestable custom of bathing in drawers. If ladies don't like to see men naked, why don't they keep away from the sight?' He was further put out when some rough waves stripped his drawers off and 'tore them down round my ankles. While thus fettered I was seized and flung down by a heavy sea which retreating suddenly left me lying naked on the sharp shingle from which I rose streaming with blood. After this I took the wretched and dangerous rag off and of course there were some ladies looking on as I came up out of the water.'

Ever since George III had set the mood by swimming off Weymouth to the accompaniment of a chamber orchestra, a string of resorts had grown up along the coasts of England, ornamented with elegant squares and piers, as sea-water swimming became fashionable for purposes of health. These were unique to England. Salt water was a novel alternative to spa waters, as a cure for almost anything. One drank several tumblers of it, or dipped in it before breakfast. Ramsgate, Margate, Brighton, Southend and Scarborough were already in vogue by the time Jane Austen came to write her last novel *Sanditon*. It was to describe the development of a new resort, but she never completed it. The novel opens with an argument between a well-established landlord, a gentleman-farmer devoted to the old rural way of life, and a speculator for whom 'the success of Sanditon as a small, fashionable bathing place was the object for which he seemed to live'. 'Every five years,' the landlord complains, 'one hears of some new place or other starting up by the sea, and growing the fashion. Bad things for a country – sure to raise the price of provisions, and make the poor good for nothing.' The speculator, who had bought up, enlarged and publicised what was once a small village of no pretensions, naturally disagrees. He cites the pure sea breezes and excellent bathing it offers. He enthuses about its fine hard sand, deep water ten yards from shore, its lack of mud, weeds, slimy rocks. The sea, he argues, cures colds, improves appetite, spirits, strength. Nobody could be really well, he protests, without spending at least six weeks by the sea every year. Although Jane Austen mocks the speculator's tastes and pretensions, she betrays a certain sympathy with his ideas. Throughout this fragment of a novel can be felt a longing for the sea, 'dancing and sparkling in sunshine and freshness'. For she herself loved sea-bathing, and once wrote in 1804 from Lyme that the 'bathing was so delightful this morning and Molly so pressing with me to enjoy myself that I believe I staid in rather too long'.

By the end of the century hundreds of towns had been developed along the sea. Houses with balconies and bay windows with seaviews replaced the old fishing bungalows. The quest for health had become a search for pleasure. Railways and Steampackets offered a new facility of movement for the masses. Here by the seashore their dull, dreary existence could be forgotten for a week or two and substituted by a world of fantasy. The aristocratic atmosphere of the Regency period, the Assembly Rooms and dance-halls, was now outmoded. Instead of Regency terraces, Victorians went wild with mediaeval castles, Venetian palaces, Tudor mansions. A taste for the exotic, inspired by the Brighton Pavilion, coloured the new style of architecture. Among the jungly ferns and palms of the Winter Gardens, the 'Indian' lounges and kiosks, the bandstands domed like oriental pavilions, the tourists could imagine themselves transported briefly to some tropical paradise. Bands of 'Nigger Minstrels' played along the esplanades and piers, that gave the illusion of decks of ships, with their bollards shaped like capstans, their lamps decorated with anchors, sea serpents, mermaids.

Mermaids proved endlessly fascinating. One, reputed to have been netted by a Chinese fisherman and purchased for $500 by Captain Eades in Java, drew hundreds of spectators daily. The eccentric Robert Hawker, later the Vicar of Morwenstow, attracted crowds of gullible holidaymakers to the Bude coast 'seated on a rock some distance from shore, wearing a plaited seaweed wig which hung in lank streamers halfway down his back. He enveloped his legs in an oilskin wrap, and otherwise naked sat on the rock, flashing

the moonbeams about from a hand mirror, and sang
and screamed till attention was arrested.'

All who visited these coastal towns could, for a
brief portion of their lives, play out whatever role they
fancied. 'Holiday time was a land of pretence,' wrote
Macqueen-Pope, recalling his late-Victorian childhood.
'They all laid claim to a social status they did not possess and nobody believed anyone, but it was part of the
fun. The men were all in professions, or were naval or
military officers on leave. If they were clean-shaven in
an age of moustaches, they said they were actors. The
girls were all of great wealth and family.' In the music
halls along the piers they sang of spurious 'Swells of
the Sea' and 'Seaside Sultans', of seaside flirtations and
marital indiscretion ('They're all single by the Seaside').
The songs reflected the transient sense of liberation felt
by those who led drab and paltry lives in the cities. Fantasies were fulfilled – 'You can do a lot of things at the seaside that you can't do in town.' There was even a plea –
'Why can't we have the sea in London?' These songs,
almost the last to extol the pleasures of coastal life till
those of the Beach Boys in the 1960s, celebrated the great
age of seaside holidays. When in 1931 Noël Coward used
in *Cavalcade* the chorus song 'I do like to be beside the
seaside', it was to evoke a vanished past, the magical
period of his own childhood before the Great War, for
an audience who now preferred Mediterranean bays and
palms to the beaches of Broadstairs.

In fact seaside life for some had passed its peak years
before. Edmund Gosse describes sadly in *Father and Son*
the impact made by his father's enthusiastically written
books on shells and anemones, with his own exquisite

illustrations, that after their publication in the 1850s tempted hordes of people to descend on the coasts, determined to disturb the antiquity of rock pools in their mad search for the paraphernalia of the aquarium which had just become the fashionable ornament of the moment. They swarmed down in such numbers that by the end of the decade the 'fairy paradise had been violated, the exquisite product of natural selection had been crushed under the rough paw of well-meaning, idle-minded curiosity. That my father, so reverent, so conservative, had by the popularity of his books acquired the direct responsibility for a calamity that he had never anticipated, became clear enough to himself before many years had passed, and cost him great chagrin. No one will see again on the shore of England what I saw in my early childhood, the submarine vision of dark rocks, speckled and starred with an infinite variety of colour, and streamed over by silken flags of royal crimson and purple.'

While the publications of the elder Gosse drew thousands down to the beaches, the enthusiasm for swimming that developed so remarkably over the century may well have been due to the enormous influence exerted by Ruskin. The attention he paid to the form of the sea in Turner's painting, the visions of Venice as a coral reef in Indian seas, his descriptions of European waterfalls and our island streams, so full of feeling for their varying sounds, flow, colour and geological structure, had perhaps the effect of his passion for rocks and mountains, that created an unprecedented craze for mountain climbing in his time. Such was its impact that the Alpine Club had been founded in the same year as his *Modern Painters* was published.

The ocean expressed the romantic spirit of the age.
Charlotte Brontë fainted at her first encounter with it.
Water was still a mysterious element, an unknown quan-
tity. Instances of drowning were so common, their effect
so devastating. It took Elizabeth Browning five years to
get over the death of her eldest brother, after he had
drowned off Torquay in a boating incident. When John
Wordsworth drowned with three hundred others on a
voyage to India, it wrecked the health of his brother
and sister, and caused Coleridge's 'unhappiest day' in
Malta. Byron lost his greatest friend Matthews in the
Cam, Swinburne his, Luke, in the Isis, Hopkins Digby
Dolden in the Nene. The most pathetic moments in
memoirs are often those that relate to drowning –
Borrow's sailor off Spain, the look of agony he cast as
the steamer hurried past him, the sight of his body sinking deeper and deeper, his arms outstretched towards the
surface; Ruskin's parents standing 'like statues' when told
of the death of his cousin Charles off the Isle of Wight –
'they caught the cap off his head, and yet they couldn't
save him'; the beautiful Miss Bathurst slipping from her
horse into the Tiber in the Countess of Blessington's *Idler
in Italy*, rising to the surface, then disappearing into its
turbid depths for ever, 'in the presence of her agonised
friends'. The German nuns who drowned in the wreck
of the *Deutschland* made Hopkins a poet, while the wreck
of the *Birkenhead* off South Africa, with the loss of
hundreds of soldiers' lives, became one of the great
imperial myths as a supreme example of self-sacrifice, of
such significance that according to Borrow the German
Kaizer ordered its report to be read out at the head of
all his regiments.

These died by accident. Others seemed to suffer from an appetite for death by water. Shelley's first wife drowned herself in the Serpentine, his mother-in-law Mary Wollstonecraft made a brave attempt to one night in the Thames, while Shelley himself made no effort to save himself off Viareggio. When Charles Kingsley was told that his brother had drowned himself in Looe pool after stealing a silver spoon at school, Kingsley's cry of anguish was remembered by many for years afterwards. On honeymoon in Venice, George Eliot's husband threw himself into a canal, after realising too late the error of his marriage. 'I am in love with moistness,' declares George Eliot's Maggie in *The Mill on the Floss*, before she finally drowns in a flood.

This love affair with 'moistness' was a feature of the age. Anything to do with water seemed to exert an extraordinary fascination. 'I associate my "careless boyhood" with all that lies on the banks of the Stour,' wrote Constable, 'these scenes made me a painter.' Like Ruskin, Walter Pater was abnormally sensitive to the slightest trace of water in painting, the pools of Botticelli with their flowering reeds, the landscape of Giorgione 'full of the effects of water, of fresh rain newly passed through the air and collected into the grassy channels', and in his eyes La Gioconda, seated among that circle of fantastic rocks as if in some underwater grotto, had been a diver in deep seas. On the day his poor cousin was drowned, Ruskin cannot help mentioning that a fresh wind had been blowing, 'exactly the kind of breeze that drifts the clouds, and ridges the waves, in Turner's *Gosport*'. Poets were amazed by the qualities of water. They were drawn to analysing its effects, its musicality, the influence of the rocks on its surface colours. Coleridge had scrutinised five kinds of waterfall, a spring with its 'tiny little cone of loose sand ever rising and sinking at the bottom, but its surface without a wrinkle', a pool 'where the stream ran into a scooped or scalloped hollow of the Rock in its Channel – this Shape, an exact white rose, was forever overpowered by the stream rushing down in upon it, and still obstinate in resurrection it spread up into the Scallop, by fits and starts, blossoming in a moment into a full flower'. G. M. Hopkins, a swimmer like Coleridge, analysed waves as if he was enclosed within them.

The German Lichtenberg was astonished by the stage at Sadlers Wells, where the whole space beneath it, like the Roman arena, was filled with water, which made it especially suitable for representing aquatic scenes and underwater ballet. Noted swimmers of the time swam for days on end, alone or racing against each other, in tanks erected in city halls, watched by vast crowds that included members of the Royal Family. Tanks were set up on the stages of music halls for underwater performances. Lurline was apparently the best of all performers in the tanks, or 'crystal aquaria' as they were called. She was an 'artiste' from the moment she stepped on to the stage until she took her departure. Her act was a revelation. In 1881 she remained underwater at the Oxford music hall for 2 minutes 51¼ seconds. Elise Wallenda, a tiny figure with a chest of twenty-seven inches and well under five feet, could successively undress, write, sew, eat and drink underwater, but her greatest feat was to remain submerged for 4 minutes 45⅖ seconds in 1898, beating the record achieved by James Finney at the Canterbury music hall, before an audience of hundreds. Both 'swimmers' were taken out unconscious, but quickly recovered.

A newspaper of the time describes Miss Wallenda taking one deep breath before submerging, then settling to the bottom, lying on her left side, 'her head resting on her left hand, with her body and legs perfectly straight and feet crossed. As time sped by the tension became painful, as the officials called out the various times before an enthralled audience. Just previous to 3 minutes being called a small bubble of air rose gently to the surface, and at 3½ minutes these became more frequent; at 4 minutes quite a stream of bubbles arose. At 4 minutes 15 seconds she appeared for the first time to show signs of fatigue. At 4½ minutes there was a movement as if attempting to rise, and at 4 minutes 36 seconds one large bubble escaped from her mouth. A few moments later she attempted to rise, but failed to do so; her trembling hand, which she had removed from her face and placed flat on the bottom of the tank, slipped away. Directly this was observed she was brought to the surface.' As a result of this near disaster, such performances were permanently banned.

All these rather static, desperate acts were eclipsed by those of Annette Kellermann, who starred in the British music hall at the turn of the century, where she dived into glass-enclosed tanks on stage and performed various intricate ballets, remaining under the surface for 3½ minutes. She was also hired for various private displays before the Duke and Duchess of Connaught and other dignitaries at the Bath Club. Her chief attractions were her novel one-piece bathing costume, and an athletic body later described by a Harvard professor as physically the most perfect out of 'ten thousand women scientifically tested'. Brought up in Australia and paralysed by polio as a child, she was introduced to swimming as a cure where she discovered like Byron that the limbs which had served her so ill on dry land 'found their true congenial element in the water'. At an early age she became the champion swimmer and diver of Australia, swimming ten miles along the Yarra river, then diving fifty feet into aquaria full of fish at the start of her professional career. Aged fourteen, she was brought over to England by her father, who, like Suzanne Lenglen's, acted shrewdly as her manager and mentor. They throve on self-publicity. Huge crowds watched as she swam through London alone, along the Thames from Putney to Blackwall, then in Paris half a million spectators gathered when she swam up the Seine. In Vienna she challenged and beat the Austrian champion, Baroness Isa Cescu, in a twenty-two-mile race along the Danube, before crossing the Atlantic to continue her sensational career in America. Beneath all this unrelenting exhibitionism she retained throughout her life an essentially romantic attitude towards swimming: 'I learn much from people in the way they meet the unknown in life and water is a great test. I am sure no adventurer nor discoverer ever lived who could not swim. Swimming cultivates imagination; the man with the most is he who can swim his solitary course night or day and forget a black earth full of people that push. This love of the unknown is the greatest of all the joys which swimming has for me. I am still looking for my chest of gold in a cool dripping sea cave – or mermaid combing her long green hair.'

For many months she swam from town to town along the English coast to prepare herself for a Channel swim, accompanied by Burgess who in 1911 became the second person to swim it, thirty-six years after Captain Webb. Webb and Kellermann remain the two pivotal figures in swimming's history. As a result of their example swimming became popular and fashionable throughout Europe and America.

One of twelve children of a doctor, Matthew Webb learnt to swim in the Severn below Ironbridge. At twelve he joined the mercantile training ship *Conway*, where Conrad's 'Secret Sharer', who emerges mysteriously from the black waters of the Gulf of Siam, had once won the swimming prize. Another cadet remarked of Webb: 'We thought very little of him as a swimmer, but admired his staying powers. He could swim for an hour without putting his foot to the floor, though in a race he was nowhere.' His first opponent was a Newfoundland dog, whose master boasted of its extraordinary stamina in the water. Webb backed himself against it. He continued floating happily in a choppy sea for over an hour. The dog however nearly drowned. It swam exhausted back to its master's boat, made efforts to climb up the side, and eventually had to be lifted out.

Webb passed straight from the training ship into the merchant navy, where he made his mark and displayed his contempt for danger with some brave and lone swims in various parts of the world. He was also employed as a mate by the grandfather of William Butler Yeats, who owned a large fleet and seems to have been, from the account of him in his grandson's autobiography, a similar type of man. In his impatience with a spineless crew, he had once swum down to the bottom of a harbour to examine a rudder, and he was famous for saving the lives of the shipwrecked. Yeats, ashamed of his lack of courage as a youth, always wanted to be like his grandfather 'who thought so little of danger that he had jumped overboard in the Bay of Biscay after an old hat'. The grandfather and Webb became close friends after Webb had shown his mettle by submerging into the Suez canal to release some hawsers, diving into some huge waves in the Atlantic in a forlorn attempt to rescue a passenger, and recovering off Natal some wrecked cargo in heavy surf. By this time he had grown into a man of herculean build, with a wrestler's body that was particularly strong 'in the loins and legs'.

After reading in a newspaper of an unsuccessful attempt on the Channel, Webb left shipping in order to concentrate on crossing it. He trained solidly by swimming various distances along the South coast, from ten to twenty miles. The journalist Watson accompanied him in a boat, and grew tired of watching his 'slow, methodical, but perfect breaststroke, and the magnificent sweep of his ponderous legs'. On 12 August 1875 he made his first attempt. Great odds were offered against the swim being successful, but there were no takers. He swam in rough seas and gave up at midnight when over halfway there, in consideration for those in the boat rather than himself, as the waves were pouring over the sides. He had not wanted to enter the water, but the advance publicity was so strong that he felt an obligation.

Twelve days later he tried again. He dived off the Admiralty pier, Dover, wearing a red costume, made of silk like Ranjitsinhji's cricket shirts. He kept up a slow and steady pace in the dark, and was soon passed by a French steamer on its way to Dunkirk. The crew came up on deck and gazed in astonishment. He continued to propel himself through the phosphorescent waves, among drifting seaweed, porpoises and stinging jellyfish. When *The Maid of Kent* passed by, the passengers cheered as a red light was held over the stern to enable them to watch the swimmer. He was later to remark: 'Never shall I forget when the men in the mailboat struck up the tune of "Rule Britannia", which they sang, or rather shouted, in a hoarse roar. I felt a sudden gulping sensation in my throat as the old tune, which I had heard in all parts of the world, once more struck my ears under circumstances so extraordinary. I felt now I should do it, and I did it.' Seven miles from the French coast the tide changed and he seemed to be driven backwards, but eventually he landed after almost twenty-two hours in the water. He quickly recovered, and merely felt a peculiar sensation in his limbs 'similar to that after the first day of the cricket season'. It was a week before he could wear a shirt collar, owing to the deep red raw rim at the back of his neck, from having been forced to keep his head back for so long.

On his return in triumph to Dover he was entertained in the mess of the 24th Regiment, the South Wales Borderers, temporarily stationed there before they were almost wiped out four years later by the Zulus at Isandhlwana. His presence in London at the Stock Exchange brought business to a close. A triumphal arch was erected in his hometown in Shropshire. Chinese lanterns festooned the trees, and bonfires illuminated the valley. A knighthood was proposed in Parliament, its strongest advocate a Mr R. H. Horne MP, who had himself once swum across the Menai Strait from Caernarfon Castle to the Isle of Anglesey. The *New York Times* reported: 'Captain Webb has achieved a vast ocean of good by giving an impulse to swimming throughout the country. The London baths are crowded, each village pond and running stream contains youthful worshippers at the shrine of Webb, and even along the banks of the river, regardless of the terrors of the Thames police, swarms of naked urchins ply their limbs, each probably determining that he will one day be another Captain Webb.' For Richard Jefferies Webb's Channel swim superseded the feats of Ajax and Hercules. He could think of nothing in mythology to equal it. Nor could Swinburne and Jowett in Oxford.

Webb then embarked on a lecture tour round the country. He possessed a certain inventive, even artistic genius. He patented a novel form of bicycle, a swimming machine, and a propeller based on a screw principle. In his youth he had painted some fine watercolours of birds and still-lifes, some of which still survive. But he never made much money, and had the reputation of being generous to a fault.

Lack of funds forced him back into the water. He took part in some endurance races, swimming for six days in a pool, fourteen hours a day, a feature of the time. He then sailed to America to challenge the American Boynton, a coastguard who had swum the Channel before him, but in a rubber suit with a paddle. He continued to use this equipment, but Webb managed to win the race. He returned to England to float for sixty hours in front of thousands of queueing spectators in the whale tank of the Royal Aquarium, Westminster. Fearne, a prominent swimmer of the time, then challenged him to a six day race in the Lambeth baths. To an onlooker they seemed like 'two great white seals smoothly, unceasingly, aimlessly swimming from end to end of the semi-deserted bath. The pace is unhurried, the two competitors scarcely seem to regard each other. There is nothing to vary the monotony of the proceeding, save at intervals the mechanical voice of the scorer calling out "Webb, ten laps" or "Fearne, four laps" as the case may be.' A race soon afterwards, with a Dr Jennings in the chilly waters of a Lancashire lake, marked the turning point in his career. Webb was so exhausted after it that he could hardly be pulled from the water. In Watson's view this race 'had a very serious effect upon Webb's constitution and he never again seemed like the Webb of old. His career from now on had a downward tendency. He had almost played his last card.' Nevertheless he left again for America to continue his floating exhibitions and contests off the East coast, and returned to England to swim his last race, from which he retired coughing up blood.

Webb was by now running seriously short of money. He had a young family to provide for. In order to recoup his losses, he determined to end his career with one last extraordinary exploit. Blondin had recently caught the world's imagination by crossing the Niagara Falls on a tightrope. Watson describes his final conversation with Webb as they rated his prospects of swimming down below them: 'We discussed Niagara. "Don't go," I said, "from what I hear you will never come out alive." "Don't care," was the reply, "I want money and I must have it." As we stood face to face, I compared the fine handsome sailor, who first spoke to me about swimming, with the broken-spirited and terribly altered appearance of the man who courted death in the whirlpool rapids. His object was not suicide, but money and imperishable fame.' Webb was warned by his friends and doctors about the deterioration of his body, but it was evidently a topic he chose to avoid. Above all he dreaded a quiet life.

Three miles below the Niagara Falls the river bends towards the Canadian side, contracts to a width of 200 feet, and rushes violently into a deep depression in the cliffside. In emerging at a right angle from the depression it forms a whirlpool. Its entrance is guarded by some ferocious rapids, their most terrible features the jagged rocks and tremendous waves thrown up by the river as it plunges down a narrow gorge at a considerable slope. It was from his memories of this whirlpool that Edgar Allan Poe conceived 'The Maelstrom'. The English flower painter Marianne North rented a house above the rapids for some months, where she was terrified by the perpetual sight of the 'savage green boiling water that seemed piled up in the centre like some glacier'. This stretch of river below the Falls attracted a succession of English swimmers. Byron's friend Trelawny swam across and back, and wrote a memorable description of his experiences. The athletic Lord Desborough, father of Julian Grenfell the war poet, on his first trip to America swam across. No Americans ventured there, as on his second visit he found that no one believed what he had done, so he swam it again. Afterwards he wrote to his wife Ettie: 'It was an awful day and blowing half a gale which made it worse for swimming, but I had to do it . . .

I hope you will not think me a beast for doing it, but I don't call it risky really.'

Another swimmer, Rupert Brooke, visited Niagara some years later. Although he did not swim there, he viewed the scene with a swimmer's eye: 'Beyond the foot of the Falls the river is like a slipping floor of marble, green with veins of dirty white, made by the scum that was foam. It slides very quietly and slowly down for a mile or two, sullenly exhausted. Then it turns to a dull sage green, and hurries more swiftly, smooth and ominous. As the walls of the ravine close in, trouble stirs, and the waters boil and eddy. These are the lower rapids, a sight more terrifying than the Falls, because less intelligible. Close in its bands of rock the river surges tumultuously forward, writhing and leaping as if inspired by a demon. It is pressed by the straits into a visibly convex form. Great planes of water slide past. Sometimes it is thrown up into a pinnacle of foam higher than a house, or leaps with incredible speed from the crest of one vast wave to another, along the shining curve between, like the spring of a wild beast. Its motion continually suggests muscular action. The power manifest in these rapids moves one with a different sense of awe and terror from that of the Falls. Here the inhuman life and strength are spontaneous, active, almost resolute; masculine vigour compared with the passive gigantic power, female, helpless and overwhelming, of the Falls. A place of fear.'

Webb sailed to America with his wife, son and daughter of seven months, and spent some days training off Nantucket beach. Then leaving his family, who remained ignorant of his intentions, on the coast, he travelled to the Falls and made a critical examination of the scene. He then called a press conference, and explained calmly what he proposed to do. He would embark in a small boat from the bank, jump off and float downriver through the rapids. It would take him two or three hours to extricate himself from the whirlpool, the diameter of which was a quarter of a mile, then once beyond its circumference he would swim to shore. He would jump into 90 feet of water, that would swiftly increase to 250 feet. He was only afraid of two awful ledges of pointed rock, which jut out from the shores into the whirlpool. He would strike out with all his strength and try to keep away from the suckhole in the centre. He would commence with the breaststroke, then swim overarm for acceleration.

Webb reckoned $10,000 was at stake. In the last twenty-three years eighty people had lost their lives accidentally in the rapids. No one had ever tried to swim through the whirlpool. The date for the swim was fixed for 21 July. This was postponed for several days to further the special train arrangements laid on by the railway companies. Ten thousand spectators were expected.

At 4 p.m. on 24 July Webb was rowed out into mid-stream, wearing the same red silk trunks he had worn for the Channel. He dived into the river, and was instantly gripped by the force of the current. He was glimpsed by the spectators holding his course in mid-channel heading for the whirlpool, which he was seen entering. At first he kept on his way swimming, then abruptly he threw up his arms and was drawn under. His last words to the boatman had been: 'If I die, they will do something for my wife.'

Some days later his body was found by fishermen four miles below the rapids. It had been delayed by the force of the whirlpool. His red silk costume was torn to shreds, and his skull exposed. He had probably hit the submarine rocks he feared at the sides of the whirlpool. He lies buried in the Oakwood cemetery at the edge of the Falls, in a heart-shaped plot of ground known as 'The Strangers' Rest'.

II

Classical Waters

Acqua Felice . . .

'The world has been empty since the Romans,
but the memory of the Romans fills it.'

L.A. Saint-Just

THIS EXTRAORDINARY ENTHUSIASM for swimming among the English, unique in Europe at the time, has been attributed to the mixture of Nordic and Roman strains in their character. The Northern sagas reveal a society in which swimming was a common accomplishment, enjoyed by men and women, who swam for pleasure in the fjords and rivers, while the heroes plunged behind waterfalls in pursuit of monsters, or down through dark lakes. In Roman society there was a similar regard for its martial and heroic qualities, inspired by the example of Horatius who swam to shore after defending the bridge. In the same war Cloelia, a Roman matron held as hostage by the Etruscans, escaped from their clutches by swimming down the Tiber. Soldiers subsequently dived into the river after their daily training on the Campus Martius. Almost all garrison towns were supplied with large open-air pools. The Roman army retained a regiment of swimming Germans, and a special company of divers as part of their forces, 'urinatores', so-called because they dribbled oil from their mouths in order to see clearly, who cleared stones from sunken hulks blocking harbours, or carried messages scratched on lead from beleaguered towns.

But it was their attitude in peacetime that was remarkable, their use of water for health and enjoyment, in baths attached to towns, barracks, and villas, that were the last to be built before the Industrial Revolution in England. Compared to the eight pools available in London in high summer, there were over 800 open to the citizens of Rome, some of spectacular dimensions and able to accommodate over 1,000 people. Gibbon comments that the 'meanest Roman could purchase with a small copper coin the daily enjoyment of a scene, of a pomp and luxury which excited the envy of the Kings of Asia.' Charles Kingsley, who loathed the tyranny exercised by the Romans, could only say in its favour that it provided 'free baths for its victims'. In Greece the Bath had been regarded as part of the Gymnasium, while in Italy the Gymnasium constituted part of the Baths. As the Empire declined, the Baths became more luxurious than ever. The more degenerate the emperor, the more sumptuous tended to be his Baths.

Almost all the emperors built Baths. Diocletian's were built by Christians over seven years. Those that were still Christian on its completion were put to death. Titus built his to divert attention from the disasters of Vesuvius and the fire in Rome. Nero's were the most extravagant and beautiful, Caracalla's the most magnificent. They were surrounded by colonnades, libraries, and palaestrae where athletes trained. The painted ceilings of the Baths of Titus were copied by Raphael for his designs in the Vatican, then obliterated on his orders, so the legend goes, while the mosaics around the Baths of Caracalla, of muscular boxers silhouetted against plain backgrounds, were to influence the work of Fernand Léger. One of its rooms, the tepidarium, became the model for the Pennsylvania railway station in New York that was destroyed in 1963, after its architect as a young man had become mesmerised by the audacity of the Bath's structure, the intricacies of light and shadow. The great central hall of Diocletian's Baths was converted by Michelangelo into a church, and the superb granite columns, each hewn out of a single block forty-three feet in height, still remain as they were in the imperial heyday. Distracted recently by the sight of these startling columns and that of a gypsy's naked breast feeding a pendant infant, I lost through her liquid fingers all the money in my possession.

High above the bathers in these pools towered colossal statuary, among them the Laocoön and the Farnese Hercules. These figures that now in the light of day appear so exaggerated would, among the shadows and glare of the torchlight in which they originally stood, have produced a mysterious and dramatic effect. The shadowy atmosphere and secret alcoves were to make these Baths, like the resort of Baiai down the coast, notorious dens of vice and corruption. Every so often emperors would be forced to issue edicts to suppress it, but normally they were the first to fall for its temptations. Swimming in fact seemed to inspire the imperial vices. Domitian swam with prostitutes, Elagabalus in pools strewn with roses among young boys, as did Tiberius in the waters off Capri, where according to Suetonius he trained them to chase him while he went swimming and get between his legs to lick and nibble him. Caligula was unable to swim, so was deprived of the opportunity for such forms of amusement. The Baths became the haunts of homosexuals and voyeurs. Those who were genitally well-endowed were said to have evoked applause in the Baths, and in the reign of Elagabalus advanced to high honours.

In the imagination of Michel Leiris, imperial Rome was to assume the form of a vast marble Bath, and in analysing the emotional fantasies of his childhood he was to attribute the voluptuous, erotic excitement he derived from its past to its cruelty and the 'bathroom aspect of its architecture, the glacial marble with its suggestion of sweating rooms, skin beaded with tiny drops, spirals of steam, naked bodies'. Perhaps the nearest equivalent these days to the steamy atmosphere of the ancient Baths, now that the New York bath-houses have gone, are those basements in certain Hamburg hotels, where on velvet sofas by the side of green marble pools naked sirens offer up their charms among potted palms and papier mâché pillars.

Excavations at Pompeii of countless public and private

pools, their walls decorated luxuriously with Tritons and Naiads, have revealed the fact that bathing was almost a passion with the Romans. They were accustomed to say of an ignorant man, 'he neither knows how to read or swim'. While the English often use cricket or boxing terms as metaphors for attitudes to life, the Romans tended to turn to swimming. In learning to swim young Romans were buoyed up with a strip of cork, and Horace's father, when advising his son that sooner or later he would have to stand on his own two feet, warns him that from now on 'nabis sine cortice' – you will swim without a cork. Once beyond this stage, their swimming was not confined to pools. The Tiber was especially popular. For those suffering from insomnia Horace recommends swimming across the river three times. He describes the young aristocrats of his day enjoying their swims there. No one can touch Enipeus in swimming downstream; Hebrus, beloved of Neobule, after some gymnastics 'bathes his oil-smeared shoulders in the waters of the river'; Lydia is reproached because under her influence Sybaris now fears even to touch the tawny river. Cicero accused Catullus's Clodia of having purposely procured a villa near the Tiber, from where she could signal to young men who came to bathe. In exile on the Black Sea, Ovid imagined 'sadly in spring-time' the youth of Rome bathing their weary limbs in the waters of the Virgo aqueduct.

All around the Mediterranean coastline there are natural pools once used by the Romans, where waves wash into the hollows of rocks. Judging by Pliny's description of beach life in the Roman colony of Hippo in North Africa, the atmosphere of resorts seems to have changed little since the imperial years: 'There people of all ages enjoy fishing, boating, and swimming, especially boys, who have leisure for such delights. They compete to be able to boast of having swum the greatest distance out to sea; the winner is the one who has left the shore and his fellows furthest behind him.' Nor have the predatory instincts of the Italian male altered much over the centuries. Separated from his lover Cynthia, Propertius wonders what she is doing far away on the beaches of Baiai, and hopes that she is fully occupied bathing rather than lying on the sand, succumbing to the seductive whispers of one of his rivals: 'May the waters of Teuthras' calm sea, yielding readily to your hands as you dip them alternately, hold you prisoner.'

Swimming was so popular that the inability of the Emperor Caligula to swim caused comment. Even under-water swimming must have been a familiar sight if Martial could laugh at someone boasting of his amours for having the face of a man 'swimming underwater'. In one letter Pliny describes the river Clitumnus, a popular bathing place, 'as clear as glass, where you can count the coins which have been thrown in and the pebbles shining on the bottom'; in another his own warm-water pool by his seaside villa, of 'extraordinary workmanship, in which you may swim and have a view of the sea at the same time'.

It is the ruins of these pools scattered throughout the Mediterranean and Northern world that more than anything else remain moving relics of their civilising influence. Through the paintings of Alma Tadema they provided the model for the stately pools of Edwardian club life, the RAC where in the opening line of Charles

Morgan's *The Judge's Story* Severidge 'swam four lengths and ate four sandwiches', and the Corinthian Club of Hollinghurst's *The Swimming-Pool Library*, 'its pillars at each corner an allusion to ancient Rome, and you half-expect to see the towel-girt figures of Charlton Heston and Tony Curtis deep in senatorial conspiracy'.

But more influential than their enthusiasm for swimming was the feeling for water that runs through Latin life and poetry, their sense of its charm and divinity that they derived from the Greeks, those rivers, lakes, and pools whose waters enchanted Hylas, Hermaphrodite, Narcissus. For Homer water was most nourishing – 'clear, light, of high value, desirable'. His heroes are obsessed with physical cleanliness, and in their view ritual washing, performed with lustral water, made a man resemble the gods. The Greeks felt that the influence of its sight and sound could restore health and vitality. They liked to see and hear water everywhere, flowing from fountains in their courtyards, in sculptured runnels through the wards of hospitals, around the running courses and gymnasia, along the sides of streets. They were captivated by their springs, gushing and sparkling from the clefts and hollows of the rocks, some famous for their coolness and copiousness, others for their purity and sweetness: Castaly, Peirene, Aganippe, Hippocrene, Arethusa – legends arose concerning their origins. Such places were linked with divinity.

Their waters became consecrated as shrines, some simple, others more elaborate like those of Castaly in Delphi and Peirene in Corinth, the latter the tears of a woman weeping for her murdered son, whose waters flow through a series of arched chambers of white marble, then run into a large pool in the open air. In the Middle Ages it formed part of the private gardens of the Turkish bey, and although the ornament and most of the marble channels that carried the sparkling water to all corners of the shrine have been erased, its basic structure still survives. Lais, a Sicilian sold to Corinth where she was revered as the most beautiful prostitute of her generation, was described as 'even more glittering than the clear water spring of Peirene'. An annual prize was awarded for a diving competition by the shrine of Dionysus nearby. Leaping into the sea from a cliff was a feature of Apollo's festival on the island of Leukas, as a trial, a sacrifice, or a cure for unrequited love. It was from here that Sappho had leapt to her death in despair. By the time of Cicero live birds were attached to the victim or performer, and rescue boats waited below.

Water flowed into the Castalian spring by the Delphic oracle through seven lions' heads over steps to a marble basin. Water was vital for the worship of Apollo and the function of the oracle. Men swam in the river before visiting it, and the Pythian priestess preceded her prophecies with a series of ritual acts that began with bathing in the Castalian spring and drinking its waters. Sanctuaries were served by priests and priestesses who were made to preserve a perfect purity all their lives. They had to bathe regularly in their waters and live apart from others, never entering a private house. Sacrifices were made where springs and rivers burst out of the ground. It was forbidden to bathe or urinate at the source of rivers, or where they met the sea. After the sanctuary of Diana in Achaia had been defiled by an act of sexual intercourse, an annual sacrifice was performed of a boy and a virgin 'with the most beautiful bodies' to the Implacable river – 'until then it had no name'. Aktaion was devoured by his hunting dogs, Sipriotes changed into a woman, Teiresias blinded after watching goddesses bathing.

For the Greeks water possessed magical, mysterious, and often sinister properties. There was a spring that made you mad, another that once tasted could make you teetotal for the rest of your life. In another Hera renewed her virginity every year. To render Achilles invulnerable his mother dipped his infant body in a river. Water caused men to fall in love with their reflections, reduced them to hermaphrodites, those indeterminate figures of androgynous beauty that haunted their artistic imagination. The Styx in Arcadia inflicted death on men and animals, dissolved glass, crystal, stone, corrupted metal, even gold. If a man or woman encountered a nymph they could become possessed, made frenzied, be taken over (nympholeptos), driven mad with desire (nymphomaniac). In lycanthropic Arcadia, after Lycaon had insulted Zeus and was transformed into a wolf for his crime, a victim was selected at an annual sacrifice to change into a wolf for nine years: 'The rite begins at a certain pool, where he must leave all his clothes on an oak tree, and swim away naked, atque abire in deserta transfigurarique in lupum – then disappear into the wilderness and be transformed into a wolf.' After nine years he swims back across the same pool, and resumes his former life.

They analysed the colours of their springs, the bluest of water at Thermopylae, the blackness of those at Astyra in Asia Minor, caused by the disgrace of their

being awarded them by the Persians in return for a
Lydian who was formally begging for mercy; the white
waters of Grecian Italy, whose immediate effect, if you
went in, was cold and you shivered, but if you stayed
in, it heated you like the most feverish drug. There
were 'delicious' springs, springs sweeter than milk to
drink, springs so acid that they consumed the pipes they
ran through. They noted that the trees and grasses which
grew around the rivers differed according to the quality
of the water – that on the banks of the Maiander sprouted
huge tamarisks, on those of the Nile the avocado, that
while poplars grew beside the Acheron, wild olives on the
Alpheios.

They were fascinated by the strange paradoxes of
water, that the well in the Erechtheion on the Akropolis
contained sea-water, and when the wind blew south it
emitted the sound of waves. Fresh water was dramatic,
a swift visitor, often subterranean in its entrances and
exits, even submarine. The extraordinary freshwater
spring still by the edge of the sea in the harbour of
Syracuse, described by Cicero as 'incredibili magnitudine,
plenissimus piscium' – of vast size and teeming with fish –
was according to legend caused by Arethusa's flight from
the clutches of the river Alpheios, who pursued her from
Greece through the Adriatic and finally united his waters
with hers in Sicily. In a passage from the *Metamorphoses*
redolent with the Latin love of swimming, the Greek
feeling for the charm of water, Ovid retold the tale of
how this beautiful nymph, worn out by her exertions in
hunting, first succumbed to the waters of the river-god:
'I came to a stream that flowed silently and smoothly, so
clear that I could see right to the bottom, and count every

pebble in its depths. You would scarcely have thought that it was moving at all. Silver willows and poplars, drawing nourishment from the water, spread natural shade over its sloping banks. I went up and dipped my feet in the stream, and then my legs, up to the knees. Not content with that, I unfastened my girdle, hung my soft garments on a drooping willow, and plunged naked into the waters. As I swam with a thousand twists and turns striking the water and drawing it towards me, threshing my arms about, I felt a kind of murmuring in the midst of the pool and, growing frightened, leapt onto the nearer bank . . . ' The Greeks were attracted to those freshwater springs that welled up from the depths and domed with their fountains the surface of the sea. They rowed out to them to take baths in their crystal water. Some islanders took the greater part of their drinking water from the sea, and placed a lead funnel over the spring from which the water mounted through a leather hose to the surface.

Greek civilisation seemed to revolve around water. The great battles with the Persians were fought near famous springs. When Lysander, the Spartan commander, was killed below the walls of Haliartus, the historian can not help interrupting his narrative in adding that he was positioned 'near the spring called Cissusa, where the infant Dionysus, according to legend, was washed by his nurses after his birth; at any rate the water has something of the colour and sparkle of wine, and is clean and very sweet to drink'. Significant events in their lives, as well as history, were associated with water. Like the oracles, the Eleusinian mysteries took place in an area of abundant natural springs. It was common for Olympic champions to be buried near frontier rivers, as was Koroibos, the Elean who won the first race in the Olympic Games. The Games themselves were held by famous springs or rivers, whose waters flowed round the courses and among the spectators. For the lyric poet Pindar the grace of athletic movement seemed like pure water running over sand. In the middle of summer, when Greek rivers are reduced to a trickle, the Alpheios continues to flow down in a torrent from the mountains into the plain of Olympia, and provides the most wonderful of bathes. It is surrounded by plane trees, like most of the spring waters in Greece, and it was under some 'spreading and lofty' plane trees that Socrates conducted his discourse on the nature of love and beauty in the *Phaedrus*, by a spring 'most lovely' that flowed under them, whose water was 'very cool, to judge by my foot, and the figurines and statues seem to designate it as a sacred place of some nymphs and of Achelous'. This once sacred stream of Ilissus now flows underground through the drains of Athens, and eventually trickles into the Kephisos before reaching the sea in a marsh which provided Byron with the woodcock he ate for lunch. 200 years ago Athens was still watered by fourteen public fountains supplied by the ancient aqueducts. Modern archaeology has unearthed only a few trickles on the sites of the ancient public springs.

When, in a mood of spiritual desolation, Romantics of the nineteenth century were to lament the loss to modern man of that Greek mythopoeic view of the world, that enabled them to humanise the natural scene and feel at home in the universe, it was to the deities of their waters that they turned in despair. It was their absence that they felt most strongly, through them that they expressed their disgust with contemporary life. In such a climate Wordsworth could not hope to hear 'old Triton blow his wreathed horn', nor Matthew Arnold 'the Dorian water's gush divine'. Edgar Allan Poe lamented that Science had 'torn the Naiad from her flood', and it was Helen's 'Naiad airs' that brought him 'home to the Glory that was Greece, and the Grandeur that was Rome'. Leopardi looked back to the times when 'the streams were once a home for the white nymphs, their shelter and their glass the liquid springs'. In 'La Bievre' Huysmans contemplates the contamination of a little river, polluted by industry, and describes the torture of the river nymph. 'Fragments du Narcisse' expressed Valéry's longing for beauty enshrined in the 'vertiginous peace' of waters – 'sans vous, belles fontaines,/ Ma beauté, ma douleur, me seraient incertaines. . . . '

While living in France, Hölderlin, who longed to restore the gods of Greece to a barren world, was observed by a young girl walking every day through her father's estate, entranced by the ornamental ponds that were surrounded by twenty-four statues of the classical deities. To each one of them in turn he paid abject homage. 'The water should be as clean as the water of Kephisos or the spring of Erechtheus on the Akropolis,' he was overheard murmuring. Contemplation of a calm sea, and the tasting of purest water, were the two images by which Winckelmann had tried to express the idea of beauty which he called Greek. Richard Jefferies describes somewhere a secluded spring to which he often walked in order to drink 'the pure water, lifting it in the hollow of my hand. Drinking the lucid water, clear as light itself in solution, I absorbed the beauty and purity of it. I drank the thought of the element. There was almost something sacred to me in the limpid water. Like this the maidens of Ancient Greece sang to the stream when they filled their urns. Even Socrates the wisest sat pondering in reverence by the stream.'

From the Greeks the Romans inherited their passion for water. The Latin poets continued to express what the Greeks had felt. 'The Romans called it acqua felice,' whispers a girl in one of Fellini's films as she listens to the sound of water murmuring through some pagan grotto, and in another a reincarnation of Aphrodite or Venus reaches up to fondle the ancient waters of the Virgo aqueduct that pour from the Fontana di Trevi. It is the felicity of their adjectives that they applied to water that lingers in the imagination, the 'lymphae loquaces' – chattering streams – of Horace's Bandusian spring, those 'amatrices aquae' – amorous waters – that have haunted English writing from Marlowe's Leander, entwined by Neptune in liquid form as he swam, to the *Rock Pool* of Cyril Connolly that describes the seduction of a 'young man flying from the Hercules of modern civilisation, bending over the glassy pool of the Hamadryads, and being dragged to the bottom'. Connolly's Palinurus drowned in Virgil's 'dark' and 'forgetful' waters. No other literature celebrates with such obvious pleasure the magic of cool water at noonday in an arid landscape. When Walter Pater in his essay on Giorgione draws attention to the presence of water in his paintings – 'the well, or marble-rimmed pool, the drawing or pouring of water, as the woman pours it from a pitcher with her jewelled hand, listening perhaps to the cool sound as it falls, blent with the music of the pipes' – he has in mind, as did the painter, the classical pastoral tradition as expressed in the Georgics, Virgil's shepherds among the flocks playing their pipes by the 'liquidi fontes et stagna virentia musco, et tenuis fugiens per gramina rivus' – the clear springs and moss-green pools, the shallow stream stealing through the meadows.

The element that to the Greeks seemed so mysterious and fugitive, the Romans attempted to regulate and control. They perfected the umbrella. Their hours were marked by the drip of water clocks, *horologia ex aqua*, which became in time sought-after status symbols, so ingenious and elaborate that automatic floats struck the hour by tossing eggs or pebbles into the air. Byron alludes to Roman water 'imprisoned' in marble, and they enshrined water in fountains and swimming pools made of glacial marble and other forms of stone quarried from all corners of the Empire, the purple-streaked Phrygian, the yellow Libyan, the green-speckled Laconian, and from Gythion, stones shaped like river-pebbles. The Greeks had built only one pool, in Olympia, and their swimming, except for the Spartans in the Eurotas, was mostly mythical or ritual. 'Three things reveal the magnificence of Rome,' records a historian from Halicarnassus, 'the aqueducts, the roads, and the sewers.' Long, arcaded aqueducts conveyed over 200 million gallons of water a day into the city of Rome. Their overflow was discharged into the sewers, subterranean canals into which the courses of seven rivers had been diverted, so vast that barges were able to pass through them beneath the streets and buildings. Even the public lavatories, where according to Carcopino men conversed and exchanged invitations to dinner, were full of water that flowed continuously in little channels around the marble seats, which were enclosed in alcoves sculptured in the form of dolphins. The rooms were filled with the noise of trickling fountains and water that gurgled out of the walls.

In *De Aquis*, Sextus Julius Frontinus, the greatest constructor of aqueducts, described with pride how for 441 years from the foundation of the city the Romans were satisfied with such waters as were withdrawn from the Tiber. Now, however, nine aqueducts conveyed water from distant parts of the Alban hills, several of them favourite bathing places. The tract is full of interesting details: the lengths of the aqueducts, the quality of the various sources of supply, an account of devious plundering of the Julia aqueduct by means of branch pipes and how these pipes were detected and destroyed. With a practicality carried possibly to excess he supplies us with information about the cost of upkeep, the builders, dates, sources, lengths and elevations of the aqueducts, the size of the supply, the number of reservoirs. Particular attention is paid to ajutages, the nozzles which assisted in the calculation of delivery. He mentions ajutages that did not fit properly and others without an official stamp. He realises that precise calculation is difficult, but adds drily: 'when less is found in the delivery ajutages and more in the receiving ajutages, then it is obvious that there is not error, but fraud'. His survey concludes with a typical touch of Roman arrogance: 'With such an array of indispensable structures carrying so many waters compare, if you will, the idle pyramids or the useless though famous works of the Greeks.'

One of Frontinus's closest friends was Pliny the

younger, at the end of whose garden with its exquisite swimming pool was a curved dining-seat of white marble, shaded by a vine. Here he would entertain on summer evenings, while from under the seat 'water gushes out through pipes as if pressed out by the weight of people sitting there, is caught in a stone cistern, and then held in a polished marble basin which is regulated by a hidden device so as to remain full without overflowing. The main dishes for dinner are placed on the edge of the basin, while the lighter ones float about in vessels shaped like birds or little boats. Here and there are marble chairs. By every chair is a tiny fountain, and throughout the grounds can be heard the sound of running streams, the flow of which can be controlled by hand to water one part of the garden or another.'

Like his friend Frontinus, practical problems of water supply and drainage always fascinated Pliny. As an administrator in Bithynia he noted that Prusa was badly in need of some public baths, that Nicomedia had squandered money on two useless attempts at building an aqueduct. He created water supplies, covered open sewers, improved communications by cutting canals from lakes to the sea. At Rome he was made responsible for maintaining the sewers and the banks of the Tiber. As with many Romans of his time, anything to do with water seemed to fascinate Pliny. Like the Greeks, he was intrigued by its curiosities. He visited Lake Vadimon, the Lago di Bassano, 'perfectly round and regular in shape, like a wheel lying on its side', devoid of boats as its sulphurous waters, 'pale blue with a tinge of green', were sacred, but full of floating islands that in high winds appeared to be racing each other across the surface. He is amazed by the intermittent spring of his birthplace in Comum, whose depth rises and falls at regular intervals throughout the day. He tries to analyse the cause. Is it due to some hidden valve, some current of air that opens and closes the outlets of the spring? Is its ebb and flow, like the sea, subject to the mysterious influence of some tide?

Most marvellous of all was the Clitumnus spring, that emerges like a miracle from out of the flat plain near Assisi and forms a chain of transparent pools, their surface broken intermittently by expiring bubbles that rise up from the gravel and sand on the bottom. On its banks once stood a temple to the river-god and shrines of other deities, and 'ash trees and poplars, whose green reflections can be counted in the clear stream as if they were planted there'. Now the temple and shrines, painted by various English water-colourists of the last century, have gone. Most of the trees have been removed, and the wild grass is neatly trimmed. The site has been acquired by an adjoining cafe and, like Horace's Bandusian spring, enclosed within wire fencing. Concrete paths direct you down to the source, which is surrounded by benches. Where in Pliny's time the stream flowed out of the pools and became a river, it was crossed by a bridge. Bathing was allowed below the bridge, but not above as it was considered sacred water. Although the bridge is no longer there, it was at about this point that I risked prosecution in swimming a few pathetic yards over shallow water, after changing furtively beneath an overhanging willow tree. Before breakfast the following morning, as the sun was rising over the Alps to the north-east, I swam from the hotel

terrace across the black water of Como to the supposed
site of another of Pliny's villas that once stood on the
edge of the lake, at the point where the waves break and
'you can fish, not merely from your bedroom window,
but even, if you wished, from your bed, as if you were
in a boat'.

The fanciful and ingenious use of water by the
Romans, so evident in Pliny's garden, was an outstanding
feature of their arenas and aquaria. The amphitheatres
were designed in such a way that the arena could be
cleared and flooded with water to form a lake, where
naval battles were re-enacted by gladiators or prisoners
condemned to death. The Romans watched exhibitions
of polar bears chasing seals, and Egyptians swimming
among crocodiles and drawing them up by nets on to
platforms. Nero filled the arena with strange and monstrous fish. Fish ponds and aquaria became fashionable in
Roman society. Treatises were devoted to their manage-
ment. Ponds became as decorative as swimming pools,
and the Roman word 'piscina' meant either a fish pond
or a swimming pool. One of the aqueducts supplied the
fish markets of Rome with fresh water, while water for
sea-water fish was conveyed up through pipes from
Ostia. Fish were pampered and often cherished more
than human beings. We hear of Romans weeping over
the deaths of their favourite fish, of slaves who had broken plates thrown into ponds to feed the lampreys. They
became an expensive commodity. Some fish might cost
more than a cow. Pike caught in the Tiber at the point
where the *cloaca maxima*, the main drain, evacuated its
contents into the river were a particular luxury, as were
lampreys fattened on human flesh. They tamed the

dangerous moray, the Muraena, named after Licinius Muraena, the noted ichthyologist and epicure. Some answered their master's call and were decorated with gold rings passed through their gills. Speculators sank large amounts of capital into excavating and constructing complicated pools by the sea, some with rock bottoms and some with sand, that required a fresh supply of sea-water with every tide. In the Lucrine Lake near Naples oyster beds were developed successfully by the wealthy C. Sergius Orata, the inventor of the shower-bath. By his seaside villa at Sperlonga, Tiberius adapted a cave in the hillside into an elaborate series of ponds fed by freshwater springs, around which were fitted marble seats from where spectators could satisfy their passion for fish, and at the same time calculate the growth of their investments.

As with bread and circuses, most emperors felt obliged to make their contribution to this mania for water, especially the two most sympathetic with the Greeks. Water supplies for private houses were constructed under Nero's orders, numerous fountains, and by his Golden House an enormous lake that according to Suetonius was more like a sea than a lake, which after his suicide became the site for the Colosseum. Hadrian united the Empire with a web of waterways whose spiritual centre was the aquatic shrine he built for his favourite Antinous who had drowned in mysterious circumstances in the Nile. Here among the hills of Tivoli the electric presence of water could be felt and heard everywhere, as it passed from canals, cascades, and pools, then sprang up through fountains into courtyards and dripped from the walls of grottos. Hadrian's Tivoli was to be the inspiration for those great water-gardens of the Renaissance. Beyond the long colonnaded swimming pool, his secluded island rotunda, and the multiple baths, Hadrian established the shrine devoted to the memory of the 'inscrutable Bithynian', whose rounded sides were obscured by a veil of water that spread over marble steps and declined gradually from basin to fountain, till it fell into a blue rectangular pool surrounded by porticos and statues of athletes and warriors.

This voluptuous enjoyment of water, the preoccupation with bathing and luxuriously ornamented baths came to be regarded by certain Romans as a Hellenistic infection. Nero's Baths were criticised for their Greekness. The Romans felt they had been contaminated by the Greek spirit rather than their example, as the fountains of the Greeks were modest and their one pool at Olympia was considered by many a sign of weakness at the time. Athletes had formerly used the river to wash off dirt and sweat. Plato thought the pool fit only for the old and feeble, and Aristophanes complained that young men were deserting the running tracks in its favour. In earlier, simpler and better times the Romans too had been content to bathe rarely. The baths had been small and squalid, dark and windowless. Moralists now began to associate cleanliness with decadence.

According to Tacitus the Baths, parties and elaborate dinners represented the corruption of Roman life. It was the sign of an undisciplined unit in Gaul that at midday its officers were all in the Baths. The moralists poured scorn on empresses who bathed in milk, and extravagant bathers like the emperor Gordian I, who bathed four or five times a day in summer, twice a day in winter. Seneca condemned the aristocrats of his day who competed with each other over the elaboration of their pools, and felt themselves overshadowed if their swimming pools were not lined with Thasian marble. He on the other hand declared himself a 'cold water enthusiast', who swam in the Tiber or in a tank 'warmed only by the sun', and celebrated the birth of a new year with a plunge into the Virgo aqueduct.

The moralists considered as grossly affected those artificial grottos created in the gardens of the wealthy, in imitation of the atmosphere of the old Greek springs, where water trickled down mossy, shell-encrusted walls and offered a retreat from society, perhaps even a source of poetic inspiration. Rather than the simple fountain houses of the Greeks, the Romans constructed elaborate hydraulic installations, monumental public fountains with façades and porticos, the greatest of which was the Aqua Julia, a grand triumphal arch with statuary and fountains that cascaded into basins and channels to distribute its waters to distant corners of Rome. In Greece itself a Roman millionaire embellished Corinth with a magnificent array of swimming pools, while another built an ornate complex of fountains in Olympia, beside the gymnasium, although it had always been watered by a sufficient and intricate system of drains and channels.

Juvenal measured the decline of Rome by the state of one of its fountains. In one of his Satires an old man, reduced to poverty and distressed by the condition of the city, decides to leave Rome to spend his last years in the countryside. Juvenal walks with him as far as the gate in a final farewell. Outside the city walls the two friends turn off the Appian Way into a little field – Egeria's Glen – to talk in peace. Once it was a sacred spot, charming and enchanted, where the ancestral priest-king Numa met his lover, the goddess Egeria. Now, relates Juvenal, the little grove has been rented out to a settlement of gypsies, and the cave of the nymph, a deep romantic chasm shaded by a cedar tree, has been disfigured by lavish decoration. The grass and simple stone have been overlaid by marble, and the spring waters enclosed in a marble basin. It might look more decorative, but the native and numinous qualities of the place have been suffocated. The divinity of its spirit had disappeared, and in describing the artifice and extravagance of what had taken its place, the leasing of its sacred waters to rapacious foreigners, Juvenal proffers some clues to the causes of Rome's decline.

After Rome's fall water gradually lost its allure. Instead of something 'clear, light, of high value, desirable', its effects came to be regarded as detrimental to health, its influence devilish rather than divine. It began to be thought of as a breeding ground for rats, a source of plague and disease. The breaststroke evolved as it kept the body flat on the surface, and the long sweeping motions of the hands prevented anything obnoxious from entering the mouth. A few centuries after the Roman occupation an Anglo-Saxon poet lamented the desolation of the abandoned city of Bath, and looked back with longing to the stately palaces and the splendid baths where 'stood the courts of stone, with a gushing spring of boiling water in welling floods, and a wall enclosed in gleaming embrace the spot where the hot baths burst into air'. With the coming of Christianity the West began to lose its interest in the sea and the tradition that had spread gradually from Greece and the Aegean. All along the Mediterranean coast villages that had once looked on the sea turned their energies inland. A maritime civilisation turned into one devoted to land, and Islam took possession of the Mediterranean. Of the 400 steam baths built by the Moors among the fountains of Granada only one survived the first hundred years of Christianity.

The church filled the sea with fantastic and imaginary monsters. For Pliny the mermaid had been exciting proof of nature's wonderful diversity, and two captured by Alexander, 'as white as snow, their hair came down to their feet round their body, and they were taller than humans have custom to be', died sadly after being brought to the surface. But now the mermaid siren, whose song appeared to Plato as an irresistible celestial harmony, the music of the spheres, came to embody for the mediaeval church the lure of fleshly pleasures to be feared and avoided by the godly, so that even today the bathers of Naples can be observed crossing themselves before plunging into the water, in order to 'paralyse those malevolent genii of the deep'.

The status of the swimmer gradually declined. No longer was he a hero, capable like the Nordic Beowulf of exploits beyond human capability. Now he needed supernatural intervention to survive. Various miracles depicted men at the mercy of the sea or rivers, powerless to save themselves until they appealed to Christ for assistance. In religious fables the fate of the 'ungodly' was compared to that of the swimmer, adrift in the vastness of the sea, denied the means of reaching safety, and finally overcome by despair.

The clash between the Christian church and swimming first occurred quite early on when a Syrian religious cult known as 'Maiouma' (from *mai*, the Semitic word for water) became popular throughout most of the Roman world in the declining years of the Empire. It involved performances by naked women in round open-air pools, before large audiences in marble seats that rose up from the pool in the form of a Greek theatre. Their strange erotic tableaux were condemned by the clerics, as were the spectators 'drowned in an abyss of sin'. Swimming, like sexual pleasure, came to be associated somehow with the devil, and was almost suppressed during the domination of Europe by Christianity. It was not until the beginning of the nineteenth century that its popularity revived.

III

The Eton Style

Appassionato per l'acqua . . .

If there were the sound of water only
Not the cicada
And dry grass singing
But sound of water over a rock . . .

T.S. Eliot, *The Waste Land*

FOR CENTURIES INSTANCES of swimming in England are rare and sporadic. Almost no one swam in the sea. A few in rivers. If there were exceptions, they tended to be aristocratic. Only those able to rise above popular superstition felt free to enter the water. Those who did were considered eccentric.

It was thought typical of Edward II's erratic and foppish behaviour that he should frolic in the water. One winter he took a holiday in the Fens 'to refresh himself with the solace of many waters' and nearly drowned while rowing about on the lakes. He then 'set off at all speed, he and his silly band of swimmers, for the parliament which he had ridiculously caused to be summoned at Lincoln'. Various Elizabethan courtiers were 'strong swimmers', like Sir Philip Sidney, or were said to possess 'perfection in this faculty'. Two so-called 'gentlemen' swam through the Armada at night and punctured holes in the sides of the Spanish ships.

An over-indulgence in swimming caused the death of the Prince of Wales in 1612. 'He retired to his house at Richmond, pleasantly seated by the Thames river, which invited him to learn to swim in the evenings after a full stomach.' In 1689 mention is made for the first time of Parson's Pleasure, the naked-bathing place on the river Cherwell at Oxford, and the first treatise on swimming was written, appropriately in Latin, by the Elizabethan scholar Everard Digby, because for many years youths 'of good birth' had been drowned in the waters of the Cam. Bystanders were amused when in 1726 the American Benjamin Franklin stripped and plunged into the Thames. He swam from Chelsea to Blackfriars, 'performing on the way many feats of activity both on and under the water', and was 'much flattered by the admiration of the company'. He taught many aristocratic Englishmen to swim, including the sons of Sir William Wyndham before they set out for their European travels, and came across such widespread ignorance on the subject that he considered staying on in England to make his fortune by establishing a swimming school.

European travel and interest in the classical world were revived by the rediscovery of Pompeii in the middle of the eighteenth century. Young aristocrats embarked on their tours, and the Dilettanti Society encouraged archaeologists to range over the Mediterranean coastline in search of remains. We hear of one being 'classically' drowned off Cape Mycale. The excavations at Pompeii revealed to a desiccated world the ruins of massive swimming baths and fountains, and traces of the old marble watercourses that extended the lengths of the gardens. Like the spring of Arethusa classical waters were restored again to the surface after prolonged submergence. Once more their influence could be felt. 'No man is now accounted a traveller', declared the *Quarterly Review*, 'who has not bathed in the Eurotas.'

With the guidance of classical writers, enthusiasts took to tracing the routes of ancient rivers and springs. Sent out to explore Greece and classical Asia Minor by the Dilettanti Society in the 1760s, Richard Chandler became fascinated by the stream of the Ilissus, into whose sacred waters Socrates and his disciple Phaedrus had dipped their naked feet as they talked. Now he would find it reduced to a sewer, but even then he was disappointed that it was little more than a trickle limping through a wilderness devoid of the fabled plane trees. The marble facing and statues, which had once preserved the sanctity of the spring, were gone. The altar of the Muses was now a church. The water was so unwholesome that the 'cattle would scarcely drink of it'. During his residence in Athens he returned to the bed of the Ilissus several times, after snow or heavy rain, hoping to see it full to the brim and 'rushing along with majestic violence; but I never found even the surface covered, the water lodging in the rocky cavities and trickling from one to another'. Chandler's descriptions are full of such elegiac sense of distinction between the present and past. He followed the course of a river in Ionia described by Pausanias, that behaved like the Alpheios in that it arose on Mount Mycale, crossed the sea and came up again beside the harbour called Panormus. He found the port of Panormus 'overrun with thickets of myrtle, mastic and evergreens', but with growing excitement he traced the spring to the gulf, 'which it enters at the head, after a very short course, full and slow'.

The sensitivity to water in any form conveyed by Pausanias in his descriptions of the history and geography of the Greek mainland during the brief golden age of the Roman Empire under Hadrian, influenced a succession of travellers over the next century. Sir James Frazer, whose *Golden Bough* begins with an evocation of the woodland lake of Nemi in the Alban hills as its savage rites became central to his theories, composed a memorable edition of the Greek author. Under his inspiration Frazer went to listen to a spring in Lilaia that according to Pausanias 'usually around midday' made a noise as it arose out of the earth 'like a bull bellowing'. Frazer only detected a gentle mumble – 'it is true I heard a rushing roaring sound, but it was only the sough of the wind in the willows'. He walked along the bank of the Ladon, whose waters were hailed by Pausanias as the finest of any river in Greece, and for beauty 'there is no foreign river and no Greek river like it'. He fails to find the sanctuary of Demeter, and muses as he walks on Milton's line 'by sandy Ladon's lilied banks'. He saw plenty of sand, but no lilies. These classical sources held for Frazer a mysterious significance. His life-work was an attempt to throw light upon the origins of feelings 'whose springs were previously unknown and therefore uncontrollable.'

The trickle of the Ilissus also saddens Morritt, the dilettanti owner of Rokeby Hall who wandered around the Eastern Mediterranean during the Napoleonic wars. Disappointing too are Maeander's 'amber waves' that are now 'muddier than any hosepond'. The hot springs of Thermopylae though 'gush out at every step', and the Alpheios still runs in a 'deep narrow bed, hemmed in by two romantic rocks'. Travelling to Troy, he traces the courses of Homer's great rivers, and finds the Simois marshy and covered with reeds and osiers, but the Scamander, that rises out of a grove of beautiful trees, is still 'everywhere clear, a quality Homer notices in a thousand places'. Not far away on the Hellespont he comes across an ancient bath which 'seen through the trees seemed as picturesque a ruin as I could imagine. Nearly all the marble sarcophagi had long been taken away to adorn fountains for the Turks or serve as cannon-ball at the Dardanelles'.

In Italy, Byron paid tribute to the waters of Pliny's miraculous Clitumnus as the 'sweetest wave of the most living crystal that was e'er the haunt of river nymph', and on reaching Rome was deeply affected by the Egerian fountain, whose embellishment had so distressed his favourite classical poet. He was reassured to find that its extravagant decoration had disappeared, and the delicate waters no longer 'slept, prisoned in marble', but bubbled 'from the base of the cleft statue'. The Etonian Henry Matthews, brother of Byron's greatest friend who drowned in the Cam, on paying homage to the site at about the same time when 'an invalid in search of health', was also heartened to find that 'time has at last realised Juvenal's wish' in the fountain restored to its original simplicity, bordered again by wild grass, a 'viridi margine'. The only marble he found that still profaned the native stone was a headless statue, not of Egeria but a male deity, the god of the stream which flowed from the spring. It is still there in its niche, though now the spring, by the Egeria Soda factory, is largely neglected, and in the absence of signposts the only guide to its whereabouts when one walks down to the river through the poppy fields is the distant sound of its chilly water as it swirls around the one channel that still survives.

While travelling south from Rome towards Naples another of Byron's friends, the beautiful Countess of Blessington, stopped off at Cicero's old villa by the sea, near where he was murdered when attempting to escape from his litter. At the bottom of an orange grove she found 'some ruins, bathed by the sea, which were pointed out as part of his villa: they probably were the baths, and never were there more pellucid ones, as I can verify; for, tempted by their seclusion and the purity of the water, I bathed therein early this morning, and felt myself invigorated by the briny element'.

It was the spectacular Baths of Caracalla that fired the imagination of Shelley. Here he chose to write his *Prometheus Unbound*, celebrating the release of the Greek spirit, 'perched upon its mountainous ruins, among the flowery glades, and the thickets of odoriferous blooming trees, which are extended in ever winding labyrinths upon its immense platforms and dizzy arches suspended in the air'. Although by Shelley's time the interior was almost in ruins, the Baths were still supported by massive surrounding walls, archways and vaulting. These were now covered by plants and trees, which softened the Piranesi-like spectacle with their overhanging gardens: 'Never was any desolation more sublime and lovely. The perpendicular wall of ruin is cloven into steep ravines filled with showering shrubs whose thick twisted roots are knotted in the rifts of the stones. At every stop the aerial pinnacles of shattered stone group into new combination of effect, and tower above the lofty yet level walls, as the distant mountains change their aspect to one rapidly travelling along the plain.'

In his excitement Shelley climbed an antique winding staircase and emerged high up on the walls, where he found spread out before him a fantastic pastoral landscape: 'Here grow on every side thick entangled wildernesses of myrtle, and the myrtelus and bay and the flowering laurustinus whose white blossoms are just developed, the wild fig and a thousand nameless plants sown by the wandering winds. The woods are intersected on every side by paths, like sheep tracks through the copse wood of steep mountains, which wind to every part of the immense labyrinths . . . '

When Shelley drowned off Viareggio, a volume of Sophocles clutched in one hand, it was the culmination of a love affair with water that influenced him to sink rather than swim. 'Arms at his side he fell submissive through the waves.' It was as though the act of swimming somehow disturbed and diluted his 'fornication avec l'onde'. Throughout his life he would plunge his head several times a day into a basinful of cold water. He never drank wine, as he found it too exciting for his brain, but almost only water. He once prolonged his stay in Pisa because of the purity of its water, which had been transported from distant hills via an old Roman aqueduct. In Comum he rented the villa in whose courtyard still flowed the intermittent spring that had fascinated Pliny.

As Shelley never learnt to swim, the pleasure he took in water tended to be confined to its surface, at least in his early years. At Eton he had sculled for long distances down the Thames for which he never lost his affection. Even as an adult he remained addicted to the 'classical recreation' of ducks and drakes. The Romans had used tiles, and Shelley would split slaty stones, carving those that were flat and thin into a round shape. When he had collected a sufficient number, he would 'gravely make ducks and drakes with them, counting, with the utmost glee, the number of bounds as they flew along skimming the surface of the pond'. He never lost his passion for launching flotillas of paper boats, freighted with coins and constructed from any correspondence he might have in his pockets, or the flyleaves of books, or even once a £10 note. 'So long as the paper lasted, he remained riveted to the spot, fascinated by this particular amusement.'

His friend Hogg described him as a 'devoted wor-shipper of the water-nymphs; for whenever he found a pool, or even a small puddle, he would loiter near it, and it was no easy task to get him to quit it'. On one of his favourite walks there was a 'pond, formed by the water which had filled an old quarry: whenever he was permitted to shape his course as he would, he proceeded to the edge of this pool, although the scene had no other attractions than a certain wildness and barrenness. Here he would linger until dusk, gazing in silence on the water, repeating verses aloud, or earnestly discussing themes that had no connection with surrounding objects. Sometimes he would raise a stone as large as he could lift, deliberately throw it into the water as far as his strength enabled him; then he would loudly exult at the splash, and would quietly watch the decreasing agitation, until the last faint ring and almost imperceptible ripple disappeared on the still surface.' In London once he talked 'rapturously' of the waterfalls of Wales, and paced round the room gesticulating as he described them, with the intensity of Keats 'rapping' the window pane as he recounted the course of a famous boxing match. To Hogg it seemed that the waterfalls of Wales and Cumberland, the English and Irish lakes, made a far deeper impression on Shelley than the normal spectator – they 'entered his inmost soul, and became integral portions of himself and his existence'.

In Italy his attraction to water intensified. 'Like the Indian palms,' wrote Trelawney, 'Shelley never flourished far from water. When compelled to take up his quarters in a town, he every morning with the instinct that guides the water birds, fled to the nearest lake, river, or sea shore, and only returned to roost at night.' When travelling to Italy for the first time, on his way through France, Shelley persuaded the coach driver to stop while he bathed in a clear running shallow stream that took his fancy. He behaved 'just as if he were Adam in Paradise before his fall'. His wife refused to join him, although he entreated her, as it would be 'most indecent', and there was no towel with which to dry herself. The voluptuous Claire Claremont, though, impulsively stripped and bathed, and one can sense in their attitudes his growing affection for Claire at the expense of his prim and domestic wife, although towards the end of her life she was to bathe daily off Sandgate. Later in the Villa Magni near Lerici, whenever Shelley joined enthusiastically in the ritual sunset swims of the population, when all the men, women and children took to the water 'sporting in it for hours like wild ducks', Mary would look grave and say it was 'improper'.

During the summer in Bagni di Lucca, Shelley would translate Plato's *Symposium* in the morning, then in the middle of the day 'bathe in a pool or fountain, formed in the middle of the forests by a torrent. It is surrounded on all sides by precipitous rocks, and the waterfall of the stream which forms it falls into it on one side with perpetual dashing. Close to it, on the top of the rocks, are alders, and above the great chestnut trees, whose long and pointed leaves pierce the deep blue sky in strong relief. The waters of this pool, which, to venture an unrhythmical paraphrase, is "sixteen feet long and ten feet wide", are as transparent as the air, so that the stones and sand at the bottom seem, as it were, trembling in the light of noonday. It is exceedingly cold also. My custom is to undress and sit on the rocks, reading Herodotus, until the perspiration has subsided, and then to leap from the edge of the rock into this fountain – a practice in the hot weather excessively refreshing. This torrent is composed, as it were, of a succession of pools and waterfalls, up which I sometimes amuse myself by climbing when I bathe, and receiving the spray all over my body whilst I clamber up the moist crags with difficulty.'

It was in this same pool in 1857 that Robert Browning

was to swim every morning at six-thirty, an experience he found so invigorating that he determined to continue it whenever possible for the rest of his life, which he did, mostly in France and off the Atlantic coast. The pale slabs of rock are still in evidence where Shelley lay reading Herodotus, and the cataract he climbed, but the torrent has been reduced to a sluggish flow by a dam and its waters stained a virulent green from the waste products of a paper factory up river and the sewage pipes of the local villages. Swimming is no longer advisable.

In Italy Shelley became intoxicated by the sea. To Trelawney it seemed that the ocean appeared to wash away all his sense of propriety – 'he behaved as if he were a merman or a fish'. He once shocked his wife by entering the dining room in the middle of lunch 'naked as a needle, glistening with salt water, bits of seaweed tangled in his hair'. Another time, bending over the side of the boat in the bay of Baiae, he looked down enraptured through the translucent water to the seabed where he could see 'hollow caverns clothed with the glaucous sea-moss, and the leaves and branches of those delicate weeds that pave the unequal bottom of the water' – in all probability the first realistic description of an underwater scene. Submarine images begin to flood his poetry – 'old palaces and towers/ quivering within the wave's intenser day' – as well as sharks and sea serpents. In Rome the ruins of the Colosseum seemed submerged beneath the sea, its dark caverns the lairs of the 'mightiest monsters of the deep'.

A contemporary noted that water was Shelley's 'fatal' element. Throughout his life he tempted fate on the water. In England he rowed down a river in a washtub until the bottom fell out, and he once descended the Rhine on a leaky raft. When caught in a storm on Lake Geneva with Byron, their boat full of water, he protested with great coolness that he had no notion of being saved, and begged the great swimmer not to trouble him. In a boat off Spezzia he suddenly proposed to his companions that they should 'solve the great riddle' by allowing the skiff they occupied to sink beneath them. There is the well-known occasion when he watched Trelawney bathing one day in a deep pool in the Arno. He astonished Shelley by performing a series of aquatic gymnastics that he had learnt from the natives of the South Seas. On his getting out, while dressing, Shelley said mournfully, 'Why can't I swim? It seems so very easy.' Trelawney answered, 'Because you think you can't. If you determine, you will; take a header off this bank and when you rise, turn on your back, you will float like a duck; but you must reverse the arch of your spine, for it's now bent the wrong way.' Shelley thereupon 'doffed his jacket and trousers, kicked off his shoes and socks, and plunged in; and there he lay stretched out on the bottom like a conger eel, not making the least effort or struggle to save himself. He would have drowned, if I had not instantly fished him out.'

One night not long before he died Shelley dreamt that his friends had drowned, and their lacerated and decaying bodies were coming to warn him of an approaching flood. A naked child rose from the moonlit surf of Lerici. In his final voyage across the gulf of Spezzia, when his boat was caught in heavy seas, an Italian captain was reported to have seen that they could not long contend with such tremendous waves, so bore down upon them and offered to take them on board. A shrill voice, probably Shelley's, was distinctly heard to say 'No'. The waves were running mountains high – a tremendous surf dashed over the boat which to his astonishment was still crowded with sail. 'If you will not come on board, for God's sake reef your sails or you are lost,' cried a sailor through a speaking trumpet. One of the gentlemen was seen to make an effort to lower the sails – his companion seized him by the arm as if in anger. The boat went down about ten miles off the coast under full sail.

Some years later Matthew Arnold was to follow Shelley to the 'soft blue Spezzian bay'. After hiring a boat and being rowed half a mile offshore, he stripped off his clothes and dived into the water. He too was to feel its fatal charm. He found himself reluctant to surface, and the sea so enticing that it was 'difficult ever to bring one's head up out of it'. He had shown early signs of such susceptibility when as a boy he disconcerted his father by spending an entire summer holiday imagining himself a corpse at the bottom of Lake Windermere.

One feels with Shelley that the inspiration behind his swimming was essentially classical – the devotion to water, the reading of Greek texts by Italian streams and waterfalls, his absorption in the myths of Narcissus and Hermaphrodite that suggest the enervating as well as seductive effects of water – and this classical impulse was to become the most characteristic aspect of romantic English swimming.

The first Swimming Society in England, formed by

a group of Old Etonians in 1828, was inspired by the classical example. It was divided into two sections: 'philolutes' (lovers of bathing) and 'psychrolutes' (lovers of cold water). They adopted as their motto the opening line of Pindar's Olympian odes – 'ariston men hudor' – water is best – and their records in the college library reveal the rivers, lakes, and streams of Europe bathed in by various members, with their comments, often classical: the Cam 'at Grantchester passable, elsewhere vile'; the Rhine 'kathara rei' – flows sweetly; Loch Achray 'achraees' – useless. A calendar refers to the birthdays of classical swimmers and later – Ulysses, Leander, Cloelia, Byron, 'the first poet and swimmer of his age, uniting the qualities of Arion with those of the dolphin that carried him', and Nicholas Persée, 'a famous Sicilian diver, who upon the instigation of the King of Naples dived into Homer's Charybdis, and returned safe, but upon repeating the experiment was never heard of again', a feat celebrated in Schiller's 'The Diver'.

Etonians appear to have been methodical swimmers. Sir George Winthrop Young, who traversed the Welsh hills in the middle of the century, lined the walks in blue on his maps, and the bathes he dotted in red. Even aged ninety he would, in all weathers, plunge before breakfast into the Thames from his lawn on the island of Formosa, and he kept a record in a minuscule hand of all his youthful bathes, in home and foreign lakes, rivers and seas.

Before a swimming pool was built after the last war, boys at Eton used the river. Part of the playing fields border the Thames, and Macnaghten, the school historian, records that these reaches of the river are as 'sacred to the Etonian as Tiber, Father Tiber, was to the Roman of another day'. 'Athens' was the point off which it was possible to dive into the river. On its boards, called the 'Akropolis', there was an inscription: 'In memory of one who spent here many of the happiest hours of his boyhood.' In his 'Distant Prospect of Eton College' the old Etonian Gray describes the boys in the Thames who 'foremost now delight to cleave/ With pliant arms thy glassy wave', a scene of naked innocence that was illustrated by William Blake, whose swimmers always seem to enjoy lyrical release from all that is mundane and constricting. There were five bathing places owned by the College on the main river, all legendary names, like Boveney Weir with its waterfall, that recur again and again in Eton memoirs, where the boys swam naked up to the end of the nineteenth century. Their banks were haunted for some years by the louche and brilliant classicist Oscar Browning who, on being dismissed for injudicious behaviour by a brave headmaster, transferred his affections to those of the Serpentine. 'On river banks my love was born,' writes Digby Dolben of a love affair he experienced at Eton, where his enthusiasm for outdoor bathing began that contributed towards the fascination he was to hold for Gerard Manley Hopkins, before he was eventually drowned.

All this Etonian tradition, with its associations of swimming with classical literature, civilised society, innocence, and friendship, was summed up in a passage from the pre-war journal of Cyril Connolly. It was written in Berlin, from where Rupert Brooke had recalled the pool at Grantchester, as Connolly looked back to the summer term at Eton, walking through the fields to

1 *Above:* Annette Kellermann aged 60, in the Yarra River

Following pages:
2 *Left:* 'Acqua Felice' – Anita Ekberg in *La Dolce Vita*, Federico Fellini, 1960
3 *Right: Night Bathers*, 1939, Louise Dahl-Wolfe

4 *Above:* 'Jantzen' poster, Grand Boulevard, Paris, 1930, Lucien Aigner
5 *Right:* Weimar diver, *c.* 1928-30, Kurt Reichert

6 *In the Park at Terni*, 1836, Carl Blechen

7 Weimar bathing scene, *c.* 1928-30, Kurt Reichert

8 Australian bathers, Gallipoli, *c.* 1916
9 *The Water Rats*, Whitby, 1886, Frank Meadow Sutcliffe

the river while trying to recollect an epigram of Rhianus because of its title 'In the Field Path' in Mackail's edition of the *Greek Anthology*: 'There is no greater expression of simplicity, security, and being at home in the world than two friends going down to bathe. Hence the occasion is a fusion of my old trinity, grace, greenness, security, and therefore derived from Eden worship, the first place where two human beings hand in hand took their solitary way. Add the particular Greek element infused into bathing and the Eton summer by the Anthology, the Phaedrus, and the chance of falling in love with boys on the way to Athens that we could not otherwise be seen with and the daydreams of their company that one would have if making the journey without them, and the whole is a perfect blend of warm Hellenic paganism, recollected boyhood, and original sinlessness . . . ' This 'walk through the fields to the bathing places' was on Connolly's list as one of those intense experiences at Eton that were to haunt his later life and root him in permanent adolescence.

In the early days non-swimmers or 'non nants' used to be introduced to the river by taking them out in a boat and throwing them overboard. Someone recollects that there used to be a man stationed at Cuckoo Weir, 'but I never heard that he taught anybody to swim. I never even saw him off the bank. He told us to strike out our arms and legs together, and that was all – imitating both as well as he could, in the air.' There was a superstition that a boy was drowned every three years, which usually held true. After one particularly tragic death swimming classes were instituted, long before anywhere else in England, under the tuition of the drawing master, the noted water-colourist William Evans, and the future Bishop George Augustus Selwyn, later a fighting cleric in New Zealand famous for swimming broad rivers in his efforts to subjugate the Maoris.

Swimming in fact became so organised that a book was published, *The Art of Swimming in the Eton Style*, by the school swimming coach sergeant Leahy, ex-champion of the Red Sea. The Eton style was a particularly leisurely stroke – 'the hands are useless for propelling the body, that office is reserved for the feet alone'. He nevertheless claimed it as the most perfect stroke in the world – 'it is only at Eton college that it is made a science of'. There was also an Eton plunge, which had two peculiarities: 'the diver must enter the water with as little disturbance as an otter leaves its lair, and he must show his head at the surface as soon as the feet have disappeared'. An early ordeal of Meredith's Richard Feverel was the rivalry of Ralph, 'an Eton boy, and hence, being robust, a swimmer and cricketer'. Poor Feverel seldom picked up more than three eggs underwater to Ralph's half-dozen, and was humiliated by him in a river race under the eye of the dashing Lady Blandish, who was always eager to spy on boys stripped for bathing.

This leisured Eton style of swimming was carried to supreme lengths of inactivity by Robert Byron. James Lees-Milne remembers him one summer off Posillipo spending the entire day in the water 'lying on his back, big belly catching the sun, made a ghastly pink for he had a white skin. Every five minutes he would make a backward motion in the water. He had with him a hired boy in a little rowing boat alongside. The boy would, when commanded, ply him with white wine through a tube, and other delicacies.' In his youth his swimming had been rather more impulsive. Motoring down to Athens in a large touring Sunbeam soon after the Great War in the company of two other Etonians, their only relief from the continuous frustrations and delays caused by officious frontier guards and burst tyres seemed to be when they immersed themselves in the Aegean, often beneath the moon, which transformed the black and sluggish water into a 'sea of opalescent silver'. Passing Greeks and a couple of *wanderwogel* Germans who were cadging a lift were amazed, as were all continentals once by the sight of English swimmers – 'Had English lunacy no bounds? We rushed into the sea, waving greetings to the moon and pretending to be Rhine maidens. The Germans saw nothing funny in it.'

At about the same period, just before the War, the great climber Geoffrey Winthrop Young spent a holiday while teaching at Eton riding a horse around Asia Minor. He was to lose in the War a leg, and his brother, who had been a beautiful diver, an arm. They were sons of the 'methodical' Sir George who had marked out his swims in red on the map and plunged off his island home on Formosa when over ninety. The purpose of Geoffrey's tour was to pay homage to the great rivers of Homer. Near Troy he almost splashed across the shallow Simois without noticing it – 'but then I checked my grey, and managed to get all his four legs into the waters at one time, pausing there out of respect'. By moonlight he walked down through fields of flowers and under oaks to the Scamander, 'running broad and hurried under the tropical moon. The great planes drooped over the quick clear water, which reflected on the surface a green and golden mosaic of their leaf. It was just so in summer that the oriental planes on our island home of Formosa in the Thames used to throw their reflections over our green bathing lawns and river. They called me irresistibly to a bathe. I managed to get a running and lucky shallow dive into the snow-chilled eddies. It was a popular turn, a new travellers' trick for the Turks' entertainment, and I had to repeat it several times.' He then walked up to the Scamander's source on Mount Ida, and enjoyed a 'long Olympian' bathe where the river emerges among a grove of oak trees.

Swimming outside England had never appealed to Swinburne. Looking back on his strange career at Eton, he mentions in a letter that his 'only really and wholly delightful recollection of the place and time was of the swimming lessons and play in the Thames'. A mother in his novel *Lesbia Brandon* laments that her dissolute son had never learnt anything at Eton except swimming, and 'that was the end of him'. Swinburne was amazed at Shelley's neglect of swimming there, when his only poem referring to Eton pleasures was a river poem. He would have wagered that Shelley of 'all verse-writing men and Eton boys' would have been the one at least 'to match him in the passion for that pursuit. I suppose', he adds, 'that he took it out afterwards in boating – whereas I never can be on the water without wishing to be in it.' Swinburne felt himself a reproduction of Shelley. Both were imaginative, frail, sensitive, rebellious, wilful, volatile. They were also ardent Hellenists, and shared a melancholy and classical preoccupation with the pain of existence, a death wish that was linked with the sea and the 'water's kiss', the 'moist limbs' of Hermaphroditus that 'melted into Salmacis'. In the cold, dark, unfathomed waters of the lake of Gaube, Swinburne is tempted to dive deeper and prolong the 'rapturous plunge that quickens blood and breath'.

No one, not even Byron, has expressed his enthusiasm for bathing more strongly than Swinburne. One of his earliest and happiest memories was of being held up naked in his father's arms and 'brandished between his hands, then shot like a stone from a sling through the air, shouting and laughing with delight, head foremost into the coming wave'. In 'Triumph of Gloriana' he compared his childhood world in the Isle of Wight to the primordial beauty of Ancient Greece; and in his biography Donald Thomas describes Swinburne as a boy swimming and floating by the hour beyond the lawns and foreshore of his coastal home there, 'lapped in the blue waters and the languid summer tides, as though in the Aegean of his Hellenic dream-world'.

He was soon to lose his taste for placid waters on being introduced to the cold Northern seas off Northumberland near Capheaton Hall, the ancestral home of the Swinburnes. Here he began to exult in rough sea-bathing. He shared his love of cold seas with a cousin, who bathed in the Arctic from the shores of Iceland at the age of seventy. On being sent to Eton he sensed that the marine idyll of his childhood was at an end. He felt like a seagull trapped in an aviary. He was confined to the 'sleepy reaches of the soft waters of the Thames'. When Herbert, the autobiographical hero of *Lesbia Brandon*, sets eyes on the sea off Northumberland for the first time, his face 'trembled and changed, his eyelids tingled, his limbs yearned all over: the colours and savours of the sea seemed to pass in at his eyes and mouth, all his nerves desired the divine touch of it, all his soul saluted it through his senses'. His father feared for his obsession, and on his deathbed 'bade someone keep Herbert from the water'.

Few have felt more painfully the longing to fling out arms and legs in turbulent water: 'I am dying for it – there is no lust or appetite comparable'; 'My craving (ultra Sapphic and plusquam Sadic) lust after the sea'. A Sapphic group in marble sculpted by Pradier, of two girls engaged in the very act, is described in a letter: 'One has her tongue up où vous savez, her head and massive hair buried, *plunging* and *diving* between the other's thighs.' Sophocles' *Antigone* fairly carried him away 'like a wave', while a painting by Hook, of a boat rowed by boys in a stormy sea, made him 'thirsty to be in between the waves'. From his dormitory window at Eton he watched lightning flashing and 'bathed' in the storm before being dragged inside by his housemaster. Watching swallows in drenching rain flying above a lake, he remarked that he had never known that they were so fond of being 'bathed in water pouring straight down from heaven'.

When Matthew Webb battled through rough seas to swim the Channel, Swinburne was electrified and wanted to celebrate the event with a Pindaric ode: 'What a glorious thing is this triumph of Captain Webb, and O what a lyric Pindar would have written on him. If only I could beg, borrow or steal the Theban lyre for half an hour I would try at an ode myself. There never was such a subject of the kind even in Greece itself: it is above all of Olympian, Pythian, Isthmian, or Nemean fame. I consider it as the greatest glory that has befallen England since the publication of Shelley's greatest poem, which ever that may be. Its hero is the only man among strangers to me personally in England that I would go much out of my way to shake hands with if permitted that honour, or, if not, even to see. Jowett himself hurrahed mildly when the news came (I had the pleasure of announcing it) and observed what a supremely great man he would have been in Greece. Man indeed – he would (and should) have been deified on the spot.' In stormy weather Swinburne himself once 'pleaded and swore' for twenty minutes at some 'keepers of the shore', until finally he 'frightened them into giving me entrance of the sea, which they had thought too fierce to be met, and swum through'.

Swinburne's mystical regard for the 'sacred spaces' of the sea, suggested by phrases like 'keepers of the shore' and 'entrance of the sea', and his urgent, compulsive desire to swim, even on winter evenings, are apparent in a letter to his sister from the South coast, written on 11 November: 'Yesterday, after a long walk that took up all the morning, of course I had to get my plunge at 4 p.m. or thereabouts, just before the sun took its plunge behind a great blue-black rampart of cloud. I saw I could only be just in time – and I ran like a boy, tore off my clothes, and hurled myself into the water. And it was but for a few minutes – but I was in Heaven! The whole sea was literally golden as well as green – it was liquid and living sunlight in which one lived and moved and had one's being. And to feel that in deep water is to feel – as long as one is swimming out, if only a minute or two – as if one was in another world of life, and one far more glorious than even Dante ever dreamed of in his paradise. (Poor great man, he only knew the Mediterranean. And I dare say he couldn't swim).' Only dangerous coasts were attractive to Swinburne. The Mediterranean bored him.

The fact that one must be 'swimming out' to experience this ecstasy is significant. Once when on holiday with Powell, another Etonian swimmer and reprobate, in Etretat, on the Normandy coast near Le Havre, to convalesce from his collapse in the British Museum, Swinburne walked down alone to the end of the beach, stripped off his clothes, and let himself be carried out to sea on the outgoing tide. He disappeared through a rocky archway beyond the point and drifted some three miles from shore when he was fortunate to be rescued by some fishermen. A passerby on the clifftop had noticed him floating away, held fast by the undercurrent, and attracted attention to the drowning figure. Swinburne was treated like a hero by the fishermen, and as they returned he recited parts of Victor Hugo's *Toilers of the Sea*, a novel full of fantastic underwater scenes where a giant octopus preys on fishermen between Guernsey and the Normandy coast. The oldest fisherman on the boat said he quite believed that there were such octopuses as could hold a strong man down and suck him to death, and in order to test his theory Swinburne 'put his little finger to the round cup-like tip of one of the suckers of quite a little one, evidently dying – when I pulled it away it hurt so that I looked at the tip of my finger expecting to see it all raw and bloody'.

Swinburne had once been acutely embarrassed at Eton when after one of his regular floggings his 'raw and bloody' body had been exposed when swimming in the Thames to the ridicule of his fellows. He admits somewhere that the pain and intense excitement he derived from flagellation released the excessive tension on his nerves. Throughout his life he suffered from an excess of electric vitality. The constant spasms, the peculiar dancing step, the mop of orange hair that sprouted at right angles from his head suggest a temperamental and excitable nature. The process of swimming in icy, violent waves, like the beatings, reduced the strain on his body and helped to restore his composure. When aged seventeen, inspired by the charge of the Light Brigade at Balaclava, he climbed the dangerous face of Culver Cliff on the Isle of Wight that was reported to be inaccessible, he became frightened after scaling some of the way and was forced to retrace his steps. He then stripped and bathed in the sea at the foot of the cliff, 'to steady and strengthen my nerve, which I knew the sharp chill would, and climbed up again'.

Flogging and swimming became for Swinburne closely associated. Both experiences were more intense at Eton than anywhere else. Perhaps the liquid resonance of the savage rite contributed to his confusion, as the lash of the thick bunch of birch twigs applied to bare buttocks is reported to have sounded 'like the splashings of so many buckets of water'. Once when lodging alone in a schoolhouse on the coast of Cornwall, he overheard a boy being flogged, 'to which my Eton ears were sensitive and sympathetic'. The same evening he rode out to the cliffs in the dark and watched the sea 'caught in a trap in Boscastle inlet, that beat and baffled itself against the steep sides of rock, heaving with rage, swollen'. He climbed down and swam, and the following day at Tintagel is nearly cut off by the incoming tide, so is forced to 'run at it and into the water and up or down over some awfully sharp and shell-encrusted rocks which cut my feet to fragments, had twice to plunge again into the sea, which was filling all the coves and swinging and swelling heavily between the rocks; once fell flat in it, and got so thrashed and kicked that I might have been in Denham's clutches. I found a deep cut which was worse than any ever inflicted by a birch.'

Denham was Herbert's tutor in *Lesbia Brandon*, who flogged Herbert when the boy was caught returning from a forbidden bathe in a dangerous sea: 'he held him down naked on his knee, pinned his legs with his foot, and drew blood from his wet skin, soaked as it was in salt at every pore'. Swimming was particularly attractive when forbidden: 'You have climbed, swam and ridden in places forbidden; you have played truant with Edward to bathe on the Witches Down; so take down your breeches' (from the unpublished *Frederick's Flogging*). Almost everything Swinburne described he had experienced himself, and these flogging scenes after forbidden bathes refer back to a time when Joynes his tutor had beaten him over the fallen trunk of a tree till the grass was stained with blood, when he was still wet from bathing after breaking bounds to swim at Cuckoo Weir on the Thames.

Swinburne took a masochist's delight in being scraped by pebbles, pounded by waves. When he swam, Herbert surrendered his body to the sea: 'Driven onto the shore, he felt the rapid lash and sting of small pebbles. He panted and shouted with pleasure among breakers where he could not stand two minutes the blow of a roller that beat him off his feet and made him laugh and cry out in ecstasy: he rioted in the roaring water like a young sea-beast, sprang at the throat of waves that threw him flat, pressed up against their soft fierce bosoms and fought for their sharp embraces; grappled with them as lover with lover, flung himself upon them with limbs that laboured and yielded deliciously, till the scourging of the surf made him red from the shoulders to the knees, and sent him on shore whipped by the sea into a single blush of the whole skin . . . '

In a letter to Lord Houghton, who had corrupted Swinburne by opening up to him his vast pornographic library, Swinburne remarked that it was a pity the Marquis de Sade had not been aware of the tortures that could be inflicted by the sea: 'I have seen last week an admirable effect of the squalls on the shores of the North Sea. In contemplating the great white and red waves of this stormy sea, and the crenellated rocks which blew out the foam from a thousand mouths and a thousand nostrils of stone, I have found punishments with which to torture a corpse.' For Swinburne water and torture seemed inextricably related, though occasionally water could provide a relief from, rather than a source of, pain. Travelling by train through Scotland along the river Spey as it wound through the fir-woods, the profusion of birch caused him to fantasise about a 'sadic revel, where the most exquisite torture inflicted on the writhing limbs of blushing adolescence would be cured and soothed by the kisses of the Naiads, the maidens of the stream'.

Sometimes in the summer Swinburne would join Jowett and a group of Oxford classicists for holidays in the Highlands. Jowett seems to have overlooked an incident recalled in the memoirs of Mallock, when one evening in Jowett's rooms in Balliol he and Swinburne were left alone after dinner as Jowett had retired to complete some work. Swinburne began to recite poetry, ranging from one poem to another, pacing the room like Shelley and intoxicated with his performance: 'His voice reached a hysterical pitch when he came to Sydney Dobell's lines describing a beautiful girl bathing. He was almost shouting these words, when another sound became audible – that of an opening door, followed by Jowett's voice which intoned in high-pitched syllables – "You'd both of you better go to bed now."'

In the Highlands Swinburne would swim up and down streams that flowed down the sides of the hills. He climbed up the sides of waterfalls and plunged into the pools above: 'the upper pool where we have been bathing regularly for days past is a most lovely basin of sheer rock, safely accessible by descent in one place only; when you jump in at the foot of the fall the impulse of the water is so strong that it sends you spinning right across the pool, and it is all one can possibly do to swim back to the other side, though but two or three strokes off'. No doubt Swinburne could dive as well as jump, as he was observed once by Gosse from an upstairs window in Chelsea emerging drunk from a cab, when he stood poised on the edge, then dived forward on to the pavement, descending upon his two hands.

Swinburne felt himself confined by lakes. He would only swim in lochs that were open to the sea, like Maree and Torridon, 'the latter the divinest combination of lake, mountains, straits, sea-rocks, bays, gulfs, and open sea . . . I had a divine day there and swam right out of one bay round a beautiful headland to the next and round back again under shelves of rock shining double in the sun above water and below. I had a nice fellow for companion, an Oxford man named Harrison.' Swinburne normally swam alone, and in Harrison seems to have found his only sympathetic swimmer. He would write subsequently from 'waterless Malvern' to Harrison when he was staying on the coast – 'I covet your sea, and *must* get a breath and taste of it somewhere this year.' In another letter he wrote sadly from the Isle of Wight that he wished Harrison were swimming alongside in his daily bathes in the sea, where he held imaginary conversations with him while swimming across the bays. He describes to Harrison how one afternoon he was 'violently beaten to and fro between the breakers in a furious reflex which flung me back off shore as with the clutch of a wild beast', while on calm days he swam across 'half-a-dozen various belts of reef, rock, and weedbed with broad interspaces of clear sea, and can observe all the forms and colours changing and passing beneath me, which is one of the supreme delights of the sea'.

Later that month, when still on the island, he wrote to Watts Dunton that he was reading the *Iliad* on the shore and the bracing effect of that and the constant bathing on his spirits had made him look fifteen years younger than he did in London. He added that he derived as much enjoyment from the sea now as he did at thirteen, and one feels that much of the impulse behind Swinburne's swimming was an attempt to recapture the charmed 'golden age' of his childhood before he was banished to Eton at that age.

When, after his health broke down at the age of forty-two, he was taken in hand by Watts Dunton and incarcerated in 2, The Pines, Putney, his enthusiasm for bathing never diminished. He swam daily in the Putney ponds while his young favourite Bertie paddled. Watts Dunton complained he was a limpet, as he would never go anywhere except for sea-bathing. Swinburne had always wanted to live in a lighthouse – 'so long as it was some miles out to sea and difficult to get at'. In order to meet his hero Victor Hugo they visited Guernsey, only to find that he had left the island three years before. Watts Dunton broke his arm in a fall from a slippery path and could only swim with one arm, 'which I find by trying can be done for a little bit, but is not satisfactory in proportion to the fatigue'. Here they enjoyed some 'delicious bathes in the most dangerous seas in the world', though no mention is made of Hugo's octopus, and they particularly relished a bay that is still a romantic place for a bathe, 'walled in with precipices', where a path leads down through the woods to a shingly beach permeated by freshwater streams.

Every autumn they would travel down to the Sussex coast, and at the end of the holiday Swinburne could hardly bear to tear himself away from the sea. From Eastbourne he wrote that he was 'better off from my favourite business of swimming', from Lancing in October that he 'had had a dip every blessed day. While swimming this morning, we could see every pebble and tuft of weed at the bottom of the water, as clearly as if the water had been air.' It was while bathing off the shore of Worthing, in November, that he composed 'A Swimmer's Dream', 'out of pure delight in the sense of the sea', and in December he was to write sadly to his eldest sister: 'I never did pine and weary after a "paradise lost" as I do after this Sussex seaboard – I thought I had outgrown such longings. But I have been yearning after my daily walk – and frequent dip – like a boy parted from his home.'

Swinburne's suicidal swim on the outgoing tide off Etretat had been watched with astonishment by Guy de Maupassant. He embarked on a boat that arrived too late to rescue him, but in gratitude he was invited to lunch where he was fascinated by his host's reptilian features, his thrilling, nervous manner, the monkey that swung from the beams, a flayed hand on the dining table that still bore traces of blood and dried skin.

The erotic, neurotic affinity with water shared by Swinburne and Shelley would have struck a sympathetic chord with the French in particular. The susceptibility of Swinburne to the suckers of octopuses is matched by the descent of Lautréamont's Maldoror into the depths of the sea out of desire for a female shark that was scavenging survivors of a shipwreck – 'his two sinewy thighs clasped tightly about the viscous skin of the monster like two leeches . . . they rolled upon one another towards the depths of the ocean's abyss, joined together in a long, chaste, and hideous coupling'.

Flaubert experienced throughout his life the same compulsion as Shelley and Swinburne to swim, as a child off Trouville and later, when writing in his house on the Seine, twice a day in the river to refresh himself and turn over phrases after the arduous nights devoted to work, 'shouting away like a demon in the silence of his study'. Like them he longed to undergo the metamorphosis of Greek myth, to be literally transformed into water with its 'thousand liquid nipples travelling all over his body'. The young hero of his autobiographical *November* wants to 'stand naked and look at himself mirrored in the streams'. His feminine, dependent, childlike nature yearned to be the 'bank moistened by the river'. Later he lies down near the sea and is tempted to let the waves wash over him – 'the voices of the abyss were calling him, the waves were opening like a tomb ready to close over him and to wrap him in their folds'.

It was on Trouville beach at the age of fourteen that he first became aware of the voluptuous older woman that was to remain his feminine ideal. He observed a woman bathing in the sea every day, tall, dark, with luxurious black hair that fell in tresses over her shoulders. He was troubled by the chance sight of her breast, 'round and full', and wanted to bite it in rage and frustration. The shape of her limbs under the wet bathing-dress fascinated him – he 'envied the waves that encircled her thighs and covered her panting breast with foam'.

The other profound erotic experience of Flaubert's youth was also related to the sea. One summer in Marseilles, when returning to his hotel from a bathe in the Mediterranean, 'bringing with him all the life of that Fountain of Youth', he was invited into the bedroom of a magnificent woman from Peru, who was staying there with two exotic companions – 'he gave her one of those kisses into which one puts all one's soul. The woman came to his room that night and started making love with him straight away. She began by sucking . . . ' He never forgot the pleasures of that night. Years later, when on his way to Tunis to gather material for *Salammbo*, he tried to re-enact the past and returned to bathe off the same beach in Marseilles. He then searched desperately for the room. He found the little hotel had been turned into a toyshop, with a barber's on the first floor. He mounted the stairs, ordered a shave, and from the barber's chair recognised the wallpaper of the bedroom.

For Paul Valéry, as for Shelley, Swinburne and Flaubert, swimming was in his own phrase a 'fornication avec l'onde'. His journal describes bathes in the Mediterranean off Seté, diving into the warm water all day long: 'my sole pastime, my only sport, was the purest of all: swimming. It seems to me that I discover and recognise myself when I return to this universal element. My body becomes the direct instrument of my mind, the author of its ideas. To plunge into water, to move one's whole body, from head to toe, in its wild and graceful beauty; to twist about in its pure depths, this is for me a delight only comparable to love.'

IV

The Byronic Tradition

*'I plume myself on this achievement more than
I could possibly do any kind of glory, political,
poetical, or rhetorical.'*

Byron on swimming the Hellespont

THIS CHAPTER IS BEING written among the shadows of a
rattan-roofed taverna smothered with bougainvillaea, by a
blue pool on top of a cliff that drops down into the waves of
the Aegean, as appropriate a place as any for a description
of Byron. If Shelley was the most pathetic of swimmers,
Byron was generally regarded as pre-eminent in his time.
Somewhere along the shore of the bay of Spezzia where
Shelley drowned there stands a plinth dedicated to 'Lord
Byron, Noted English Swimmer and Poet'. His crossing
of the Hellespont so impressed a physician from Bologna
that he insisted on testing the physical powers of endur-

ance of the 'celebrated aquatic genius'. It was one of the qualities that made him a legend in Europe, and enabled him to distance himself from the literary society he despised, those who were merely 'all-author', 'the would-be wits and can't be gentlemen: I leave them to their daily "tea is ready"/ snug coterie and literary lady'.

During his childhood Byron had swum in Scotland in the Dee and Don rivers, and later at Newstead Abbey in the lake and a cold subterranean pool he had created in a cellar where the monks had once embalmed bodies for burial. In his early poetry there are references to swimming at Harrow, plunging in from the 'green declining shore'. Sometimes he would hire a pony to reach a bathing place about two miles away as he found it too far to walk, but usually he used the 'duck puddle', an oblong pool fed by a brook once described as a 'confined pond of stagnant fluid standing on a bed of deep soft ooze, much frequented by watersnakes'. This was later extended into a lake to form the most delightful open-air pool in England, 500 feet long and a hundred wide, fed by a spring, crossed by a bridge and surrounded by trees and flowers. Like 'Forty Years On', one of the Harrow songs was to celebrate the enduring effect of its charms: 'Ah! long in the sober hereafter,/ Shall linger in ears far away,/ The sound of that innocent laughter,/ The splash of the spray'.

No one before Byron had recorded the thrilling sensation of swimming, of being rolled along on the 'swift whirl of the new breaking wave', plunging down into their 'green and glassy gulfs', when as a boy he 'wantoned' in the breakers. Lame as he was, swimming gave him some of the most exhilarating moments of his life, though he always wore trousers to conceal his disfigurement. Only in swimming could he experience complete freedom of movement, the principle to which he devoted his life. His Achilles tendon was contracted, forcing him to walk on his toes and producing an odd mincing gait. 'I delight in the sea,' he once said to Medwin, 'and come out with a buoyancy of spirits I never feel on any other occasion. If I believed in the transmigration of souls, I should think I had been a merman in some former state of existence.'

Bathing was one of those 'keenly felt pursuits' whose principal attraction was the 'agitation inseparable from their accomplishment', that like gaming and travel satisfied the 'craving void' he so often felt in his life. 'What is the reason that I have been, all my lifetime, more or less ennuyé?' he once asked, and confessed he only found release from the mood through 'violent passions, a dose of salts, and swimming also raises my spirits'. It seemed to act as an immediate antidote to boredom. When the inhabitants of Ithaca enthusiastically proposed that Byron should visit some of their local antiquities, Byron turned 'peevishly' away, muttering to Trelawney: 'Do I look like one of those emasculated fogies? Let's have a swim.' And after a long bathe Byron clambered up some rocks, and fell asleep under the shade of a wild fig tree at the mouth of a cavern.

Byron was extraordinarily proud of his swimming. The Countess of Blessington accused him of boasting about it. When Polidori, his annoying and rather vain companion in Italy, had the temerity to ask Byron in what ways he was inferior to him, Byron loftily replied: 'I think I named four things – that I could swim four miles – write a book, of which four hundred copies should be sold in a day – drink four bottles of wine – and I forget what the fourth was, but it is not worth mentioning . . . ' Like Swinburne he suffered from an excess of nervous energy, and swimming, like his boxing lessons with Mr Jackson, helped to induce that state of 'languid laziness' which he preferred to all others. Water [...] the fascination it did for [...]helley, confine himself to [...]nd champagned till two – then supped, and finished with a kind of regency punch composed of madeira, brandy, and green tea, no real water being admitted therein . . . ' – although on one occasion he quoted Pindar's 'ariston men hudor' – water is best – to indicate that he was temporarily not drinking.

For Byron swimming was primarily a muscular activity. Unlike Shelley and Swinburne, he was not intrigued by what lay below the surface. There are no descriptions in his work of underwater scenes. On his final voyage to Athens he would make himself a 'man forbid, take his station at the railings, and sit for hours in silence', but it was the 'billows' melancholy flow' that held him rather than visions of the submarine. The depths only attracted him if some sinister history was involved. One of the fascinations of the Castle of Chillon was that 'close to the very walls' the lake is 800 feet deep, and here he found far below the water level the signatures of prisoners engraved on the walls of dungeons. Public executions in London had made little impression on him, but he could never remember 'without a shudder' his servant's report of how sixteen beautiful adulteresses had been sewn up in sacks on the orders of the Turkish

Viceroy and thrown at night into Lake Pombotis, to be violated by eels and watersnakes. The complex emotions felt by Byron for this morbid scene were no doubt close to those experienced by Gustave Moreau, when he painted some majestic slave girls writhing in soldiers' arms before being dropped as fodder into a pool of lampreys to create the Roman delicacy, those strange fish with suckers instead of mouths, whose horny gums and rough tongues tear up their victims and in making love devour and disembowel the female. Byron was to exorcise its frisson in poetry. Leila, the lover of the Giaour, is tied in a sack – 'sullen it plunged, and slowly sank'. It was the fate that Gulnare of 'The Corsair' dreaded, and Byron was to prevent a girl he knew from suffering this form of execution off the Piraeus. Like Swinburne he was fascinated by the drowning of Hadrian's Antinous and Sappho's leap to her death in the sea from Leucadia's 'far-projecting rock of woe'. He stared long at the cliff as his boat passed below it on his passage to Greece.

Wherever Byron swam became almost a sacred spot. Engraved in stone above the archway leading to the bay of Portovenere are the words: 'This Grotto was the inspiration of Lord Byron. It records the immortal poet who, as a daring swimmer, defied the waves of the sea from Portovenere to Lerici.' Rose Macaulay paused in her travels at a point in the stream dividing Portugal from Spain where Byron and Hobhouse were once said to have swum, and at Estremoz the Spanish pointed out a pond in a quinta outside the Portalegre gate where Byron had another bathe.

The poet Leigh Hunt's first view of Byron was of him swimming in the Thames, 'rehearsing the part of

Leander, under the auspices of Mr Jackson the prizefighter. I had been bathing, and was standing on the
floating machine adjusting my clothes, when I noticed
a respectable-looking manly person, who was eyeing
something at a distance. This was Mr Jackson waiting for
his pupil. The latter was swimming with somebody for a
wager. I forget what his tutor said of him, but he spoke
in terms of praise. So, contenting myself with seeing his
Lordship's head bob up and down in the water, like
a buoy, I came away.' On one occasion Byron swam
three miles down the Thames from Lambeth through
the Westminster and Blackfriars bridges. He was once
so impressed by a girl who swam well that he proposed
that they should jump together into the Serpentine. He
also enjoyed the Medway in Kent – 'a small river not
above eight feet in depth constitutes my Lavarium here'.
Off the coast of Hastings a year before Waterloo he 'renewed his acquaintance with his old friend the Ocean,
and I find his bosom as pleasant a pillow for an hour
in the morning as his daughter's of Paphos could be in
the twilight'. At Brighton he found himself stranded far
out to sea, swimming against the wind and the outgoing
tide. Crowds gathered on the shore to watch his return,
accompanied by Hobhouse whose futile efforts nearly
drowned him.

In Italy he rode and swam daily from the pine-forested
shores of Ravenna, and in Venice off the Lido, where in
1933 Robert Byron, a quasi-descendant, was to find the
worst bathing in Europe, in water that 'tasted like hot
saliva, and cigar ends floated into one's mouth'. One
evening Lord Byron swam during a storm. His lover
of the time, Margherita the Herculean baker, offered

prayers. As night approached, she remained petrified on the marble steps descending into the Grand Canal, her arms extended towards the sea. When he eventually returned, she upbraided him: 'Was this a time to go to the Lido, dog of the Madonna!' One night he was observed leaving a palace on the Grand Canal, but instead of entering his own gondola he threw himself into the water, dressed as he was, and swam to his lodging. To avoid the oars of the gondoliers he carried a torch in his left hand.

The most famous of his Venetian feats was when he accepted a challenge to a swimming contest from the Cavalier Angelo Mengaldo, a man of similar romantic and egotistical disposition who in Napoleon's retreat from Moscow had swum the Danube and Beresina rivers under Russian gunfire. They were joined by one of Byron's close bachelor friends, Alexander Scott. The race began at the Lido and they swam towards Venice. At the entrance of the Grand Canal Scott and Byron were far ahead of Mengaldo, and that was the last they saw of him. He had climbed into a gondola halfway across the lagoon. They had beaten him 'all to bubbles', as Byron put it. The Englishmen carried on. Scott retired after the Rialto bridge, while Byron continued down the whole length of the Grand Canal, landing at his palace stairs after swimming for three hours and forty-five minutes. Venetians dubbed him the 'English fish'. 'I was in the sea from half past four till a quarter past eight without touching or resting,' he told Hobhouse, adding 'I could not be much fatigued, having had a *piece* in the fore-noon, and taking another in the evening at ten of the clock.' He had recently written to Moore after one of his coastal bathes: 'I am just come out from an hour's swim in the Adriatic, and I write to you with a black-eyed Venetian girl before me, reading Boccaccio.'

Byron's final voyage to assist in the liberation of Greece was delayed by an illness caused by his bathing in the chilly sea off Genoa, which penetrated his ears as he dived for Genoese lira on the bottom through 'clear but deep water'. When originally in Greece he had ridden down daily through the olive groves to the Piraeus in order to swim across the bay, and Lady Hester Stanhope was to catch her first sight of Byron there, diving from the molehead as her brig sailed into the harbour. The Greeks he found swam naked, while the Turks did not.

Swimming was a bond that united Byron with his friends, and acted as a catalyst for his emotional attachments. He swam with the boys who attracted him, across the Piraeus with Nicolo Giraud and in Falmouth harbour with a youth to whom he gave the name L'Abbé Hyacinth. Neither, he complained, was very adept. He was forced to rescue from drowning in the Cam the Trinity choirboy John Edleston, the object of a 'violent, though pure, love and passion'. His last attachment, the young Greek Lukas, could not swim. When on their way to Missolongi the ship ran aground on the Scrofes rocks, Byron got ready to support his body heroically through the waves. Rejected by Lukas just before he died, he was to write some lines in his misery reminding him of the moment when he 'bade' the boy cling to him 'through every shock – This arm would be thy barque or breast thy bier'.

When staying, during holidays from Harrow, with

his greatest friend there, Edward Noel Long, they used to jump from a pier into the strong current of an estuary that carried them far out to sea, forcing them to return in a vast semicircle. Later, when at Cambridge together, they would dive into the Cam's 'not very translucent wave', into water fourteen feet deep, for plates, eggs, and coins they had dropped to the bottom, or cling to tree stumps on the riverbed. 'We were rival swimmers,' Byron was to write sadly after Long was shipwrecked and drowned off Spain in 1809 on his way to fight in the Peninsular War.

Of his three closest friends, the two Etonians and brilliant classical scholars, Charles Matthews and Scrope Davies, were both keen swimmers. One feels with the pedestrian Hobhouse that he was slightly on the edge of the circle, a companion Byron quickly tired of on his travels, because he tended to avoid water if he could. In fact Byron complained that he never even washed. Matthews, who sparred wonderfully but could never win a fight, was rather envious of Byron and Scrope Davies's brilliance in the water. Although he swam well, it was 'with great effort and labour, and too high out of the water'. His friends warned him that he would be in trouble 'if ever he came to a difficult pass in the water'. Their prediction proved correct, as he later became entangled in some weeds while swimming in the Cam and drowned. Scrope Davies on the other hand, a fellow of Kings and avid gambler who eventually had to escape to France to avoid his creditors, once won a bet of 5,000 guineas by swimming from Englehurst, the seat of Lord Cavan on the Southampton river, to the Isle of Wight. Only this morning, in an overseas edition of an English newspaper, there was a brief mention of a swimmer of nineteen who had a 'life-long ambition' to swim from a beach near his home at Stubbington, Hampshire, to the Isle of Wight, and drowned in the attempt.

One evening Scrope Davies and Byron dined at the house of Lord Delvin, then proceeded at midnight to a gambling house, where they lost all their money, and being in 'bad humour' they stripped and plunged into the sea. This proved another instance of swimming's ability to cure Byron's malaises, for after half an hour's swimming they emerged in their dressing gowns to 'discuss' a bottle or two of champagne and hock in their quarters.

Byron only knew the adventurer Trelawny during the final two years of his life. They met in Italy where they soon established a close friendship, and it was in the company of Trelawny that Byron sailed to Greece for the last time. All but Hobhouse of his close friends had either drowned or died destitute. Byron recognised in Trelawny a kindred spirit. They were both rebels with aristocratic forebears, born into a system to which they were temperamentally unfitted, and viewed life in tragic and dramatic terms. They had each experienced dismal marriages in England – Trelawny to a 'weight he could neither endure nor shake off' – and in swimming they found release from the discipline and constriction they loathed. Trelawny had already wrecked a promising career in the Royal Navy by beating up a lieutenant who had made his life a misery. He escaped to the interior of an island in the Indian Ocean, and was granted refuge in a bungalow among lemon trees and jasmine with a pool, where he 'splashed and sang and played a thousand antics, sending the spray into the air in a bright shower'. During his years in the Indian Ocean Trelawny was compared by the admiring natives to a shark, and his exotic wife Zela, clothed always in striped cotton, to the little blue-and-white pilot fish. It was a brief tropical marriage, but while it lasted, before she was supposedly devoured by a real shark, swimming was their 'diurnal habit' and they were almost amphibious.

Trelawny looked and behaved like one of Byron's heroes, and as a result adopted rather a patronising attitude towards him. He remarked on Byron's strange tiptoeing gait 'verging on the ridiculous' and the fact that he could hardly mount a horse without assistance, but he did concede that his 'flexible body, open chest, broad beam and round limbs' were 'built for floating'. He always knew how mortified Byron would feel if beaten, and admitted to often holding back to enable him to win. After losing to Trelawny in a race to a yacht moored three miles offshore, Byron asked him humbly what was the furthest distance he had ever swum. Trelawny, who was prone to self-glorification, replied instantly: 'for five hours in the water off Patagonia. The heave of the sea was in my favour, there was no wind, and the water was calm. The others with me were drowned.'

Trelawny arrived in Italy in time for Shelley's fateful voyage, and had tried to teach him to swim before he drowned. When the body of Shelley's Etonian companion Williams was being prepared for cremation on the shore, his face reduced by fish to a 'livid mass of shapeless flesh', Byron could stand it no longer: 'Are we all to resemble that?' He stripped, flung himself into the sea and swam far out into the bay, followed by Trelawny, to test the force of waves that had over-powered his friends. About a mile from shore Byron was dreadfully sick, but Trelawny could not persuade him to return. After an hour in the water they eventually swam back. Later, during Shelley's cremation, when his corpse fell open, the heart was laid bare and the brains 'visibly seethed, bubbled, and boiled as in a cauldron', Byron again could not face the scene. He swam off to his yacht, anchored almost two miles offshore, and back again, while the combination of sea and sun peeled all the skin off his body 'after going through the process of one large continuous blister'. Once again he had sought relief from moods of gloom and revulsion in swimming, just as after his mother died, rather than attend her funeral he had boxed vigorously with a servant in the Newstead drawing room.

During their voyage to Greece, Byron and Trelawny every day at noon would jump overboard 'in defiance of sharks or weather'. When they paused for some days in Cephalonia, every afternoon they would cross the harbour in a boat and land on a rock to bathe. Even there their rivalry continued. Trelawny wagered that he could swim from the island of Ithaca across to the nearest point of Cephalonia, a distance of about six miles. He persisted in the attempt until late in the evening, when the darkness forced him to climb back into the boat. After their arrival in Greece, where Byron remained in Missolongi and Trelawny travelled overland to link up with the guerrilla fighter Odysseus, they never met again.

Trelawny eventually returned to England, to Putney where he bathed daily, not in the ponds on the common like Swinburne, but in a garden pond attached to the house he rented from Benjamin Leader, the Victorian landscape painter. From there he moved to Usk in Wales with his new wife Augusta, and would swim naked and sit for hours in a lake up to his neck in water reading a book. He finally retired to a cottage in Sompting, within sight of the sea on the Sussex coast, where Swinburne was thrilled to meet him during one of his autumn holidays. In a letter to Harrison in 1872, his swimming companion in the Scottish lochs, Swinburne describes one of his extraordinary experiences in the sea, then continues: 'This talk of swimming reminds me to tell you that before leaving for London I made the acquaintance, and may say, I think, that I gained the friendship of a very famous old veteran of the sea, in that and other capacities, the one Englishman living I was really ambitious and anxious to know.' He was to say the same of Matthew Webb after his Channel swim three years later. Trelawny swam continuously from the Sussex coast up to the day he died. 'I have Shelley's mania for water,' he confessed, 'I should have pitched my tent on the shores of the Mediterranean – the bay of Spezzia would have done. I liked it when it was desolate – now it's as bustling as Leghorn. I pursue my old habits as Indians do: an American, seeing me coming out of the sea, said "Why, that is an Indian."'

It was during a trip to America in 1833 that Trelawny accomplished his most memorable swim, across and back the same ghastly stretch of water below the Niagara Falls that Webb was to swim down to his death in the rapids and whirlpool. His letter, written from the Eagle Hotel, Niagara, describes in dramatic detail the experiences that Webb never lived to relate. It was a hot and cloudless August day when he sauntered along the brink of the rapids, then descended the long spiral staircase that led down to the riverside. He came to a solitary hollow about a mile below the Falls and two miles from the whirlpool. Here the turbulent water had mined the banks, broadened the riverbed, and dark limestone rocks shelved steeply down into the water. On either side of the river the cliffs rose perpendicularly two or three hundred feet, and even at this distance from the Falls he found the waters in midchannel 'still boiling and bubbling and covered with foam, raging along and spreading in all directions. Pieces of timber I threw in spun around in concentric circles. Then turning and twisting against the rocks like crushed serpents, the streams flowed on to the Rapids and formed dangerous whirlpools two miles lower down. Above the Falls this river is a mile broad, where I was now it was less than half a mile, above and below me not more than a quarter, so that flowing through a deep ravine of rocks it was very deep even to its brink, and in the centre they say above a hundred feet.'

Despite the ferocity of the scene, Trelawny 'hastily' cast aside his clothes, 'with nerves throbbing and panting breast, and clambering up to a ledge of rock jutting over a clear deep pool, I sprang in head foremost'. Like all the English champions he used the breaststroke, 'his back bent inwards, his head reined back like a swan's and the chest thrown forward'. He became so confident that he gambolled around in midstream and dashed down the river towards the whirlpool 'to try my strength in those places where the waters are widest. I floated for some

time over the eddying whirls without much difficulty
and then struck through them right across the river.'

After reaching the bank on the far side he realised
how close he now was to the Rapids 'which no boat
nor anything can live in'. Plunging into the river again
he felt cramp affecting his toes and fingers, and his body
drifting rapidly downstream held fast by the current. He
began to panic: 'I now remembered the terrible whirlpool
below me, I could make no progress, the stream was
mastering me. I seemed to be held by the legs and sucked
downwards, the scrumming surf broke over and blinded
me, I began to ship water. In the part of the river I had
now drifted to the water was frightfully agitated, it was
broken and raging all around me. Why did I attempt
to cross a part of the river that none had ever crossed
before? I heard the voices of the dead calling to me, I
actually thought, as my mind grew darker, that they
were tugging at my feet. I saw the waters of the Rapids
below me raging and all about hissing. I thought now
how much I would have given for a spiked nail so fixed
that I could have rested the ball of my toe on it for one
instant and have drawn one gulp of air unimpeded, to
have swallowed the water that was now sticking in my
windpipe.'

He began to feel that Niagara 'as a requiem' was
a fitting end to his 'meteor-like career', as it was to
prove for Webb. He gave up struggling against the
waters that hurled him along, but after a while he
felt the surface becoming smoother. He had been flung
from the vortex and was floating towards the rocks. 'I
heard the boiling commotion of the tremendous Rapids
and saw the spume flying in the air a little below me,

and then I lay stranded, sick and dizzy, everything still seemed whirling round and round and the waters singing in my ears.' What mortified Trelawny was the proof this swim provided of his declining powers, when there was a time when he could have forced his way through 'ten times these impediments'. No longer could he flaunt his 'vaunting crest – my shadow trembling on the black rock as reflected by the last rays of the setting sun shows me as in a glass, that my youth and strength have fled'.

It was not just Byron's friends who shared his mania for swimming. His admirers were also affected. The flamboyant German, Prince Hermann von Pückler-Muskau, was not only Byronic in the externals of his existence, in his raffish extravagance that lost him his family estate, relentless seductions, the frantic pace of his career. He also combined an aristocratic attitude to life with a belief in universal freedom, and was affected by a wanderlust tinged with melancholy and nostalgia for the past and his own youth, and intensified by numerous romantic bathes. The journals of his travels in England and Greece are haunted by Byron's shade. Riding past Newstead Abbey, Pückler-Muskau was to note sadly that the family seat was now much neglected. He discussed Byron with Goethe in Weimar, and was impressed by the character and 'invincible enterprise' of Trelawny on meeting him in Greece. He was even drawn to Trelawny's abandoned Greek wife, then had an affair with Lady Hester Stanhope, to whom he appeared 'not only a great man, but one essentially different from all others'. Byron she had rather dismissed when meeting him briefly after she had watched him diving from the mole into Piraeus Harbour.

Pückler-Muskau followed Byron by swimming in the Piraeus and elsewhere in Greece, but it was oriental rivers that he relished, beyond the scope of Byron's travels. In the river Jordan he bathed 'voluptuously', and swam obsessively in the Nile while his servants beat the water with their oars to ward off crocodiles. In Byronic fashion he rescued his Nubian lover from a crocodile off the banks of the Nile, and swam across the cataracts to free from servitude some beautiful slave girls. In England the closest he got to water was when he galloped along the shore at Brighton by the waves of a moonlit sea, whereas as a young cavalry officer he had once vaulted on his horse over the great bridge across the Elbe and swum ashore, to the amazement of the crowd.

In the middle of the Russian winter Alexander Pushkin would rise early, run down to the river, break the ice with his fist and plunge into the freezing water. When in Moscow he swam in the classical marble pool, where Russians still swim naked. He shared Byron's fascination with the sea and waves. When travelling to the Crimea, at the sight of the sea, he ordered the carriage to stop: 'Sophia and I jumped out and ran to the shore. The surface of the water was covered with waves, gentle, caressing waves, pursuing me back and forth as I ran.' Watching the girl play in the surf, he longed, like the waves, to lap her feet with his lips. All day long he would swim in the sea, and at night would lie awake for hours listening to its sound. His obsession with Byron began in his youth in St Petersburg. He increased his intimacy by having an affair with a girl who had once been Byron's mistress, just as Scrope Davies had made a speciality of taking on his friend's discarded lovers. 'I will introduce you to a Greek girl who received Byron's kisses,' Pushkin wrote in a letter. 'I feel as though I was communing with the English poet by reverently caressing her flesh.'

An incident in the Dnieper, when he watched two prisoners chained together swimming to freedom across the river, was the inspiration for his poem 'The Robber Barons', and caused him to imitate their action by swimming the river himself. He ended up racked with fever 'in a jew's hovel, delirious without a doctor, and with only a pitcher of lemonade for a remedy'. Pushkin's enthusiasm was remarkable as he lived at a period when few Russians swam. In acknowledgment a friend once wrote to encourage him to resume his poetry, and compared his efforts to those of an athlete contending with the sea: 'You were born to be a poet. Try to be worthy of it. I am standing on a deserted shore, and I see an athlete struggling in the waves. He will not drown, if he uses all his strength. Swim then, athlete!'

Swimming for Pushkin was an impulsive, daring, decisive gesture. When encouraging his best friend Pavel Nashchokin to abandon his tenacious gypsy lover in order to marry his first wife, he wrote: 'You are evidently a man of passion and in an impassioned state you are able to do what you would not even dare to think of in a state of sobriety, just as once when drunk you swam across a river, though you didn't know how to swim. The present affair is like that – take off your shirt, cross yourself, and splash off from the bank. We shall follow you in a boat, and somehow or other you'll scramble out onto the opposite side.'

For Byron too the difficulties of love had been associated with swimming. When trying to extricate himself
from a love affair that was causing him great anguish,
he wrote that 'before I sink I will at least have a
swim for it, though I wish with all my heart it were
the Hellespont instead, or that I could cross this as
easily as I did ye other'. Looking back to his messy
affair with her daughter-in-law Caroline Lamb, Byron
wrote in disillusioned mood to Lady Melbourne: 'It is
true from early habit one must make love mechanically
as one swims. I was once very fond of both, but now
as I never swim unless I tumble into the water, I don't
make love till almost obliged.'

The infatuation of Edgar Allan Poe with Byron caused
him to consider taking ship for Europe in order to fight
for Greek independence. He liked to be photographed
in Byronic poses and affected a Byronic cloak. It was
all part of the aristocratic posture he chose to adopt.
He had attended a boarding-school in England that
was to haunt his memory, and his alter ego William
Wilson is educated at Eton. In Poe's short story 'The
Assignation' his identification with his hero is evident.
A young man modelled on Byron dives into a Venetian
canal to rescue a young girl, after the 'quiet waters
had closed placidly over their victim'. On emerging,
his cloak, 'heavy with the drenching water, becomes
unfastened, and, falling in heavy folds about his feet',
reveals to the spectators the elegant figure of a young
man 'with the sound of whose name the greater part
of Europe was then ringing'. The rescuer is also a
self-portrait of Poe. His own 'singular eyes' and 'forehead of unusual breadth' merge into the features and

character of Byron, and both men were notable swimmers.

At the age of fifteen, emulating his hero, Poe had swum six miles up the James river against the current, a feat on which he was to pride himself for the rest of his life, as Byron did his swim across the Hellespont. When, long after the event, an article appeared in a newspaper comparing his swim with Byron's, Poe was rather offended: 'The writer seems to compare my swim with that of Lord Byron, whereas there can be no comparison between them. Any swimmer "in the falls" in my days would have swum the Hellespont, and thought nothing of the matter. I swam from Ludlow's Wharf to Warwick (six miles), in a hot June sun, against one of the strongest tides ever known in the river. It would have been a feat comparatively easy to swim twenty miles in still water. I would not think much of attempting to swim the British Channel from Dover to Calais.' Among his friends watching in admiration on the riverbank was a boy whose beautiful mother dying of consumption was the model for Helen with the 'Naiad airs', and another, the hero-worshipping Ellis, who was rescued from drowning by Poe as Edleston was by Byron. Poe's swim in the James river 'that outstrips the normal bounds of possibility' was to fascinate Baudelaire. No doubt it was those long, lone swims of his boyhood over the shadowy, mysterious depths of rivers, that made Poe in Marie Bonaparte's words a 'poet of water', the element towards which he was orientated, that polarised his imagination – the dark lake whose waters closed over the house of Usher, the fatal well below the pendulum, the descent into the Maelstrom.

Byron had swum the Hellespont with a Mr Ekenhead on 3 May 1810. It is little more than a mile wide, but the current makes it so arduous that he doubted whether 'Leander's conjugal powers must not have been exhausted in his passage to Paradise – I attempted it a week ago and failed owing to the North wind and the wonderful rapidity of the tide, though I have been from my childhood a strong swimmer, but this morning being calmer I succeeded and crossed the "broad Hellespont" in an hour and ten minutes.' He was later to write that 'I plume myself on this achievement more than I could possibly do any kind of glory, political, poetical or rhetorical.' From now on he would 'disdain Datchet', a village on the Thames where he had once engaged in a swimming contest. He described his feat in numerous letters, often twice to the same person and three times to his mother, as if he wanted to eradicate the memories of her derision of his club foot when he was a boy. Medwin mentions a well-rehearsed conversational ploy that was often repeated whenever the subject of swimming arose. Byron would turn round to Fletcher his manservant, to whom he occasionally referred, and ask: 'Fletcher, how far was it Mr Ekenhead and I swam?' Fletcher would dutifully reply: 'Three miles and a half, my Lord,' and Byron would resume with a description of the swim.

The strait between Sestos and Abydos is not particularly wide but very deep, and it suggests the superficiality of Byron's imagination as well as nerve that he should be one of the first to swim over dark waters and great depths, at a time when the submarine world was still a matter of conjecture and relatively unknown. His genius was for the surface of life. Byron would have liked, like

Keats, to have seen 'far into the sea, the shark at savage prey', to have leapt, as Keats professed to have leapt in 'Endymion', 'headlong into the sea, and thereby become acquainted with the soundings and the quicksands', but he knew his capabilities. Despite attempts to achieve some form of mystic union with the spirit of a place – 'Are not the mountains, waves, and skies, a part of me and of my soul, as I of them' – he realised that he could never really lose his own 'wretched identity' and expressed his limitations characteristically in swimming terms: 'Swimming long in the abyss of thought,/ Is apt to tire: a calm and shallow station/ Well nigh the shore, where one stoops down and gathers/ Some pretty shell, is best for moderate bathers.'

No doubt Byron was attracted by Leander's combination of nocturnal swimming and dangerous loving. When Trelawny, in his eagerness to see Claire Claremont, embarked one night from Genoa in a heavy squall though everyone advised him to stay and avoid the danger, he repeated to himself and 'hardened his resolution' with Ovid's lines on Leander: 'Nor adverse winds nor raging seas can ever make him stay, whom Love commands.'

Leander's nightly swim to Hero, from Abydos to Sestos, was a constant source of inspiration for English writers, notably Marlowe, Leigh Hunt, and Keats who characteristically wrote a sonnet on a gem depicting the swimmer. When still a schoolboy in London, Coleridge was once walking down the Strand revolving his arms in imitation of Leander swimming the Hellespont. A passerby presumed that this was a novel method of pickpocketing and after apprehending him was so struck by Coleridge's scholarly explanation that he gave him a ticket to a circulating library in the city – a crucial moment in Coleridge's career as he took full advantage of the opportunity to flood his imagination with its contents. The pathetic tale of an athlete dying young was to strike a chord in A. E. Housman: 'By Sestos town, in Hero's tower/ On Hero's heart Leander lies . . . ' In his youth Charles Kingsley painted and drew Leander swimming through the waves. Turner too was haunted for years by the myth and made numerous sketches of the scene before his final painting, where Hero flashes her lamp on a fountained terrace while Leander's body is washed up on the moonlit sands below. He had been encouraged by Etty's popular painting of the subject that was exhibited widely around England. Henry Scott Tuke considered his large pastel of Leander his best work, and offered it to the Tate on his death to hang near Turner's masterpiece. The most famous of rowing clubs was to adopt the swimmer's name, and perhaps some mysterious influence of his romantic Christian names 'Leander Starr' prompted Jameson's desperate raid. In Blixen's *Out of Africa* an 'English gentleman of the Victorian age' dines out on the fact that once he had swum the Hellespont.

Four years ago I flew to Turkey to swim the Hellespont. I left it rather late. Less than two days of the holiday remained when we rounded the bend on the road from Troy and there it lay below us in the evening light, like a great Italian lake with the hills of Gallipoli to the north and a narrow tributary connecting it with the sea. The perpetual blue skies were for the first time streaked with clouds. A bleak wind ruffled the surface and the current, which was always strong, was now forcing the water to race through the narrows. A few hours later, in desperation as time was running out, I waded across the pebbles into the waves at the narrowest point of the channel where the ferry leaves the Gallipoli peninsula to return to Cannakale. I soon realised my mistake. Even Byron had known that here, where the waters that flow down from the Black Sea are compressed within shores only a mile apart, the current is twice as strong as elsewhere and will sweep you in no time miles downstream and out into the open Aegean beyond Cape Helles – 'If Mr Ekenhead and myself had thought of crossing at the narrowest point instead of going up to the Cape above it, we should have been swept down to Tenedos.' Within seconds of entering the water I was enveloped in waves and dragged sideways, but managed to cling to some rocks from where I groped my way back to the shore, to the vast amusement of the passengers lining the decks of the departing ferry.

The following morning I searched for a boatman in Cannakale. My pathetic experience the previous evening had put a stop to any romantic notions of swimming across alone. The water was still rough, my daughter wanted to swim with me, and the channel was now crammed with a continuous flow of boats and tankers of every size and nationality. Someone along the quays mentioned a Mr Ibrahim Soydins who specialised in Hellespont crossings. He was not in his office, but pinned to the wall above his desk were some rather daunting instructions from an American professor who had swum across in 1973. We had arrived unfit and unprepared, but now we were warned that in order to join the 'glowing ranks' of those who had crossed

the Hellespont, the 'Gods and Kings, Poets and Lovers, Heroes and Armies all looming tall and straight
through 5,000 years of history', we would have had
to have swum, for two months at least, 2,500 metres
a day, mixed with some weight-training sessions four
times a week. To become mentally fit he advised reading Homer – 'it should provide you with an overflow
of inspiration' – and *Paideia, the ideals of Greek Culture* by
Werner Jaeger, particularly the chapters on 'Culture and
Education of the Homeric Nobility' and 'Ionian and
Aeolian poetry'.

We eventually tracked down Ibrahim in the Archaeo-
logical Museum, where we found him lecturing on Greek
fragments to a party of American tourists. He warned us
about the conditions, but after some bargaining a deal
was struck up, and the swim was arranged for six that
evening. Our plane was due to leave before dawn the
following morning from an airport 300 miles away. He
would in the meantime obtain permission from the military authorities on Abydos for us to dive into the water
just off the peninsular, as it is now a military base and
heavily fortified.

At the appointed hour we found him on the quay-
side changed for the occasion into a nautical uniform
and peaked yachting cap emblazoned with anchors. He
had hired a long fishing-boat with an engine and crew
of three. Throughout the crossing he was to stand like a
figurehead on its prow, his arm raised in the direction of
our course. As the boat sailed upstream along the Asiatic
shore we sat on the deck rubbing in some jelly he had provided as a protection against cramp and jellyfish. Carved
as a memorial on a hillside was the date 18. 3. 1915. It

was the day the *HMS Goliath* was destroyed. Littering these straits are the remains of various British warships sunk as they tried to force their way through in that fateful year. As we were unable to land, the boat halted just offshore and we dived into the sea. The surface was still choppy, but shafts of sunlight were beginning to break through the clouds and illuminate the seabed. This soon dropped away, and halfway across plunged down to formidable depths.

I swam sidestroke to avoid looking down. My dread of deep water stems from a voyage to India at the age of six, when the ship was delayed for some days in a port on the Red Sea. While waiting to continue the voyage we took a rowing-boat out beyond the reef, and I still remember the experience as clearly as a nightmare. As we rowed out from the shore across the shallow water the bottom dropped down suddenly at the edge of a steep marine cliff, and we found ourselves floating in clear smooth water over rocks rising up from an apparently unfathomable depth to quite near the surface. It was a fearful sensation as the boat rose and fell between them, and I could not look over the side without feeling extremely giddy, as if suspended on some aerial height, leaning over a tremendous gulf. The sight as a child of those submarine peaks rising abruptly from the sea-bed has marked my imagination for life.

Here in mid-channel, when I did try the crawl for a few yards and was forced to look down through the green water, I became aware of a silvery shape suspended about twenty feet below. It hovered there every time I chanced to look down. No doubt it was only some discarded packing-case swaying slowly in the current, but to me at the time it had every semblance of the underbelly of a shark as it turns on its back to strike. We had been assured that there were no sharks in the area, but they are notorious for emerging in the unlikeliest places and Byron himself had encountered some large fish in the middle of his crossing. It was at about this stage of his swim here that Patrick Leigh Fermor noted a 'strange fluctuating and hissing noise' under his submerged left ear. He too was swimming sidestroke. This he presumed to be the shifting and grinding of enormous masses of pebbles and silt at the bottom of the sea, revolved by the clash of conflicting currents, but he found out subsequently that it was caused by the presence of Russian submarines.

To allow for the current the boat kept us on a course a long way east of our objective, the ancient site of Sestos which is now marked by a grove of cypresses surrounding a villa on the shore, like one of those mysterious scenes in Böcklin's paintings. We were holding our course well until not far from the other side a Russian tanker almost a mile long loomed from the west and passed in front of us, while we marked time in the waves and its crew stood by the railings to stare in silence. By the time it had gone we found that we had been driven by its wash and the current far out of our way downstream. We were being dragged past a promontory with a lighthouse, after which the shore retreats northwards and the Hellespont widens considerably. This was our last chance, so we started thrashing through the waves. Gradually the water became lighter, and we felt seaweed, then the reassuring touch of rocks and sand. A lorry driver halted on the road to watch us land, far down the shore from the shadowy grove of cypress trees. Back in Cannakale my daughter was ceremoniously presented by our guide with a purple-ribboned medallion and her photograph taken for the local press. I received nothing, because I was neither blond nor young and had bargained too hard over the price.

On my return to England I was disappointed to read that Byron had found his crossing of the Tagus estuary at Lisbon a far more hazardous adventure, so the following summer I felt obliged to book a holiday in Portugal. Byron had been disconcerted by the powerful tide and the counter-current, a wind that was blowing freshly, and although the distance is about the same as the Hellespont, he spent almost twice as long over the crossing. Conditions there can be treacherous. George Borrow once took a small boat across the estuary. A storm suddenly arose, the waves swept over the sides, and he thought his last hour had come. When selling bibles to the incredulous Spaniards, Borrow had swum in the deep pools among the sandbanks somewhere near the source of the river: 'One night, as I was bathing myself and my horse in the Tagus, a knot of people gathered on the bank, crying: "Come out of the water, Englishman, and give us books; we have got our money in our hands."'

All our passports and much else were stolen on our first evening there, so when reporting our losses to the British Embassy I asked the naval attaché about the conditions. He warned me against the swim for various reasons, and advised me to visit the marine institute to study the directions of the various tides. I decided not to as I was rapidly losing my nerve. If I became too rational and delved too deeply into the intricacies of the currents, I would never make the attempt. Surely, with Byron, it had been an instinctive, impulsive gesture. I did however make a decision to swim on the incoming tide, preferring to be swept upriver than out into the Atlantic, and studied the times of the tides in the local paper.

My daughter wisely refused to accompany me on this occasion, so I left her to paint in that most elegant of zoos and drove down to the shore in the early afternoon. Byron's swim had ended at Belem tower so I determined to start there. The embankment sloped down about ten feet into the water. Scum and litter frothed at its edge, among patches of tar and oil. I left my clothes in the car and wore a pair of shorts with some escudos in a pocket, to enable me to return on one of the ferries that criss-crossed the estuary. I climbed down a ladder and five yards out was startled by a tug on my legs as if I had been gripped hard by a tentacle. It was only the effect of the current, but it was enough to make me retreat hastily back to the shore. By now a large crowd had gathered on the parapets of Belem tower, and I was loath to disappoint them and myself. So once more I struck out through the marginal current, keeping my head well above water to avoid ending up, like Pushkin in the Dnieper, racked with fever. Nothing was visible through the surface, not even my hands, which was a relief as I had no wish to set eyes on the huge robalo fish I had noticed nosing along the riverbed around the pillars of the pier and sucking up everything in their path.

My destination was a line of oil refineries on the

other side which once in Byron's time had been full
of orange groves and vineyards. After an initial crawl
I relapsed into a stately sidestroke, which allowed me
the leisure to look back at the shore through the palisade
of masts in the marina. Behind the railway, the oblong
factories and rectangular blocks of flats were occasional
glimpses of the old baroque balconies and twisting towers
that William Beckford had once admired. This perverse
and exotic voluptuary, adored by Byron who was always
trying to catch up with him, had exiled himself here to
escape the consequences of some homosexual scandal in
England. It was along this shore that he rode every day
and sometimes swam. He had installed in his extravagant apartment floor-length mirrors that reflected the
bodies of young men swimming in the river below,
and looking down at night from his veranda on the little
beach he would long to stretch himself on the sands by
moonlight and devote all his wild imaginings to 'some
love-sick languid youth' reclining by his side. 'Alas,'
he mourned, 'will my own youth pass away without
my feeling myself once more tremblingly alive to these
exquisite though childish sensations.'

By now I was well over halfway across and drifting
towards the suspension bridge, trying hard to distract
my mind from what lay around and beneath me with
memories of Beckford and others, when my thoughts
were disturbed by the wail of a siren like those I imagined
sounded at Alcatraz whenever a prisoner escaped from
the island. Shortly afterwards a patrol boat bore down
on me. References to Byron made little impression. I
was dragged from the water and subjected to an hour's
interrogation. Apparently no one was allowed to swim

in the estuary unaccompanied by a boat and without the harbourmaster's permission. The river was considered too dirty and dangerous. Anyone spotted in it was either a drug smuggler or a stowaway, and treated as such. From the boat the further shore seemed disappointingly close. But perhaps it was just as well. There was an ocean liner approaching fast from under the bridge, and there seemed little likelihood of my avoiding it.

V

Characteristics of the
English Swimmer

Swimmers into cleanness leaping . . .

WHILE THERE WERE MANY in England who practised
swimming as a form of competition or relaxation, for
some it became an obsession, an urgent, compulsive in-
dulgence that could tingle the nerves and transport
them in Swinburne's words to 'another form of life'. One
reads of Coleridge jumping into the waves without
warning when well into his fifties, of Benjamin Haydon
'rushing' down to Brighton in September where, as he
relates in his diaries, he 'rolled in the sea, shouted like
a savage, laved his sides like a bull in a green meadow,
dived, swam, floated and came out refreshed'. When

swimming once far out into a bay, Robert Browning felt his limbs slip their fetters and his body in flight like a butterfly.

The passion for bathing really began with the Romantic generation, and 'swim' was a word that particularly appealed to its poets. It recurs as the key word in various well-known lines. On reading Chapman's *Homer*, Keats felt 'like some watcher of the skies when a new planet swims into his ken'. The arena 'swims' around Byron's dying gladiator, and in 'The Lime Tree Bower my Prison' Coleridge 'stood, silent with swimming sense'. The word suggests a state of suspension, a trance-like condition. There is the strange adverb 'swimmingly' that implies unimpeded progress. Like Narcissus many of the swimmers suffered from a form of autism, a self-encapsulation in an isolated world, a morbid self-admiration, an absorption in fantasy.

Like those opium addicts of the nineteenth century analysed by Alethea Hayter, these swimmers felt themselves to be pariahs, elect outcasts, insulated from their fellow men. They too often experienced through their swims the classic constituents of an opium dream: 'the feeling of blissful buoyancy, the extension of time, contrasts of temperature, the bliss of the outcast'. Anyone who submerges some way below the surface into deep water can experience those nightmare visions of de Quincey's, inspired by drugs and the prison etchings of Piranesi, of sinking down through huge vaulted airless spaces, among rocks and columns that rise up from the ocean floor in a limitless and yet claustrophobic expansion of space, alone, but not unobserved; there is a sense that one is always under surveillance, invisible enemies and predators are somewhere hidden beyond in the shadowy gloom and remote recesses; the sensibility sharpens; the slightest touch or sound can cause alarm in this silent world.

'I have often been asked', begins de Quincey's *Confessions*, 'how it was, and through what series of steps, that I became an opium-eater. Was it gradually, tentatively, mistrustingly, as one goes down a shelving beach into a deepening sea, and with a knowledge from the first of the dangers lying on that path: half-courting those dangers, in fact, whilst seeming to defy them?'

For de Quincey the processes of taking drugs and swimming seemed somehow related. He admits later to having consumed so much opium in his life that he 'might well have bathed and swum in it'. The effect of opium inclines the imagination towards visions of moving water-fountains, waterfalls, sea waves, and de Quincey felt himself in his dreamworld sink to the ocean depths, 'with the weight of twenty Atlantics on him'. Crabbe's experience of almost drowning in the river Waveney when a young man caused him to dream that he walked unharmed and breathing in the depths of the sea over which great tidal waves had rolled. The cities of opium-affected writers are often sunk deep in stagnant seas, the inhabitants isolated from each other, unable to communicate.

Swimming, like opium, can cause a sense of detachment from ordinary life. Memories, especially those of childhood, can be evoked with startling strength and in vivid and precise detail. In a recent autobiography James Hamilton-Paterson describes his nocturnal dives across the coral floors of the Pacific, off an island in the Philippines where he spends a third of every year. As he floats far below the surface through the black water, memories revive of the 'dotty militarism' of his prep school, the dormitories named after famous generals, Kipling's 'If' framed and hung over the dining-hall door. His mind becomes dislocated. He begins to appreciate William Burroughs's 'A psychotic is a guy who feels in touch with the underlying real.' 'For psychotic,' he comments, 'write swimmer.' Phrases from Nietzsche, Schopenhauer, de Chirico stream through his mind. Back in London he shrinks from the ordered, structured rhythms of everyday life. At dinner parties he feels uncomfortable and unable to communicate to a cynical audience the attractions of his other life beneath the waves.

These earlier swimmers seemed absorbed, like the opium takers, by the strangeness and novelty of their experiences. The ecclesiastical terms used by de Quincey to describe his addiction, the 'pure paradises' and 'celestial pleasures' of the drug, its 'martyrs', 'altars', and 'priests', recall the mystical phrases adopted by Swinburne in relation to his swims, the image of the 'sacred' sea as a 'paradise lost', 'another and better world' where one 'lived and moved and had one's being'. Both the opium addicts and the swimmers tended to be solitary, remote figures, who felt themselves superior to dull, conventional minds. The descriptions of their experiences are like those of a man who has just explored an unknown territory, and returns to astonish us with his discoveries. On the whole they reject the material world, respectability, the industrial system and contemporary society. They were generally out of harmony with their age, idealists who felt deeply the futility of life, the contrast between what life is and what it ought to be. It was as though water, like opium, provided the swimmers with a heightened existence, a refuge from the everyday life they loathed.

Sometimes the title of a book can give a 'swimmer' away. For instance Barbellion's *The Journal of a Disappointed Man* – the diary of an employee in the insect department of the British Museum, slowly dying from multiple sclerosis that 'cut me off from everything'. Hypersensitive and self-conscious, forever fascinated by the 'Gothic architecture of his own fantastic soul', he despised society's 'drill, routine, orthodoxy, conformity' and all those absorbed in the petty cares of a commonplace existence, 'the happy men with firm step'. By night he would wander the streets of London, looking with hungry eyes through windows disclosing happy, comfortable interiors, and curse his colossal discontent, his dingy lodgings, cramped and confined, his mawkish, gauche, morbid, fastidious nature that caused him to refuse invitations to dinner because a man had watery blue eyes, to hate a man with a slight mannerism or affectation in speech, and to fall out of love because of the shape of a girl's thumbs.

It is not long into the journal before so alienated a man is undressing in a cave by the sea and bathing in the pouring rain, plunging up to his armpits in green salmon pools – 'what did I care about the British Museum or Zoology then? All but the last enemy and object of conquest I had overcome – for the moment perhaps even Death himself was under heel – I was immortal – in that minute I was always prostrate in the stream – sunk deep in the bosom of old Mother Earth, who can not die!' While swimming he revels in the 'sensuous enjoyment of his animal existence'. Even the sight of others swimming causes him extraordinary pleasure. Sitting alone on a beach above a rock pool, he watches three children racing across the sands to bathe, a man dive from a boat and a horseman gallop his mare down to the beach to 'plunge about in the line of breakers'. The dying Barbellion then turns his head again to the rock pool 'with a great thumping heart of happiness. I kept my head down so as not to overindulge my spirits.'

Likewise the reclusive naturalist Richard Jefferies, who felt repelled by his own species, and the wolfish struggles of a competitive society. When an invalid for the last five years of his short life he 'envied the man swimming fifty miles from shore' and looked back nostalgically to his childhood bathing in Coate Reservoir near Swindon, where the 'water did not seem to resist him, it parted and let him through. Between the strokes he glided buoyantly, lifted by the water as swallows glide on the plane of the air. All this portion of the water was in his power, and its elasticity as his strokes compressed it threw him forward. He did not see where he was going, his vision was lost in the ecstasy of motion, all his mind was concentrated in the full use of his limbs. The delicious delirium of strength – unconsciousness of reason, unlimited consciousness of force – the joy of life itself filled him.'

Arthur Hugh Clough, Arnold's favourite pupil at Rugby, never got over the 'electric shock' that the great headmaster communicated to his more susceptible minds. Regarded by Arnold with an 'affection and interest hardly less than I should feel for my own son', he became convinced in later life that the intense devotion to schoolwork, all Arnold's insistence that life is a 'serious and solemn thing', had left him a wreck physically and mentally. And then at Oxford all his moral certainties disintegrated under the Tractarian influence of his tutor. His life thereafter lacked definition. He never felt able to resolve these perplexities, face up to 'this eager rivalry of life, this cruel conflict for preeminence', and ended up in someone's words 'tying up parcels for Florence Nightingale'. Like the sensitive Barbellion, he found it difficult to socialise, 'to herd with people that one owns no care for', and in London returns to a 'lone room, while all within him yearns for sympathy'. As well as Barbellion's fastidious tastes he shared his awkward self-consciousness, and felt the gentry with their 'slightly mercantile' airs and accents looked down on his 'bookish and maladroit' manners.

Clough's poetry and letters suggest that it was principally through swimming that he found release from the indecision of his 'thought-riddled nature'. It freed him from the troubles and perplexities of the intellect, and restored contact with the vital, instinctive elements of his own being. He cursed his questioning, reasoning intelligence, and envied those who accepted their faith and believed merely because their fathers did before.

On the beach of the Venice Lido his Dipsychus, who longs for a life of heroic action, cries out exultantly to his doubting, hesitant spirit:

> Oh, a grand surge! We'll bathe; quick, quick! undress!
> Quick, quick! in, in!
> We'll take the crested billows by their backs
> And shake them. Quick! in, in!
> And I will taste again the old joy
> I gloried in so when a boy.

At Rugby Clough's swimming became legendary, particularly after he swam from Swifts, the bathing place of the Sixth form, to the mill on the Leicester road and back again between roll-calls. Most of the boys were content to use a minute brick building which covered a small, slimy, cement pool of clean but cold water, in the far corner of part of the Close known as Pontines. When at Oxford he mentions in his letters his regular bathes before breakfast in Parson's Pleasure on the river throughout the winter, before reading hard for the rest of the day. On 5 November he writes that 'I had a bathe this morning at our mutual friend "Parson's Pleasure" – the temperature both of air and water in no wise however resembling that which you experienced there, it being the coldest morning yet that I have bathed this year.' In April he laments that the 'beauties of the pool have been diminished by filthy lucre-speculators of a bathing-house, and I have therefore deserted it. But a substitute is to be found.' And he transferred his allegiance to some other cold baths in Holywell.

He would bathe in the countryside around Oxford

during those wanderings across the 'warm green-muffled' Cumnor hills commemorated in 'The Scholar Gipsy', Matthew Arnold's tribute to Clough and all he stood for. With his friends he would bathe on their holidays in the secluded streams of Wales, and in Scotland, where they went like Swinburne with their tutor to study Classics, they found in the glen of Clunie a little stream which 'dashes through the granite just beside us and gives us a pool to bathe in'. Here, whatever the weather, they swam daily in the early morning, then read, and waited for breakfast – 'and at four, after the bathing again, the dinner'. Clough's mock-heroic poem 'The Bothie of Tober Na Vuolich' describes their discovery of a stream that springs from a loch 'unexplored in the folds of great mountains'. They follow it for miles through alders and pine forests, to a point where the 'boiling, pent-up water' forced its way through a massive block of granite and fell into a basin:

> Ten feet wide and eighteen long, with whiteness
> and fury
> Occupied partly, but mostly pellucid, pure, a
> mirror;
> Beautiful there for the colour derived from green
> rocks under;

Here among the cliffs and pendant boughs:

> You are shut in, left alone with yourself and perfection
> of water,
> Hid on all sides, left alone with yourself and the
> goddess of bathing.

Below the slabs of rock there was a tiny beach, and:

There they bathed, of course, and Arthur, the Glory
  of headers,
Leapt from the ledges with Hope, he twenty feet,
  he thirty . . .
And they looked, and wondered, incredulous, looking
  yet once more.
Yes, it was he, on the ledge, bare-limbed, an Apollo,
  down-gazing,
Eyeing one moment the beauty, the life, ere he
  flung himself in it . . .

These bathing scenes were admired by Thackeray, who
wrote to Clough: 'Your description of the sky and the
landscape – and that figure of the young fellow bathing
shapely with shining limbs and the blue sky for a background – are delightful to me. I can imagine to myself
the Goddess of bathing in a sort of shimmer under the
water – was it as clear as Romamund'a Well?' In paying
tribute to its 'proper idyllic feeling that is half sensual and
half spiritual', Thackeray shows he recognised beneath
the jocular, mock-heroic tone Clough's feeling for the
numinous qualities of the atmosphere, his respect for
the goddess of bathing, Artemis, shimmering under
the water, whom Clough describes elsewhere beneath
a waterfall watched by Actaion, yielding her 'ambrosial
nakedness' to the river-water overflowing to receive her.
  Swimming and water became for Clough symbols
of the innocence and boyhood for which he always
yearned. 'And why does childhood ever change to man?'
he once lamented. One reads of Clough later in life, on
holidays from the Civil Service, bathing obsessively off
the Isle of Wight. When dying in Florence the doctor

deprived him of his 'favourite occupation, swimming'. At Rugby he had looked back to his early years by the sea in Charleston, Carolina, the rambles along the shore when, during his father's long absences, a strong bond of sympathy developed between him and his mother as she 'poured out the fullness of her heart on him'. Watching Arnold's children playing in their garden made him long for his own brother and sister and their bathes from the beach on Sullivan Island off the Carolina coast where they spent their summer holidays – and Edgar Allan Poe some months in the army. When the family left Clough aged nine at his Chester prep school and returned across the sea to Carolina, his sister wrote that this was practically the end of Arthur's boyhood. 'For while the tired waves, vainly breaking/ Seem here no painful inch to gain' of 'Say not the Struggle', written in Rome towards the end of his life, would seem to refer to the inactivity and indecision of his adult life, whereas 'Far back, through creeks and inlets making/ Came silent, flooding in, the main' and 'Westward look the land is bright' suggest the revitalising waters of his American boyhood. In periods of dejection he would long to be enclosed in 'circling waters crystal clear, that calm protecting atmosphere', to sink down into the sea 'without a shore', or descend to the ocean floor with a rope on his loins 'through the fissure' and swing across the enchanting shell-sprinkled cavern.

It is generally accepted that in the area of the unconscious, water in any form and immersion in it suggests a hidden desire for a return to the security and irresponsibility of the womb and its amniotic waters. The long river-swims of Edgar Allan Poe's boyhood, the recurrence of funereal, stagnant waters in his writing, the Maelstrom 'whose depths I positively felt a wish to explore', symbolised for Marie Bonaparte the 'lost and always sought-for mother with whom his necropholist soul forever longed to unite'. His mother had died when he was very young. 'When someone likes doing something very much,' runs one of Lichtenberg's aphorisms, 'he almost always has some interest in the thing that is greater than the thing itself.' Freud alludes to the large number of dreams, often accompanied by anxiety, where the subject's desire to be immersed in water is based upon fantasies of pre-natal memories. He mentions somewhere what he called a 'pretty' water dream, dreamt by a woman patient – 'At her summer holiday resort, by the lake of –, she dived into the dark water just where the pale moon was mirrored in it' – that signified for Freud the patient's desire to return through the buttocks that gave birth (the pale moon) to the dark waters of the uterus. Late in life, when under the influence of Freud and Jung, the American Jack London was to express his search for a mother's love in a short story about a deracinated, Oxford-educated Hawaiian who dives down into a submarine cave in the Pacific to search for his ancestral bones. Two fathoms below the surface he enters a hole, that grows larger as he travels slowly along the passage until he emerges into a dark cavity, where the water is very cold. Hart Crane dived to his death in the Bay of Mexico to be reunited, so they say, with the sea, which always served for him, as for Swinburne, as a symbol of maternal regression and integration.

If there is any truth in the psychological implications of water, it is backed by the fact that almost all the swimmers already mentioned were strongly attached to their mothers and felt alienated from their fathers. Byron, deserted by his father, suffered from an intense, smothering relationship with his mother. After wonderful, carefree childhoods, they were nearly all sent at an early age to boarding-schools from which they recoiled in shock. It was there that they encountered for the first time, and in its intensest form, the pressure to conform. Byron was very unhappy until his final year at Harrow. Shelley at Eton was mocked for his 'wild and marked peculiarity', as was Swinburne. 'Away from home and the sea and all common comfortable things, stripped of the lifelong clothing of his life', the swimming hero of Swinburne's *Lesbia Brandon* felt on entering Eton 'as one beaten and bare, like one torn alive out of life or all that was sweet in it'. Trelawny was deposited in a severe boarding-school by his irascible father, who encouraged the headmaster to beat him continuously. Poe, like Clough, was sent after a childhood in America to a prep school in England where his Southern pride led to his isolation and unpopularity. Coleridge's experiences at Christ's Hospital caused him nightmares throughout his life.

When Charles Lamb arrived at Christ's Hospital, he too felt dispirited and 'alone among six hundred playmates. O the cruelty of separating a poor lad from his early homestead! The yearnings which I used to have towards it in those unfledged years! How, in my dreams, would my native town (far in the West) come back, with its church, and trees, and faces! How I would wake weeping, and in the anguish of my heart exclaim upon sweet Calne in Wiltshire.' It is significant perhaps that his only relief from the anguish he experienced was the exhilarating bathing excursions to the New River – 'How merrily we used to sally into the fields, and strip under the first warmth of the sun, and wanton like young dace in the streams, how faint and languid, finally we would return, toward nightfall, to our desired morsel, half-rejoicing, half-reluctant, that the hours of our uneasy liberty had expired.' Even towards the end of his life, in the long warm days of summer he would remember those bathes when 'we would live the long day like otters, never caring for dressing ourselves when we had once stripped'.

To think of the West Country would also make Charles Kingsley weep. A boarding-school brought to an end his idyllic seaside life on the Devon coast, the 'fairy gardens' of his childhood, where he often returned later in life to bathe every day as he did as a boy. Much has been made by German psychiatrists of the archetypal myth of *The Water-Babies*, the story of Tom the chimney-sweep whose longing 'to go and see the sea and bathe in it likewise' transforms him into a water-baby under the maternal care of 'Do as you would be done by', who picked him up from the seabed and 'talked to him, tenderly and low, such things as he had never heard in his life'. Kingsley's wife described how the process of writing the book was an act of inspiration rather than composition, that seemed to flow naturally out of his brain and heart: 'one spring morning, while sitting at breakfast, I reminded him of an old promise: "Rose, Maurice, and Mary have got their book, and Baby must have his." He made no answer, but got up at once and went into his study, locking the door. In half an hour he returned with the story of Little Tom. This was the first chapter of *The Water-Babies*, written off without a check.'

Kingsley once described himself as running not forwards in life but backwards, 'as fast as he could'. His acute nostalgia for the happiness of childhood runs through his descriptions of the bathes he used to enjoy when he was a parson in Eversley, Berkshire, where the stream trickled off the moors, 'in a lonely woodland bath, with the hum of bees, and the sleepy song of birds around me, drinking in all the forms of beauty which lie in the leaves and pebbles, and mossy nooks of dank tree nooks, and all the lowly intricacies of nature which no one stops to see. And all over, as the cool water trickled on, hovered the delicious sense of childhood, and simplicity and purity and peace, which every temporary return to a state of nature gives. A woodland bathe to me always brings thoughts of Paradise. I know not whether they are foretastes of the simple bliss that shall be in the renovated earth, or whether they are back glimpses into the former ages when we wandered – Do you remember? – beside the ocean of eternal love.' From Snowdon, Kingsley wrote that he was enjoying a state of 'utter animalism. There is a pool at the bottom of the garden into whose liquid ice Froude and I take a header every morning.' Kingsley's swimming there reminded Thomas Hughes of a 'great Newfoundland dog out for an airing, plunging in and out of the water, shaking himself over the ladies' silks and velvets'.

Kingsley's obsessive swimming and tale of a poor, dirty chimney-sweep transfigured by water derive from his preoccupation with cleanliness. He felt that bathes and cold baths make one morally good. Tom scrambled down the crag and flung off his clothes crying: 'I must be clean.' One of his heroines dies 'burbling of clean water'. Like Shelley, Kingsley never drank anything but water. In letters to his wife he reveals his anxiety, after making love to her, to 'wash off the scent of her delicious limbs', also his plans to build her a rustic bath in the garden. Among the classical remains of Nimes he was struck by the Roman ladies' bath 'in a fountain bursting up out of the rock, where, under colonnades, they used to walk about, in or out of the water as they chose. All is standing, and could be used tomorrow, if the prudery of the priests allowed it. Honour to those Romans; with all their sins, they were the cleanest people the world has ever seen.'

At a crucial point in the autobiographical *Lavengro* George Borrow feels somehow dirty, dissatisfied with his lack of direction and moral certitude, convinced that the ideals of his youth had vanished. He stands idly one Sunday by a stream. His companions leave him to go to church. As he gazes on them walking away, he feels almost inclined to follow. He does not stir however, but remains leaning against an oak. After some time he sits down at its foot with his face turned towards the water and falls into deep meditation. He recalls the early Sabbaths of his life – how carefully he said his prayers, combed his hair, and brushed his clothes. He thought of England's 'grand liturgy, the sonorous minstrels', the sober evening walk and how glad he was when at the end of the Sabbath day he had done nothing to profane it. 'And when I had mused on those times a long while,

I sighed and said to myself, I am much altered since then; am I altered for the better? And then I looked at my hands and my apparel, and sighed again. I was not wont of yore to appear thus on the Sabbath day.'

For a long time he continued in a state of deep meditation, till at last he lifted up his eyes to the sun, then lowered them to the 'sparkling water, in which hundreds of the finny brood were disporting themselves; and then I thought what a fine thing it was to be a fish on such a fine summer day, and I wished myself a fish, or at least among the fishes, and then I looked at my hands again, and then, bending over the water, I looked at my face in the crystal mirror, and started when I saw it, for it looked squalid and miserable.'

Immediately he rose to his feet and said to himself: 'I should like to bathe and cleanse myself from the squalor produced by my late hard life. I wonder if there is any harm in bathing on the Sabbath day. I will ask Winifred when she comes home; in the meantime I will bathe, provided I can find a fitting place. But the brook, though a very delightful place for fish to disport in, was shallow, and by no means adapted for the recreation of so large a being as myself; it was, moreover, exposed, though I saw nobody at hand, nor heard a single human voice or sound. Following the winding of the brook I left the meadow, and passing two or three thickets, came to a place where between lofty banks the water ran deep and dark, and there I bathed, imbibing new tone and vigour into my languid and exhausted frame.'

At another stage of his travels around England described in *Lavengro* he walks to Salisbury and his swim in the stream becomes a form of ritual, an act of consecration before he climbs a hill and looks across to behold towering to the sky the finest spire in the world – 'on arriving at its banks, I found it a beautiful stream, but shallow, with here and there a deep place, where the water ran dark and still. Always fond of the pure lymph, I undressed and plunged into one of these gulfs, from which I emerged, my whole frame in a glow and tingling with delicious sensations.' When later in Spain he watched some friars swimming a mile out beyond the firth of the Guadalquivir, he strangely disapproved of their behaviour. 'Swimming is a noble exercise,' he commented, 'but it certainly does not tend to mortify either the spirit or the flesh.'

A scholar gypsy like Clough, solitary, secretive, and self-absorbed, Borrow was in the habit of fleeing from society – 'when people addressed me, I not infrequently, especially if they were strangers, turned my head away from them'. Beneath his cold exterior he was drawn to whatever was wild and extraordinary. Like de Quincey he believed himself an outcast, and gravitated by instinct into the company of those on the edge of human society – gypsies, snake-catchers, prizefighters, criminals, murderers. He would no doubt have added swimmers, as he considered them the antithesis of the gentility he loathed. Its postures, he claimed, were exposed by swimming: 'the world – at least the genteel part of it – acts very wisely in setting its face against swimming: for to swim you must be naked, and how would many a genteel person look without his clothes'.

Like other swimmers his later years dragged compared to the wonder and delight of his childhood. The memory of it would make him shield his eyes and weep. Devoted to his mother, Borrow was considered useless by his military father who was bewildered by his total lack of ambition and discrimination in adult life. Like Trelawny's father, he preferred the elder brother, who was described by George as a 'beautiful stream hastening to the ocean, sparkling in the sunshine', while George in contrast was a 'deep dark lagoon, shaded by black pines, cypresses and yews, a wild and savage spot'. Borrow always seemed mesmerised by water. He would look down on streams for hours, and on London Bridge was almost tempted to dive into the 'maelstrom' of the Thames, 'the grisly pool, which, with its superabundance of horror, fascinated me'. In Spain his sympathy was aroused by the sight of a distraught mother forever gazing into the pool where she had lost her son. When wandering in Wales, where he lodged with an 'Esther Williams', he looks down into a deep lake, and imagines its prehistoric past when crocodiles lurked in its depths and dragged down drinking animals – 'Would that I might swim far out into that pool, dive down into its deepest part, and endeavour to discover any strange things which beneath its surface may lie.' In the manner of Byron he liked to swim in places that excited his historical imagination, like the still blue pool in the midst of a garrulous stream where the galley of a Viking earl was once moored as he searched for a home in England, 'when Thor and Freya were yet gods, and Odin was a portentous name'.

After Borrow's death one of his neighbours recalled how he used to wander about the countryside by himself, his 'great delight being to plunge into the darkening mere at eventide, his great head and heavy shoulders nodding in the rays of the sun. Here he hissed and roared and spluttered, sometimes frightening the eel-catcher sailing home in the half-light, and remembering suddenly school legends of river sprites and monsters of the deep.' In his youth Borrow had saved a boy from drowning, after dashing from a steep bank into a stream in full dress, where there were twenty others who might have saved him by putting out a hand 'at no inconvenience to themselves'.

Later in life he was involved in a sea rescue that made him famous, as it was widely reported in various newspapers. 'Intrepidity,' ran one headline, with the following account: 'Yarmouth jetty presented an extraordinary and thrilling spectacle on Thursday, the 8th inst., about one o'clock. The sea raged frantically, and a ship's boat, endeavouring to land for water, was upset, and the men were engulfed in a wave some thirty feet high, and struggling with it in vain. The moment was an awful one, when George Borrow, the well-known author of *Lavengro* and *The Bible in Spain*, dashed into the surf and saved one life, and through his instrumentality the others were saved. We ourselves have known this brave and gifted man for years, and, daring as was this deed, we have known him more than once to risk his life for others. We are happy to add that he has sustained no material injury.'

When living in Great Yarmouth, where this incident took place, Borrow would swim almost every day in the sea. The time of year or the weather seemed not to affect him. One winter he wrote that he was very unwell, but hoped that cold bathing in November would

be of benefit. He would record in a notebook, daily,
the length of time he could stay underwater after his
first dive and the point on the other side of the river
he could reach before surfacing. He used to dive five
fathoms down and bring up handfuls of sand to prove
he had been to the bottom. Once, when walking along
the bank of a river with Robert Cooke, the publisher
John Murray's partner, Borrow suggested a bathe. He
immediately stripped, 'took a header into the water and
disappeared. More than a minute had elapsed, and as
there was no sign of his whereabouts, I was becoming
alarmed, lest he had struck his head or been entangled
in the weeds, when Borrow suddenly reappeared a considerable distance off, under the opposite bank of the
stream, and called out: "What do you think of that?
There, if that had been written in one of my books,
they would have said it was a lie, wouldn't they?"'
On another occasion he was pursued by the police to
the edge of the Thames after some riotous behaviour,
from where they thought there was no escape, but he
plunged boldly into the river and swam fully clothed to
the opposite shore.

Even when older he remained as enthusiastic as
ever. At the age of sixty-nine he was seen off Lowestoft
Beach swimming across the difficult current to the
Ness Buoy. When over seventy he would walk from
the centre of London to Putney, where he wandered
around Wimbledon Common and Richmond Park in
the company of Swinburne and Watts Dunton, discussing literature and life and bathing with them in
the Penn pounds 'with a North East wind cutting
across the icy water like a razor'. He would run

about the grass afterwards like a boy, to shake off the waterdrops.

Towards the close of the century swimming was to become a particularly exhilarating, predatory pursuit for homosexuals, who were made to feel at the time somehow outside the common run of humanity. The most passionate swimmer among them was Frederick Rolfe, the self-styled Baron Corvo, a name and title he adopted to give the appearance of being an exiled nobleman. He is the supreme example of the swimmer who suffers from a form of autism, a morbid self-admiration and absorption in a fantasy world of his own creation. No one, he regretted, admired as much as he did the distinction of his mind, the boyish slenderness of his body and its 'firm muscular whiteness'. A failed priest, he had contracted his first name Frederick to Fr. in the hope that it might be read as 'Father'. He pretended to be rich as the result of a fictitious income from a Duchess Sforza-Cesarini, but in reality lived a life of extreme poverty, first in a lonely London garret where he wrote and exercised with dumb bells for ten years, then finally in Venice, on a leaking boat in the lagoon that was constantly attacked by swarms of voracious rats.

A man of self-confessed 'queer character and unending contradictions', he adopted the austere and exclusive habit of a priest, and a priest's precise and pedantic diction, with the occasional injection of words of his own invention. In fact he did everything he could to distance himself from the low, coarse, half-educated and uncultured bores by whom he felt himself surrounded. He considered himself different from other men, and took up the defiant stand of Corvo versus the rest of the world. On the publication of Edward Carpenter's progressive pamphlet *Towards Democracy* he thought of responding with 'Towards Aristocracy' – 'It's a matter of principle with me not to yield an inch to dirty Demos.' He shared the swimmer's hatred of gentility, common humanity, those who would consider his way of life 'mad, that is to say from the common point of view of the profane vulgar who wants hot water before breakfast, and tea-and-crumpet precisely three hours before dinner, linen stiffly starched, and sock-suspenders meticulously aired'. His own desires were otherwise. He was for fresh air, and open skies, and 'lovely loneliness'. While other men were content with so little, he was not content with anything at all.

All Corvo's novels are disguised autobiographies, or expressions of his fantasy life. Just as the reclusive Borrow professed himself a lover of nooks and retired corners, forever wandering about in search of strange crypts, crannies, and recesses, Corvo in his lonely lodging felt kinship with the crab, because of its instinctive gravitation towards some 'sure and secret cranny of his own, some hidden crevice beneath a shelving rock, where nothing could dislodge him, and wherefrom he might watch the world and seize the flotsam and jetsam floating by'. Encased in a carapace of secrecy and mystery, scuttling sideways to avoid humanity, Corvo was ready to pounce on his enemies or possible friends.

To establish his identification he called the most autobiographical of his novels *Nicholas Crabbe*, which traces his tragic search for the ideal, permanent friend. Crabbe pounces on him one day while surveying the swimmers in the Serpentine. He was sitting on a bench watching a 'continuous stream of pink humanity' descend from a distant diving-board, when presently a 'tiny form like a flash of pearl-coloured flame dashed up it: issued from it: descended: and disappeared in the water; and a shining head moved toward the opposite shore. Crabbe fixed his gaze on that. He conceived an image of the complicated effort and energy which produced the movement, straining his eyes so as not to lose sight of the little white dot even for a moment. The white head went on, nearer to none, avoiding all. At a few yards from the other side, it turned eastward. The boy evidently was a splendid swimmer, and Crabbe noted that he used the breaststroke all the way. At length he turned southward again, bearing straight toward the place where he had left his bundle. He dived, and swam a few strokes beneath the surface, from time to time. As he came up out of the water, Crabbe noted his manliness, and the airy poise of his winged gait, light-limbed, mercurial. He shot out both eyes, and stared at him up and down . . . '

From then on Crabbe and Kemp, his new-found friend, walked every day to Highgate Ponds, at or before sunrise, and back again after 'long swimming'. Kemp was slowly going blind and had to be guided by hand as far as the springboard. After that he set his course by his friend's voice. They were the admiration of the early bathers. Kemp's poor sight was in fact a reflection of Corvo's own. Corvo's eyes were very weak, and without glasses he was quite helpless. Whenever he bathed, he would enter the water first, and a friend would stand on the side of the bath, shouting to direct him and warning him when to turn.

All Corvo's heroes are swimmers. In *The Desire and Pursuit of the Whole* he finally finds his perfect friend, his other half for which he always yearned, in a girl, though endowed with the body of a noble boy. She attempts to drown herself in the middle of the night and slips straight overboard 'as smoothly as a well-licked torpedo'. He flashes down after her. Through the black water he sees the 'rippling rings of her disappearance', and dives through them to save her. His last unfinished novel starts with its hero Septimus Scaptia, a fifth-century bishop, rowing out across the Venetian lagoon to find an unfrequented and deep canal for swimming. Eager to impress the boys whom he felt were laughing at him, the bishop lays aside his books, slips out of his 'dalmatic, and performs a neat header from the ship's poop'.

Hadrian VII, the fantasy of a neurotic Englishman who becomes elected Pope, begins with him entrenched in his London lodgings, a pathetic figure surrounded by Corvo's fencing-foils and dumb-bells. There is some brown packing-paper tacked to the wall, on which are pinned various photographs, of Hermes, Sebastian and Donatello youths, an unknown Rugger XV, and mentioned last of all a 'group of divers in the clear of the moon'. After his election, when bored with the claustrophobia of Catholic ceremonial, Hadrian VII manages to escape for a few weeks in the summer to a vast barrack of a palace above Lake Nemi. Below the palace, halfway down the cliff, there is a little ruined shrine. Here he would spend the day in a low cane chair, alone with some cigarettes and a copy of Pindar. One morning, when his eyes were turned to the distant shore, a 'tiny slip of pink shot from sunlight to shade: another followed: two tiny splashes of silver spray arose, and vanished: two blue-black dots appeared in the rippled mirror. Hadrian envied the young swimmers. He remembered all the wild unfettered boundless joy of only a little while ago. He wondered what the world would say if the Pope were to swim in sunlit Nemi – or in moonlit.' Swimming across the volcanic Nemi last spring, its black waters restored after being drained by Mussolini in the recovery of Caligula's ceremonial barge, I looked up at the long palace whose gardens still stretch down to the lake, but the ruined shrine and low cane chair had disappeared.

It was in his last years in Venice that Corvo's character came into its own. Here he felt free to exercise his individuality without restraint, refining his powers of deceit and preying on the gullible. J. C. Powys once observed him in a narrow canal, lying among leopard skins in the back of a 'floating equipage that resembled the barge of Cleopatra'. After years of chastity he now cut free with a vengeance, and led a life that was beyond his means and daring in England. He was charmed by the sight of the boys diving 'terrifically' from the bridges of the canals, and in the smaller waterways the respectable mothers of large families 'placidly brooding for coolness sake up to their necks in water, among crabs on their bottom doorsteps'. In England when working in Oxford he had swum 'coldly', like Clough, at Parson's Pleasure at seven every morning, and while schoolmastering miserably in Broadstairs his only pleasure was bathing in the sea, which, in mid-November, he claimed to have done every morning since his arrival. His experience of

swimming had already been sufficiently emotional for
him to declare, when embarking on his history of the
Borgias, that 'a delicious feeling came upon me, which
comes upon the swimmer who stands ready to plunge
on the brink of a new stream. It is the grand sensation
of enquiry, of experiment, of daring discovery.'

But the warm waters of Venice and the profusion of
naked boys inspired Corvo to fresh heights of enthusiasm. We read of him swimming half a dozen times a day,
beginning at 'white dawn, and ending after sunset which
set the whole lagoon ablaze with amethyst and topaz'. He
would often get up in the middle of the night and pop
silently overboard to swim for an hour 'in the clear of a
great gold moon, or among the waving reflections of the
stars'. He describes in detail one particular bathe: 'Soon
after sunrise I awakened: it was a sunrise of opal and fire:
the boys were deep in slumber. I took down the awning,
and unmoored quietly, and mounted the puppa to row
about in the dewy freshness in search of a fit place for the
morning plunge. I am very particular about this. Deep
water I must have – as deep as possible – I being what the
Venetians call "appassionato per l'acqua!" Besides that,
I have a vehement dyspathy against getting entangled
in weed or mud, to make my toenails dirtier than my
fingernails. And being congenitally myopic, I see more
clearly in deep water than in shallow, almost as clearly,
in fact, as with a concave monocle on land. I took sounding; nowhere could I touch bottom; and this signified that
my bathing place was more than four metres in depth.
Then I plunged in to revel in the limpid green water.'

Once he fell overboard while smoking a pipe, but after
swimming strongly underwater 'came up unexpectedly

far from his boat, looking extremely solemn, with his pipe still in his mouth. On climbing back into the sandalo, he calmly knocked the wet tobacco out of his pipe; refilled from his rubber pouch, which had kept its contents dry; borrowed a light; and with the single word "Avanti" went his way. Such impassivity charmed the Venetian onlookers; word went round of this incident which, coupled with his aquatic fervour, gained him membership of the Bucintoro Swimming Club.' And that, one feels, would have gone some way to compensating him for all the inadequacies and unhappiness of a disappointed life.

Corvo tried to encourage the Cornish painter Tuke to journey to Venice and paint these lithe gondoliers and swimmers poised in the air and water like 'showers of aquamarine on a sapphire sea'. He felt he was the only painter alive who could do them justice. Tuke's paintings of boys bathing off the coast of Cornwall, against glittering backdrops of sun and sea, were exhibited almost every year at the Royal Academy towards the end of the nineteenth century. Under the influence of Tuke's *The Bathers* Corvo himself painted a picture of numerous nude boys playing around in the moonlit, phosphorescent waves of St Andrews Bay, and wrote 'A Ballade of Boys Bathing': 'Breasting the wavelets, and diving there,/ White boys, ruddy, and tanned, and bare.' 'White' at the start of the line is significant. Although these writers and painters venerated the sun, they were averse to bronzed bodies. Tuke would never allow his models to sunbathe. He only painted white skin. When Corvo's Robert Kemp emerged from the Serpentine, Nicholas Crabbe was struck by the 'pure diaphonous whiteness' of him, his ivory skin. The poet Martin Armstrong watches a young swimmer and muses sadly: 'To think that the glory must leave his head,/ And his young, white body must all forsake him.' English women on European beaches protected themselves from the sun under sunshades and parasols, in order to keep their skin white and distinguish themselves from foreigners.

Tuke used to bathe in the early morning throughout his life, even in winter. He would swim at six-thirty before working, then again with his models in the late afternoon. He particularly liked painting shallow water that shelved gradually, revealing the seabed below the swimmers through the blue and green surface. His influence was enormous. His portrait of the adolescent T.E. Lawrence changing to swim on the beach hung in the music room at Clouds Hill in the last years of Lawrence's life, when he used to motorcycle to Southampton every evening to test his powers of endurance by swimming assiduously in the public pool. *Midday Rest* hung over Ranjitsinhji's bed in his palace in India. He also coached Tuke's cricket. The most erotic of his paintings, *Summer Dreams*, was bought by T. C. Worsley, who shocked the authorities at Wellington College by hanging it above his fireplace. After bathing once in a lake, Barbellion the 'Disappointed Man' clambered back into the boat and stood up to dry himself in the sun 'like one of Mr Tuke's young men'.

Although happily married, Tuke was acquainted with a number of the so-called Uranians, homosexual writers of the period, many of whom looked to his work for inspiration. It was due primarily to Tuke that numerous bathing poems were composed at the turn of the century, describing waves yearning to clasp and circle swimming boys. One poet contemplates Gainsborough's elegant *Blue Boy* and wonders whether he ever longed to be wild and dishevelled: 'Did you e'er strip to the winds and go swimming?/ Run on the seashore exaltingly bare?'

The most individual of these poets was Ralph Chubb, who claimed that an early memory of watching some boys playing naked in the sea marked his temperament for life. According to D'Arch Smith he was so affected by the death beside him in the Great War of a curly-haired blacksmith's son that he determined to free English youth from the cynical manipulation of the elderly and bourgeois. He appealed to the 'young swimmers' of England: 'My staunch young brothers, I know you! Your bard has arisen at last! When you sweat at the mills I am with you, when the siren hoots, and off you run with your towel and strip to the skin and plunge from the black lockgate in the pool and wash off the grime and sweat.' His 'Ballad of the Forest' describes a visit he made to a secluded bathing-place where boys and young girls stripped naked to swim unmolested until they are discovered by two scandalised adults and driven from the water. In 'The Water Cherubs' he expresses his longing to join again on the beach the group of naked bathing boys that he had seen so long ago.

This was the age of the voyeur, of observers who adopted the role of lonely witness rather than joyous participant in the Byronic manner. A poet watches some boys 'slothfully' stretch their alluring limbs in the water, but declines to approach them: 'Awhile I watch them splash and dive and duck,/ Then saunter off and curse

– and bless my luck.' Before their eyes the bodies of
boys are transformed by the touch of water. Neapolitan
ragazzi become sea creatures with silvery scales, boys
on grimy barges 'the youth of Greece'. Gerard Manley
Hopkins, a devotee of Frederick Walker's painting of
'Bathers' and drawn, like Byron and Saki, to young men
who loved swimming, described in his 'Epithalamium'
a listless stranger whose mood is transformed when he
comes across some boys bathing naked in a 'marbled'
river, 'boisterously beautiful'. Embarrassed perhaps by
his emotion, he climbs down to a neighbouring pool,
where he strips and swims in the 'flinty, kind cold
element', among 'warbling water' and 'chancequarried,
self-quoined rocks'.

Although married, John Addington Symonds considered it permissible to 'imagine delights beyond his
grasp' and indulge his sense of 'plastic beauty' in men
by visiting the public baths. When in London he would
stroll out in the early morning or late evening along the
Serpentine – 'there I feasted my eyes upon the naked
bathers'. It was from the banks of the Serpentine that
Corvo's Crabbe first set eyes on his Divine Friend, and
Kairns Jackson wrote in Corvo's honour the 'Ballade of
the Serpentine suggested by some lines of the Rev. F. W.
Rolfe'. In the summer afternoons at Oxford, Corvo was
observed, after his morning swim, 'sitting under the
Parson's Pleasure willows on a decrepit chair, rolling
cigarette after cigarette in his nicotine stained fingers',
and surveying the naked bodies with 'unbecoming satisfaction'. Corvo admitted to making a point of visiting
Oxford during Eights Week, because 'as a physical epicure I liked to see how England's most recent flesh is

coming on'. Parson's Pleasure was also an object of furtive curiosity for Walter Pater, the aesthete who when
asked once what he would like to have been, if not a
man, replied: 'A carp swimming for ever in the green
waters of some royal chateau.' It was while watching
in the Harrow school pool the bodies of divers 'curving
for their plunge' that J. A. Symonds first became aware
of his erotic inclinations, and the sight of a Harrow boy
emerging from the sea at Folkestone, of 'superb intellect
and refinement', made a profound impression on Wilfred
Owen on the last day he ever spent in England, as he lay
on the beach reading Shelley.

In poems of the Great War sympathetic young officers watch with foreboding the recruits in their charge
'chaffing and splashing and plunging into waterholes',
boys 'bursting the surface of the ebony pond', as they
exult in life perhaps for the last time. A casualty of
the war, H. H. Munro (Saki), an inveterate, punctilious bather in European rivers and London clubs, was
brought up by two aunts whom he loathed. His symbolic breakaway from their influence occurred when he
swam naked at Etretat, where Swinburne had swum out
on the outgoing tide. In the short story 'Gabriel Ernest',
a revelation of his guilt and anxieties, Saki personified
his homosexuality in the form of a swimmer, a 'strange
tongued' werewolf who 'feeds on child's flesh', whom
he first set eyes upon lying 'on a shelf of smooth stone
overhanging a deep pool'. As he lies there drying his
limbs luxuriously in the sun, his hair parted by a recent
dive, he seems innocent enough, and Saki presumes him
to be a bather from some neighbouring pool. Then he
notices his uncanny, tigerish eyes, and when the boy

plunges into the pool to swim across to him, he recoils in horror. 'I can't have you staying in these woods,' he protests. 'I fancy you'd rather have me here than in your house,' the boy replies. He becomes alarmed at the prospect of harbouring this 'wild nude animal' in his 'primly ordered' home. He makes no mention on his return of his discovery in the wood, but the following day, on entering the morning room, finds the boy 'gracefully asprawl on the ottoman'. 'How dare you come in,' he screams, 'supposing my aunt should see you,' and when he hears her footsteps, he makes frantic efforts to obscure as much of the boy's anatomy as possible under the folds of the *Morning Post*.

In an age of heavy formal clothing, the sight of the naked swimmer appeared as a revelation. When R. L. Stevenson as a boy watched his father running down the sands into the North Sea, he felt 'somewhat horrified at finding him so beautiful when stripped'. There is a strange account of Rajah Brooke's rather whimsical methods of selection for his Civil Service in Sarawak. On leave in England for a few months one summer, he was watching some boys bathing in water meadows near Totnes in Devon. One boy particularly impressed him, who had far outdistanced the others. As the boy stood naked and dripping in the meadow, Brooke approached him and was so taken by his charm that he adopted him and had him educated to be a future administrator on the island.

In the last few years of his tragic life, while suffering from the effects of a car crash at twenty from which he was never to recover, the bizarre and mawkish Denton Welch would walk along the banks of Kentish rivers in pursuit of boys bathing and diving off the platforms of locks. He would sit down on the opposite bank and stare 'frankly' at them. Their physical strength and exuberance represented everything that he lacked as an invalid. 'It could only last a year or two, that animal magic,' he mused, as some lusty and rough boy performed an erotic striptease on the riverbank, conscious of Welch's staring eyes. Sometimes he would be shocked when the trace of an 'educated' accent betrayed a swimmer as a product of the 'dreaded gentry', but he would be reassured by the sight of hob-nailed boots and dirty clothes.

The swimmer became for Denton Welch an object of hero-worship. Like Corvo he hoped to find among them the perfect friend. His shrill, nervous, feminine nature searched for a complement in figures that exuded physical power and confidence, with 'thick beautiful necks' and 'barbarian hands'. There is the curious short story 'When I was Thirteen', based probably on a personal experience like almost all his writing, that relates a momentary infatuation with an undergraduate while on holiday in Switzerland. His elder brother, who happens to be at the same university, tries to steer the young boy away from his influence. 'He's not very much liked,' he tells him, 'although he's a very good swimmer.' The expression on his face implies his disapproval, but his words only serve to reinforce the boy's interest.

After a childhood spent in China, Denton Welch was sent to boarding-school in England, where he suffered abuse for his effeminate appearance and irregular behaviour. Holidays were spent with dull relatives in respectable hotels. It was during this frustrated period of his life that an ecstatic river swim described in the autobiographical *In Youth is Pleasure* seemed to wash away all his humiliations and open up visions of a happier, more liberated existence. One holiday, when standing on a riverbank, he watches a scarlet canoe race round a bend towards him. It was paddled by a man and two boys. They were singing and laughing. He envies them their freedom and excitement, in contrast to his own confinement, in hotels with relatives, or in a school 'like any criminal in gaol'. The degradation of his life appalled him. He runs to the boathouse, hires a canoe, and notices some swimming-slips hanging behind the counter. 'And how much are those things?' he asked. 'He had a fierce desire for them. They seemed to him at that moment a very potent symbol, something very free, daring.' In a state of great agitation he pushes the canoe out into midstream and paddles over to a miniature beach on the side of the river. There he 'jerked his shirt off his head excitedly. When he pulled up the slips and felt the connecting string between his legs, he gulped and trembled and went rigid. He stood like this on the muddy little beach, exulting and tremulous,' then slowly entered the dark water.

It was as though the intensity of his experiences during these lone swims somehow revived in Welch memories of the independence and happiness of his carefree years as a boy in China during and after the Great War – 'before the preparatory school doors shut behind him and split off forever his childhood, so that it gleamed always for him as the only unsullied part of his early life'. One of his earliest recollections there was of his elder brothers bathing naked in the rock pools, 'looking beautiful against the trees and sky'. He was too inexperienced to join them. 'Painfully' he learnt to swim, after being pushed in by his mother. He became gradually a devotee of the 'delicious' water of oriental pools. He would sometimes swim with his shirt and shorts and sandals on, 'beating about with my hands and shouting out my delight'.

His parents sailed away one summer on a trip to Java and left the brothers with friends on a plantation. The first morning there Welch was up early. He walked down the garden on the mountainside, from one terrace to another, threading his way among the bamboo groves and luxuriant ferns that were irrigated by a network of streams – 'the springs bubbled straight up through rocks and sand. There were bamboo pipes leading from some of these. I followed one line down through terraces, and suddenly I was in a little clearing with a swimming pool before me. The pipes were steadily filling it. I knelt down and put in my hand. It was stingingly cold.' After tea in the afternoon they went down to bathe. 'The pool was now full of the bright, bitter spring water. By this time I had learnt to swim and I felt proud as I did my energetic breaststroke. In the days that followed I would rush down early to the pool in my black cotton bathing suit and let the water slowly envelop me. I would swim and turn and feel the hot sun burning on me.' Sometimes they would be carried by coolies through the forest in sedan chairs. When they noticed a stream or rock pool, the coolies would set them down, and they would undress and stand in the water, 'their toes curling round the smooth pebbles'. Nearby was an empty house among some overhanging trees with a swimming pool in which they bathed, 'dank and dark with rotting leaves. It was ghostly and horrible and exciting.' One day his mother returns. He kisses her 'frantically'. The next morning, when he got up early to bathe and his mother came with him, 'I danced about with nothing on. I rolled in the water, feeling it hug me closer without the cotton suit between. It was glorious freedom.'

He was obsessed by his mother – her beauty, her clothing, her underwear and jewels. It was his mother who awakened his passion for Greek and Roman sculpture, when she showed him a collection of photographs she had formed when at school in a Florence convent. In a book of Greek myths she once gave him he comes across a picture of Prometheus spreadeagled on the mountainside, being devoured by the eagle. He reacts with a mixture of shame and admiration, and closes the book quickly. He now began to feel he was an Ancient Greek, 'free and fierce and like a clever animal'. He wanted to appear naked in public. In later life he was to transfer to his swimmers this early admiration for the heroic figures and nudity of Greek sculpture, when they stood in the shallows like 'truncated statues fixed to a base in the bowl of a fountain', or after pulling their shirts over their heads seemed to be a 'white pillar of marble growing out of the tree trunk of their trousers' as if involved in the gradual metamorphosis of an Ovidian myth. Welch even admires himself when after swimming once in his clothes, he looked with interest at the 'Greek sculpture effect' caused by the thin wet shirt clinging to his ribs and chest.

When Denton Welch returns to China after his schooldays at Repton are over, it has lost much of its magic. His mother had died. A swimmming pool he used once to enjoy, beyond a tennis court and decaying summerhouse, is now empty and 'dead leaves chased each other round the sloping sides'. Thrust now into the adult world of country-club life, he feels uncomfortable, disillusioned, and self-conscious. When he dives into the blue waters of the club pool, among the pink bodies, he hits his head on the bottom. On rising to the surface dazed and sore, he hopes that his legs had not spread apart grotesquely and indecently like those of others around him. In his youth he had watched his brothers bathing in the rock pools, naked and beautiful. Now he becomes aware of the swollen stomachs of middle-aged men, with their 'hanks of hair in the most improbable places', bloated women with buttocks like 'full wine skins' and their 'waxy, hairy, blue-veined thighs'. A girl invites him to swim through her legs. They look so vast and thick through the water that he feels hardly able to swim through. A party one night in a private pool becomes a nightmare. He recoils from the black water. Someone tries to duck him and he almost screams. He strikes out and hits the man on the mouth. He is forced by the man underwater – 'feeling my hand pass over a cold, contracted nipple, I tweaked it viciously and tore at the flesh and hair on his chest'.

During one of those long summer afternoons as he lay on the riverbank watching boys bathing, Denton Welch was reading *The Philosophy of Solitude* by John Cowper Powys, the novelist who had witnessed in Venice Corvo's fantastic equipage, and like him was a self-confessed mystic. The essay Welch would have found sympathetic as it advocated the need for withdrawal from modern society. To defy the influence of science, the damage it has caused by undermining the mind and the will, man according to Powys must resort to a 'passionate loneliness' and look for inspiration in mythology and memories of his own mystical experiences. Like George Borrow, Powys longed to escape from the 'tribal activities' of school and organised society. They were both solitary and brooding, deprecated ambition, success, the effects of science, anything mechanical, and cultivated their exiled state of mind in pursuing their obsession with the Celtic past and mythology. They shared an abhorrence for everything an English gentleman represents, and a sympathy for the down-trodden, tramps, the Celtic fringes of society. Their lives were devoted to sensual, mystical, elemental sensations that found expression in their swimming.

'It has now become a kind of religious rite with me,' Powys writes in his autobiography, 'like muttering a Latin psalm, to revive the feelings with which I swim out of my depth. I turn it into a mood in which, with the pride of the devil, I defy the world! It was certainly towards the non-human condition of floatingness and flowingness that I struggled, when, by swimming out beyond my depth, I felt as if I resolved myself into air and sky and sea! One of the most daring things I ever did was to swim out into the deep sea from Chesil Beach! I had heard my father speak of doing this, and so I must needs do it too, although Bernie himself, a very good swimmer, refused to swim so far. Indeed I have never in my life seen any mortal person bathing off Chesil Beach.'

Powys describes at length and vividly the 'ichthyosaurus ego' that provided the impulse for much of his swimming. He related it to his concept of 'loneliness' as the 'soul's strongest link with all the earlier stages of evolution'. In a state of 'loneliness' a human being feels himself drawn backward, down the long series of his avatars, into the earlier planetary life of animals, birds and reptiles and even into the cosmogonic life of rocks and stones. Through swimming he was transported back to that world of weird ritual and mythology described in his novels. Just as Borrow, when gazing into the Welsh lake, had longed to plunge far down into its black waters and associate with the prehistoric creatures that his imagination supposed still lurked there, Powys took delight in swimming far out of his depth with his head 'elongated above the waves', when he felt as 'primaeval as an ichthyosaurus'.

Swimming also made Powys feel like an enthusiastic young girl, as he always did when affected by experiences and people that attracted him. It transformed him into one of those sylph-like creatures with delicate, adolescent limbs that continually preyed on his mind and drew him irresistibly to the beaches of Brighton. There he would for years, even after his marriage, pursue his 'maniacal quest for provocative feminine forms basking in that blazing sunshine'. He would 'gloat like a satyr on hundreds of bodies as they bathed or extended themselves for his delight along the sand, fastening his feverish gaze on any leg, knee or ankle that chanced to be revealed'. He was to discover that he was not the only one affected, as he became aware of certain other men who had evidently reached a point of obsession far beyond his own, whose eyes that had lost all human expression shocked and terrified him – 'No heartless seducers of women, no neurotic perverts that I have ever encountered have had such a look of being hopelessly damned as these elderly gentlemen betrayed in their curiously high-coloured faces, as if they lived on the heart's blood of women, as they hunted and stared and eternally stared and hunted!'

In his novel *Weymouth Sands* a girl with 'high Mongolian cheekbones' can not resist her passion for watching boys bathing. She is married to a dry philosopher. While he sits on the beach engrossed in his speculations, she lies shivering and open-mouthed as her 'whole nature flowed and writhed like a passionate sea-Undine round the glittering bodies of the naked lads'. Powys's compulsive voyeurism extended beyond the beaches of Brighton. It caused him to accept lectureships in America merely in order to gaze at naked women in the slot machines of Philadelphia, to feast his eyes on their sylph-like limbs in burlesque shows, and watch from the dark streets of New York secretaries as they undressed in their illuminated apartments 'like tropical birds'.

In America Powys swam with Theodore Dreiser and Edgar Lee Masters in the freezing waters of a Columbia County grotto. He derived a perverse pleasure from seeing Dreiser's shocked expression on entering the chilly water, as he wanted to cause him a physical jolt, to wrestle with him 'as I felt surging waves of magnetic attraction between us'. In San Francisco he watched George Sterling, the aesthete and friend of Jack London, diving for waterlilies in the ponds of Golden Gate Park. A letter from Virginia describes an inn where he stayed on a marsh, by a sea-estuary among 'reeds and black decaying tree trunks and indescribable mud – and on the other side of the water black cypresses and the House of Usher. The place heaved and palpitated with the life of putrescence like a horrible great heart.' Here he bathed, from a shore that was covered with dead turtles, among the shrieking cries of fish hawks, in saltwater that 'tasted of Death'. Powys in fact loathed estuaries. He was put off by their sinister tidal currents, the perverse mingling of sea and river fish. Yet the masochistic strain in his nature always compelled him to swim in them. By the mouth of the river Arun in Sussex he was perturbed by its 'strange double nature' that resembled some 'monstrous offspring of an unnatural mating'. None the less he used to bathe there on starlit nights with his brother Llewellyn, on one occasion submerging so long under the swift dark tide that their companions gave them up for dead.

Powys had learnt to swim in the Sherborne school bath, at the time one of the largest bathing pools in England. There he was dangled on the end of a rope 'like a newt' as he used his arms, not to swim, but to cling frenziedly to the cord suspended above him. The only master in the school he found at all sympathetic was an 'athletic' Epicurean, who appealed to him because he bathed quite alone in the pool not only in the summer months, but throughout the winter. It was in the changing rooms by the pool that Powys's voyeuristic obsessions evolved, where he made sure that he changed and dried next to a 'notoriously beautiful' boy in the school – 'my delight in the boy's loveliness was so intense that when I stole timorous, nervous, furtive, and yet ardently satyrish glances at him, as having undressed at my side he stood for a moment in his bathing drawers meditating his plunge into those blue-green waters, I was totally lost to the world'. It was an experience he was never to forget. When, over eighty, he was writing to a friend about a book that he had not 'dipt' but 'dived' into, the aquatic imagery he had used took his mind back to the diving-board by the Sherborne school bath, where on the brink he would 'hesitate long, partly from fear but also because of the lovely figure of – Minor, with whom I was in love'.

Powys, like almost all these swimmers, was hardly a typical schoolboy and suffered for it. He used to run twenty miles home to tea to enjoy a momentary release from the ridicule and bullying he had to endure. His autobiography mentions his longing at the time to return to the security of the maternal womb, which he compared to the 'snug, secluded' retreat beneath the sea of Jules Verne's Captain Nemo. It was in the presence of water that he could occasionally find consolation and become totally lost to the world, by the swimming pool and the ponds surrounding Sherborne that became for Powys, during his walks in the area, 'holy' places. They reminded him of an aquarium he had been given as a child, in which he arranged an underwater landscape of hills, gorges, and forests and in so doing became aware of the power of the individual mind to create its own enclosed world, independent of the attitudes of others. In later life he would take pains to 'dip' as a form of ritual his 'sacred' walking-stick in every historical stream he encountered, descending once long flights of steps down to the Guadalquivir. On recovering from tuberculosis, his younger brother Llewellyn ran down over the sounding shingle to 'dip his hands into the sea'.

After bathing once in a forest pool, Llewellyn wondered if John could supplicate the nymphs of the pool on his behalf, for John alone he felt had access to those 'deep, cool wells where the gods themselves let down their buckets'. The sadistic instinct that fuelled Powys's erotic imagination throughout his life, ever since he had been fixated at the age of three by a picture of an eagle seizing a lamb, he described as a 'demon swimming up from the depths'. Those characters in his novels who are prepared to pull off their boots and plunge into the depths of the sea immediately establish an ascendancy.

The 'ichthyosaurus ego' advocated by Powys, that draws one back through earlier stages of evolution, as a resistance against the indifference and vulgarities of contemporary life, lay behind the swims of those who searched in remote places for what they felt civilisation had lost. Although they did not revert to the prehistoric world of Powys, their bathes in far flung corners of the world expressed their spiritual quest for a more uninhibited, instinctive, pagan existence. Their attitude was that of the Irish priest in George Moore's novel *The Lake*, who comes to realise that he has succumbed gradually to the dead wisdom of codes and dogmas, his body neglected and devoid of emotion. For years he had resigned himself to a 'frog-like acquiescence in a stagnant pond.' He finally makes the decision to confront the world and travel to America, in order to 'cling to his own soul, to cherish what is inly'. He lays aside his priest's clothes on a patch of white sand by the side of the lake, and is transformed suddenly into a figure of pagan beauty. He steps from stone to stone, and stands transfigured on the last one 'as on a pedestal, tall and grey in the moonlight – his buttocks hard as a fawn's, and dimpled like a fawn's when he draws himself up before plunging after a nymph'. In the dark water he turns on his back to look up at the moon. He is reminded of baptism, when naked he came into the world.

Those lone women travellers of the nineteenth century suggest in the emotional intensity of their descriptions that their swims meant more to them than mere refreshment in a hot climate. They seem, rather, to symbolise their release from the restrictions imposed on them by a masculine society at home, gestures of contempt for the conventions they had left behind. In England they were barred from most baths. When on the beach, they were subject to incessant and demonic male scrutiny, as we learn from Powys. Far away in the tropics they seem to be washing themselves finally free of the suffocating world they had abandoned, revelling in a newly awakened sensuality that they had always been denied. One hot night in West Africa, when sleep was impossible, Mary Kingsley steals out of her hut past her sleeping companions and paddles a canoe across a dark lake, alone among the stars and the flashing fish leaping out of the water. She finds a miniature rocky bay with a soft beach of sand, strips off her clothes, swims in the black water and dries herself on her cummerbund.

From an island in the Pacific Ocean, Constance Gordon Cumming writes to her sister in Scotland, on the excitement of stripping off her layers of Victorian frills and exposing her naked white body for the first time to the pleasures of tropical sun and water: 'You can hardly realise what an enchanting feature in our travels is our daily bath. No humdrum tub, fitted by a commonplace housemaid, but a quiet place on some exquisite stream, sometimes a clear babbling brook, just deep enough to lie down full-length beneath an overarching bower of great tree-ferns and young palm-fronds, all tangled with trailing creepers, and just leaving openings through which you see peeps of the bluest skies, and tall palms far overhead . . . sometimes I come on such irresistible places when I am scrambling about alone, where the tall reedy grasses are matted with large-leaved convolvuli, and not a sound is heard save the ripple of the storm over the stones, or the rustle of the leaves in the faint breeze, that I just slip in and revel, and go on my way rejoicing.'

Until middle age Marianne North had led the typically cloistered life of a Victorian middle-class spinster, dedicated to the care of her deaf and demanding father. On his death she determines to devote the rest of her life to painting the flowers of this 'lovely' world, and leave her house in Hastings for ever. She sets sail for America. There she rents a house on the East Coast washed on three sides by the sea. A few steps from the back door there is a sandy little bay, 'the very ideal of a bathing place', where she mentions swimming for the only time in her lengthy travels, though not however naked: 'We bought some stuff to make bathing-dresses at "John Loring's, one-price-dry-goods-warehouse" in Boston. Mrs S. had chosen one of scarlet serge. I one of dark-blue grey, so that we looked much like two large lobsters in the water, one boiled, the other unboiled, but spectators were not common.'

Many of these travellers were inspired by the example of Shelley's mother-in-law, Mary Wollstonecraft. When wandering alone around Scandinavia she had discovered bathing as a remedy for her ill health. She used to row herself out across the sea to some sheltered rocks to preserve her privacy while swimming. The tradition was carried on by Rose Macaulay, in her lone compulsive bathes from the fabled shores of Spain and Portugal, naked whenever possible, sometimes at dawn below the climbing gardens and arcaded terraces, but more often at night, looking back from the warm, dark, 'shot-silk' waters to the twinkling arc of lights that followed the line of the palm-fringed crescent beaches.

One never reads of D. H. Lawrence swimming in England, not even in the Garsington pool, an old fish-pond below the sloping lawns, converted by Ottoline Morrell into a romantic rectangular pool fed by a natural spring. The Morrells' tennis court had already inspired the setting by Bakst of a Nijinsky ballet. A small island in the middle, surmounted by a sarcophagus, was used as a diving-board, from where Juliette Huxley dived, 'her long yellow hair making her look like a water nymph or a picture of a silvery saint by Crivelli'. Ottoline Morrell drifted among the bathers in a peplum-style tunic, while Dora Carrington posed naked on the pedestals of sur-rounding statues. Not even such an atmosphere could tempt Lawrence into the water, though he could sneer at the sight of Bertrand Russell in a bathing costume – 'Poor Bertie Russell! He's all Disembodied Mind.' Perhaps, as an advocate of primitive, elemental man, Lawrence was ashamed of exposing his own 'bony, pinched, pigeon-breasted' body, his skin that always remained white when for him a brown skin was the only beautiful one. To the Greeks a 'white unsunned body was fishy and unhealthy' he once asserted. His avoidance of swimming is surprising when bathing scenes in his novels, observed by women with disgust or amusement, provide brief moments of male happiness, a symbolic release from sexual inhibition, unhappy marriages, and frustrated love.

When however Lawrence travelled to Mexico in pursuit of a more primitive, sensual existence, his physical shyness fell away and he succumbed in idiosyncratic fashion to the sensations of swimming that he loved to describe. There in the cool of the Chapala evening he was seen by Witter Bynner leading Frieda, 'she in her bathing dress, he in shorts, to a shallow neck of the inlet leading to the station. The shallows were only waist-deep, the shore an almost solid jumble of sharp rocks and stones, with interstices of mud and slimy reeds; but here the two figures would arrive each afternoon. They would pick a painful way into the water, hand in hand, teetering and wobbling, till they were submerged to the hips, whereupon with the utmost gravity and with hands clasped as they faced each other, he would start them bobbing up and down, a bit deeper each time, till shoulders were covered and then he would bob gradually up again, free himself, shining white, and stumble back to shore.' Frieda would laugh aloud at the absurdity of the display and his solemn dedication to the ritual.

Whatever his philosophy about the noble savagery of the Mexican Indian, in reality Lawrence objected strongly to the young Mexicans who played around them while they attempted to swim – 'Don't you realise how dirty these little chits are?' he would scream. 'You let them swim on your shoulders and clutch you round

10 *Class* – Marjorie Gestring, 1936 Olympic Games, John Gutmann

11 *Left:* Johnny Weissmuller,
1930, George Hoyningen-Huene

12 *Below:* Esther Williams

13 Busby Berkeley's waterfall sequence from *Footlight Parade*, 1933

14 Sutro Baths, San Francisco, *c*. 1900

15 'Roman' pool, Hearst Castle, San Simeon

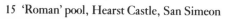

16 *The Swimming Hole, c.* 1883-5, Thomas Eakins

17 *Watson and the Shark*, 1778, John Singleton Copley

18 *Above: Diving Girl and Octopuses*, 1814, Katsushika Hokusai
19 *Below:* Japanese Crawl, 1936, Leni Riefenstahl
20 *Right:* High-diver, 1936, Leni Riefenstahl

21 *Houlgate, September 1919*, Jacques Henri Lartigue

the neck and rub their dirt into you. You don't know what diseases they have, what you might catch. It's outrageous, it's reckless, and it's a silly spectacle. People are talking.' His attitude to his wife's bathing revealed another paradox. Although his novels described the voluptuous behaviour of naked swimmers, here by the Mexican shore he demanded that Frieda should change in their hotel, not on the beach – 'then hesitantly,' Witter Bynner relates, 'as if afraid of his own remark but unable to restrain it, he whispered the strangest sentence I ever heard from him: "It's not a question of being considerate of any of you. *It's what people will think.*"' His inherent puritanism insisted that she swam in calico bloomers run up by himself. Perhaps in the back of his mind was the bitter memory of her naked swim, soon after they eloped, across a river to offer herself to a puzzled but compliant woodcutter, merely in order to shock Lawrence and establish her sexual freedom.

'How I hate civilisation', wrote Rupert Brooke in a letter from San Francisco on his way back to England from the Pacific, 'and houses and trams and collars.' The islands provided relief from a world grown 'tasteless, habitual, and dull'. Brooke had always been fascinated by the vagabond and wanderer as human types. The spiritual vagabond, he had noted while still at Rugby, was a rebel against the 'safeties and little confines of our ordinary human life'. In the South Seas he became captivated, like Lawrence in Mexico, by the romance of living with people who felt rather than thought, who were simple rather than complex. Swimming there summed up his preference for the instinctive to rational life, the savage to civilised society. Floating hour after hour over the warm lagoons of the South Pacific, or diving down to the coral reef in vain pursuit of the radiant butterfly fish, he felt his intellect decline, his body become more active, 'the senses and perceptions more lordly and acute'.

A letter home mentions that he felt it was better to 'leap by moonlight into a green and silver cool strange sea than to write rotten little poems'. He imagines his friends in London rushing from lunch party to lunch party – 'Won't you come and swim two minutes underwater catching turtles', he implores them, 'or dive forty feet into a waterfall.' On Tahiti, Brooke lived in a shack with a wide veranda over a blue lagoon, near a wooden pier with 'deep clear water for diving, and coloured fish that swim between your toes'. He bathed naked in pools under waterfalls, in volcanic lakes, and watched the 'loveliest people in the world diving thirty feet into the green sea'.

When he toured Canada, to escape from its dullness, what he considered its materialistic instincts, he would bathe in the lakes all day, diving off rocks into the 'clearest and sweetest of blue waters', or lie for hours quite naked on beaches of golden sand. It was the 'brisk touch' of the clear water as one dived that embodied for Brooke the essence of Canada, 'that every swimmer knows – colourless, faintly stinging, hard and grey, like the rocks around, full of vitality and sweet'. Like Byron he was drawn to deep and dangerous water, swimming once off an extreme rocky point where the streams of two rivers, the St Lawrence and the icy Sanguenay, met and swirled, and the current was exceptionally strong. He seemed to feel the two-mile-deep body of black water moving against him, that was 'as cold as death. As my head came up I made one dash for the land, scrambled out onto the hot rocks, and lay there panting. Then I dried on a handkerchief, dressed, and ran back home, still shivering, through the woods to the hotel.'

Swimming represented for Brooke a symbol of youth in a world dominated by the older generations he despised, of life at its very best and most emotional – 'from now on the edge will go off our longings and the fierceness off our feelings, and we shall no more swim in the Cam – and we shan't mind much'. His earliest verse, written at the age of ten, describes a huge wave breaking over the seafront. Later he was to spend two months over a poem in which he assumed the identity of a fish 'rippling with dark ecstasies'.* He bathed extensively in England, in the streams of the New Forest, the little rock pools of the Teign, and the great creamy breakers of Cornwall. When in Clevedon he would hire a boat to row out beyond the mud-flats, from which he would dive into the sea. Once, on the rocks off Lulworth,

* Richard Jefferies had once written an essay 'Mind under Water' to describe his empathy with fish. Many of these swimmers reveal a remarkable sympathy with life under-water, as if in touch with their distant marine existence, traces of which emerge in our bodies at the embryonic stage – lamprey's kidneys, gills – only to disappear at birth. Borrow longed to be a fish, as did Denton Welch on hot nights in China. Shelley returned crayfish to the Thames after buying them and Haydon was astonished by the paradox of his cruel treatment of women, his consideration for fish. The 'ichthyo-sauran' Powys transferred tadpoles from shallow to deep pools in a drought, waded far out into New York harbour to put a 'diseased tortured fish' out of its misery. Corvo felt himself a crab, Kingsley 'made up principally of fish bones'.

Brooke and some friends were reading Keats when his copy fell into the waves and drifted out on the strong tide. They hired a rowing-boat, but the rocks were too treacherous, so Brooke was forced to strip and plunge into the sea to retrieve it from the 'roaring vortex'. It was though for the pool at Grantchester that he longed when sweating 'sick and hot' in Berlin – 'And there the shadowed waters fresh/ Lean up to embrace the naked flesh'. Unlike Clough he had hardly swum at Rugby, although Jex Blake had had built there in 1876 the first covered pool in any school. A school friend remarked that he had not yet developed there that passion for bathing with which the friends of his Grantchester days associated him. He would read whenever they walked or bathed. Even in his first few terms at Cambridge it seemed to him a 'wicked waste of time to walk or swim – two things which came soon afterwards to give him as much pleasure as anything in the world'.

Once he had acquired lodgings above the river in the Vicarage at Grantchester, his correspondence becomes irradiated with descriptions of his swims. Cricket, the game he excelled in at school like Byron, is only mentioned twice, in references to his own final batting average of '2.something' and the school's neglect of left-hand bowling talent. About a mile along the river there is a pool where Byron reputedly swam. Just above, where the water was held up by sluice-gates, Brooke used to bathe, often like Byron at night, by the light of a bicycle lamp propped up in the grass on the edge of the river. It was here that he swam naked with Virginia Woolf, in the dark water 'smelling of mint and mud'. Now the wooden sluice-gates have been replaced by a concrete weir, so the water level has been reduced, and what was once a round deep pool is a narrow stretch of water choked with silt and weeds.

'Come prepared for bathing', Brooke would write to his friends, 'and clad in primitive clothes.' He became like Byron the centre of a circle of swimming friends, those 'flower-crowned, laughing swimmers'. Virginia Woolf remarked that under his influence the country near Cambridge was full of young men and women walking barefoot, sharing his passion for bathing and fish diet. When temporarily smitten by Brooke, Rose Macaulay swam naked with him in Grantchester just as Virginia Woolf had done. George Mallory, who while climbing would always 'fling' himself into Welsh pools or Himalayan streams, used to dive naked from the punts into the river. Even the great Cambridge philosophers of the time were infected by his enthusiasm. One reads of G. E. Moore on Dartmoor suddenly stripping off his clothes whenever he came across one of those cold, black, soggy pools and plunging in. Wittgenstein, at Cambridge soon after Brooke, swam in Byron's pool and was fond of drawing an analogy between philosophical thinking and swimming: 'Just as one's body has a natural tendency towards the surface and one has to make an exertion to get to the bottom – so it is with thinking.' Bertrand Russell bathed by moonlight with Rupert Brooke off Lulworth, and in his autobiography records his last 'friendly' encounter with Asquith the Prime Minister, which he felt the 'most surprising' incident of his whole life: 'I was walking on a hot summer's day in Oxfordshire, along the banks of a small river and I got so warm that I thought I would go in and bathe. And

I went in and bathed. The place seemed completely lonely, and I bathed without a costume. When I came out, who should I find standing on the bank but the Prime Minister. A great surprise to me. It was no occasion for dignity, or for serious discussion of great political problems. I put on my clothes as quickly as I could while he conversed in an amiable manner. And that was the last time I had a friendly, comfortable relation with Mr Asquith.'

When Brooke compared the mood of England embarking on war to that of 'swimmers into cleanness leaping', it reveals his admiration for the wild eccentricities of Noel Olivier as much as his own delight in the 'abandoned gesture'. Brooke never learnt to dive properly. He tended to hurl himself into space and splash down flat on the surface. Noel's sister however had married Hugh Popham, the Cambridge diving champion whose acrobatic dives fascinated Brooke, while Noel herself once shocked the headmaster at an old Bedalian weekend by diving naked off the high board in full view of everyone. On one occasion they bathed in a country river, ignoring the rustics, and Noel, 'not to be put off from her high dives, picked her way along the parapet between rows of wrists and elbows, politely asked for standing room in the middle, and made a perfect dive into the pool. With florid, expressionless face, the nearest labourer shook his black Sunday coat sleeve free of the drops which had fallen from her heel.'

After leaving Cambridge Brooke wrote enviously to Geoffrey Keynes: 'I loathe you for bathing in beautiful Grantchester. I splash occasionally in municipal baths made fetid by the middle classes.' When working at the

Bodleian he would get up in his country cottage long before dawn and bathe as he walked down to Oxford in the streams among the Cumner hills once favoured by Clough. The days of these extempore naked swims were numbered. The drowned body of the eminent classicist Llewellyn Davies was found in a pool near Kirby Lonsdale in the spring of 1905, where he had evidently bathed 'on his way to the railway station'.

Like Byron, Brooke died by Greek waters, when engaged in a war to liberate the 'holy land of Attica' from the Turks. It was confirmation that he was close to dying when on the beach of some Greek island one of his friends suggested swimming out to the ship about a mile away. Brooke said he wished he could join them, but he did not feel strong enough. 'So the others plunged in, and he followed seated among their clothes in a fisherman's boat.' On his death Henry James contrasted Byron's bitterness, his lack of harmony with his age, with the fact that Brooke 'took for his own the whole of the poetic consciousness he was born to, and moved about in it as a stripped young swimmer might have kept splashing through blue water and coming up at any point that friendliness and fancy, with every prejudice shed, might determine. Rupert expressed us all, at the highest point of our actuality.' When he was buried, the waters off the shore of Skyros lay almost motionless over a bottom of white marble, and the sea appeared to Arthur Asquith more beautifully green and blue than he had seen it anywhere.

Gallipoli was a swimmer's war, and brought to a bitter conclusion the English infatuation with Leander. Many of the invaders swam to shore behind the boats.

Survivors recall looking down through the clear water and watching the wounded struggling to regain the surface. Swimming now in the rocky shallows off the peninsula, by the thin beaches of tawny sand, and looking up to the cliffs and surrounding hills, it is easy to appreciate their agonies. Pinned down for months among the gullies and ravines, the soldiers took great risks in cleansing their bodies daily in the sea, as a brief respite from the maggots that obscured the bottoms of the trenches, the lice, scorpions, centipedes and other miseries. The Aegean became their only source of pleasure and health. The diversion on Suvla Bay, which could have proved the turning point of the war, was abandoned because Stopford's IX Corps prolonged their bathing rather than assist the Australians consolidate their brave initiative.

To Compton Mackenzie the scenes on the beaches resembled a seaside resort on a fine bank-holiday: 'Even the aeroplane on top of the low cliff eastward had the look of an "amusement" to provide a sixpenny or threepenny thrill; the tents might so easily conceal phrenologists or fortune-tellers; the signal station might well be a camera obscura; the very carts of the Indian transport, seen through the driven sand, had an air of waiting goat carriages.'

The novel *Tell England* by Ernest Raymond, who served at Gallipoli as an army chaplain, was inspired by the spirit of Brooke's 1914 war sonnets. Its two heroes, whose friendship forms the theme of the book, combine to form a fictional extension of Rupert Brooke – the athletic Rupert Ray, whose final length wins the swimming relay for his house at school, and Edgar Gray

Doe 'with his hair, paler than straw, reaching down beneath his shoulders, and with his brown eyes and parted lips wearing a feminine appearance'. After surviving Gallipoli where his friend dies, Rupert Ray writes in his notebook on his last night alive, in a trench on the Western front: 'We are given now and then moments of surpassing joy which outweigh decades of grief. I think I knew such a moment when I won the swimming cup for Bramhall' (his house at school).

Brooke never had a chance to swim the Hellespont, but he did enjoy several swims in the Dardanelles before he died. It was not Leander's swim, but memories of the Athenian expedition against Syracuse that 'flashed irresistibly' through his mind as he embarked for the campaign. The New Zealander Freyberg, the future Field Marshal, who accompanied Brooke's coffin a mile through the olive groves then helped dig his grave, was welcomed by Brooke on his arrival at Gallipoli because of his reputation as an Olympic swimmer. He was subsequently to swim two miles along the shore naked at midnight to distract the Turks with flares he ignited on various beaches. Another casualty of the war, Patrick Shaw Stewart, the Etonian classical scholar who was in charge of the firing party at Brooke's burial, was captivated by the 'association-saturated spots' that he could see around him as he swam one evening in the warm waters off the peninsular: 'The flower of sentimentality expands childishly in me on classical soil. It is really delightful to bathe in the Hellespont looking straight over to Troy, to be fighting for the command of Aegospotami, and to restate Miltiades' problem of the lines of Bulair.'

It was in the life and work of Rupert Brooke that the classical feeling for swimming and water exerted its utmost charms for the last time. Water possessed for him magical, cleansing properties, and swimming became a means of purification. His body was 'washed by the English rivers', his divers leapt into 'cleanness', and the 'soft caress' of the waters of Tahiti 'wash the mind of foolishness'. Before returning to Grantchester one June, he wrote to Geoffrey Keynes: 'Shall we bathe? I haven't bathed since November. There's a lot to wash off. Have you any care for syphilis of the soul? It may be there is a herb growing at the bottom of the river just above the pool at Grantchester, and that if I dive and find it and bring it up – it will heal me.' His last word as he lay dying was a plea for 'water'.

The process of stripping naked and plunging assumed for Brooke the form of a rite, a sexual and physical awakening and metamorphosis, a link with the local deities and naiads of the stream. Canada he found too impersonal, as it was devoid of any mystery or trace of the divine: 'The maple and the birch conceal no dryads, and Pan has never been heard amongst these reed-beds.' The native swimmers of the South Seas seemed to him like 'Greek statues come to life – to see them strip and swim a half-flooded river is an immortal sight'.

So often one finds the swimmer transformed into a figure of pagan myth, and used as an expression of romantic protest against the bitter experience of life. The sense of the classical Golden Age merged in the minds of these swimmers into the unruffled, radiant years of their childhood, whose loss so many of them mourned, that made Byron and Borrow and various others weep. It was this intense nostalgia nourished by a classical education that provided the incentive for the intoxicating swims of Clough and Swinburne, Shelley's submissive descent into the Mediterranean and Byron's bathing along its shores. Those who have been immersed, as so many of these swimmers were, in classicism, in the tears and tragic sense of transience that underly so much of classical sentiment, tend to look back, perhaps more than others, to a long lost state of perfection, both in society and in themselves. 'We are all Greeks,' protested Shelley. When Charles Kingsley, whose swims in the Berkshire chalk streams restored him to his childhood, set eyes on the classical Mediterranean for the first time in Southern France, he ran ecstatically through it for miles. He felt he was 'coming home'.

This classical spirit, that prompted Shelley to read Herodotus before plunging into Italian rivers, Corvo Lucan on the Venetian canals, his Hadrian VII Pindar above Lake Nemi, Swinburne and Powys Homer 'with barbaric devotion' by the sea, remains the most romantic and significant characteristic of English swimming. After Rupert Brooke it lost something of its intensity. One can sense though its presence in the work of Iris Murdoch, one of the last of the English river swimmers, where she translates her own memories into the lyrical experiences of those characters in her novels who swim to 'faint far-away light' in canals that tunnel through mountains or caves by the sea, across the surface of rivers or down through mysterious lakes, who long to get to the sea, and when they reach it, go down to it at midnight and dip their hands in as a form of ritual. It survives still in those swims of Patrick Leigh Fermor's through the

legendary rivers and caves that were reputed to link the
upper world with Hades, and in his final tribute to his
friend Kevin Andrews, who drowned in 1989 when
'after a day of reading the Religio Medici, he set off to
swim from the Southernmost Cape of Kythira to Avgo
Island: six miles there and back. A sudden storm blew up
with a seven-Beaufort-scale wind; night fell, and after a
long search, and helicopters flown over from Crete, hope
was finally abandoned. He vanished, forty-two years to
the day after first setting foot in Greece, heading for an
islet full of seal-caves and gulls in a legendary reach of
the Aegean.'

Born in Shanghai like Denton Welch, of an English
father and American mother, Andrews' life had been a
reincarnation of Borrow's in the Greek countryside. As a
scholar gypsy he had roamed the plains and hills dressed
in a shaggy goatsherd's cape with a wooden flute in his
pocket. Once, at an elegiac stage of his career, when he
was leaving Greece for the first time and felt his youth
was at an end, he had taken a train to Mount Olympos.
He got out at night by the shores of the North Aegean,
then walked down among the waist high esparto grass
to a beach 'where the stones showed clearly under the
water as I went in to wash off the day's dust and soot
in a foaming sparkle of phosphorus. I swam under water
through filtered moonbeams under the cold, yellow light
spilling all over the surface, and then fell asleep by the
little splash and fall of the Aegean a few feet away; on
the other side the masif of Olympos reared up into the
stars.'

When swimming one languid afternoon far out in the
Corinthian gulf, Robert Byron once sensed a momentary

lifting of the veil, some mysterious insight into the secrets of the ancient world: 'There is a unique rapture about a Greek bathe. The mystery of Ancient Greece unfolds itself. Those petty wars, those city states. Those burdens of the classroom.' No doubt it was those same 'burdens of the classroom' that have left me somehow obliged, when passing near lakes Trasimene and Sirmio, the bays of Salamis and Syracuse, the Spartan Eurotas and the Olympian Alpheios, to swim and submerge in their waters, as some form of tribute to the local deity, and spend much of my life in pursuit of interesting pools.

VI

German Romanticism

Der Taucher

WHILE THE ENGLISH dominated swimming in the nineteenth century, it was the Scandinavians who excelled at diving. When Noel Olivier was diving naked into the Bedales pool, and her brother-in-law astonishing Rupert Brooke with his displays from the high boards of Cambridge, diving was a relatively new art. For most it was merely a means of entering the water, until the Swedes swept the board at the 1900 Paris Olympics where they were forced to plunge into the Seine. The skills of their divers were celebrated in the paintings of Eugene Jansson who, after a lifetime depicting the bleak nocturnal suburbs of Stockholm, devoted the last ten years of his life to a dramatic series of male figure subjects. Set mostly in the Swedish Navy's bathhouse at Skeppscholman, these show nude or semi-nude sailors plunging and bathing in the pool, exulting in their muscular and frenzied movement.

The Swedes introduced the art of diving to England at the turn of the century. Their impact was enormous. The crowds were amazed at their daring and graceful evolutions, as they watched one diver after another hurled into space from a pagoda platform sixty feet high, with such force and spring that their bodies were carried about thirty feet away from the diving tower, the head thrown backwards, the back sharply hollowed, arms flung out to form a horizontal line through the shoulders like the spread wings of a bird, a position maintained until about six feet from the water. At the height of its flight the body appeared to pause in the air. It seemed to the spectators an 'idealistic' manner of reaching the water, for it was just like the action of the swallow when flying.

Like Diaghilev's 'Ballet Russe' that took London by storm a few years later, these swallow dives made an impression on the arts of the period, particularly in the depiction of classical figures. As Bellerophon falls headlong towards the sea from the flying horse Pegasus in Riviere's painting of 1906, his arms are spread wide. Corvo photographed naked boys plunging into Lake Nemi, their 'heads thrown back and arms raised and held wide'. Aware of his weakness in drawing figures, Corvo would project slides of these photographs on to empty canvases, and draw round the outlines of the diving figures. Then after adding a bow and quiver he would call the finished product *Cupid in Flight*. The Nereids in the romantic paintings of Arnold Böcklin, the Swiss German artist, that plunge off rocks into the waves, arms extended and bodies arched, display all the influences of the fashionable swallow dive.

The Germans gradually took over the ascendancy from the Swedes, mainly through Walz and Zurner, though the Swedes managed to win back their titles briefly when the Olympic Games were held in Stockholm in 1912. Diving had its origins in the great gymnastic movement inspired by Friedrich Jahn, in reaction to the series of crushing defeats inflicted on Prussia by Napoleon at the beginning of the nineteenth century. In the summer equipment would be moved to the beaches of the Baltic and acrobatics performed over water. Gradually they were combined with water. Gymnasts who turn to diving consider it far more difficult. With no support, nothing to grip or hold on to, they experience the effect, in the space of at most two seconds, of being lost in space, with no idea where they are in relation to the board, the water, or the side of the pool.

This sense of disorientation was conveyed by Hans Ertl, Riefenstahl's cameraman at the Berlin Olympics of 1936, by positioning his camera in the pool, half-submerged below the diving platforms, in order to confuse the viewer over the angle and direction of the dive. It was a method of filming that he had formulated at the Winter Olympics, when he crouched in the middle of the track and revolved his camera as the ski-jumpers shot over him 'like eagles, only to sheer off at the last moment because the intended prey was inedible'. He would also dive down with the submerging divers and after adjusting his lens film them returning to the surface through the water. Much of the sequence was shot in an empty stadium, after the Games had ended, sometimes by searchlight till late at night, from angles and positions that would never have been allowed during actual competition.

Riefenstahl's *Olympische Spiele* gave final expression to the Nordic passion for diving. The film was a product of the cult of physical athleticism and open-air nudity that was such a marked feature of German life at the time. The Nietzchean belief in nature as a source of primal energy for mankind was the inspiration for the devotion to swimming in the Weimar Republic, when according to Spender 'the sun – symbol of the great wealth of nature within the poverty of man – was a primary social force. Thousands of people went to the open-air swimming baths or lay down on the shores of the rivers and lakes, almost nude, and sometimes quite nude, and the boys who had turned the deepest mahogany walked among the people with paler skins, like kings among the courtiers. The sun healed their bodies of the years of war, and made them conscious of the quivering, fluttering life of blood and muscles, covering their exhausted spirits like the pelt of an animal.'

On the misty shores of the Baltic, where in the opening of Riefenstahl's film the movements of female gymnasts merge mysteriously with the ripples of the sea and the waving grass, Spender would undress in the early morning beneath the pine trees. 'Let us go into the water now,' someone would murmur, and they would wade far out to find a deep channel and swim for an hour, 'shouting only an occasional word across the sea to one another'.

Nakedness was the 'democracy of the new Germany', the Weimar Republic, the nakedness that for George Borrow had signified the virtue of the swimmer, that set him apart from the cant and self-deception of the bourgeois. Off Regan Island in the Baltic, where Caspar Friedrich had painted, Isherwood splashed around with the blond German boys; in Berlin he plunged into the great lake at Wansee or the Wellenbad, an enormous indoor pool with a mechanism for creating waves. Like Corvo and others by the Serpentine, boys gathered there in search of friendship, that 'Sacred German concept'. The open-air baths were vast and surrounded by Greek statues, crowded in all weathers by men in bathing slips whose brevity shocked Weissmuller on a tour of Germany in the Twenties, when fresh from New York State where the law, until 1938, stipulated long drawers for men that covered the chest. Auden acknowledged that 'Sunday meant lakes for many, a browner body, beauty from burning', though he did not care for the beach and preferred rainy weather. Little has changed. It was not long ago that I was swimming on a dark February evening in a series of open-air pools above Kassel with a group of joyous naked Germans beneath the falling snow.

This identification with the mysterious forces of nature affected the photographs of List and the paintings by Heckel and Mueller, of dreamy, angular nudes lying by riversides, or wading into the blue lakes from which all human life once evolved, images of primaeval innocence and unfulfilled longing for a life of beauty and universal harmony. They reflect an effort to recapture, through primitivism, a happy state that no longer existed. The figures in Munch's *Bathing Boys* assume, as they become more immersed in the clear blue water, the shapes of strange amphibian creatures, the forms of frogs or turtles that recall man's prehuman origins.

It was the intensity of this belief in the regenerative powers of nature and athleticism that made Riefenstahl's filming of the Berlin Olympics an act of almost religious devotion. In its most memorable sequence, a prolonged succession of divers arch their bodies among the clouds, their arms extended in the attitude of Icarus and we watch them fall and rise again through the water. Of all the passages in the film, it is these diving figures that reveal her admitted sympathy with the Greek idea of the grace of the human body and its liberation through movement. From a series of fragmented images she contrived a cinematic invention that bore little relation to what was actually seen in the Olympic pool. It reflects her view that the games were as much an aesthetic exercise as competitive, though the emotional effect of the music and editing seems to be trying to convey rather more than merely her self-confessed passion for physical beauty and preoccupation with the bold and heroic in life. There is a suggestion of something more remote, an allusion to the old German Romantic belief in the aristocracy of the spirit, the mood of yearning and restless search for self-fulfilment beyond the mundane and trivial, 'compelled to go forth from here and ever forth as far as the sky is blue'.

One can sense that this passage in the film was intensely personal. The figures of the divers merge into that of the romantic heroine she herself played in her 'mountain' films, a pure, innocent and simple girl who lived among the clouds, her mystical aspirations untouched by the corruption of the valley people below. More thought and preparation went into this sequence than any other, as if Riefenstahl believed it contained the core of what she wished to convey. It was reserved for the climax of a film in which she wanted to demonstrate 'the complete domination of the body and the will by the individual, and create an extraordinary atmosphere that is lifted above ordinary life'. Towards the end of the sequence, as the laws of gravity seem suspended and the divers appear to enjoy complete freedom from all earthly restrictions, Riefenstahl deliberately underexposes their forms, so that their features become indistinguishable and their bodies reduced to silhouettes of impersonal, mythical figures as they form intricate patterns against the background of a cloudy, ominous sky.

Reifenstahl had wanted to begin the film with a swimming scene, of Naiads emerging from the sea with the Olympic flame. 'And for that end the Aegean sea was very beautiful, picturesque, wonderfully surrounded by cypresses, pines, and bright yellow sand. And that is the way that Böcklin painted it in his pictures. And it would develop a conception of the beauty of the sea, Romanticism. Above all in Böcklin's *Isle of the Dead*, many motives were contained that should have been contained in my film.' The whole film reveals a strong relationship with the Romantic as well as the Neo-classical tradition. Like Hitler she wanted to revive the German sense of myth and magic, mystical aspirations that she symbolised in the image of the diver.

Earlier in her career Riefenstahl had been a dancer, in a fanciful and abandoned manner like Isadora Duncan, and on first meeting Hitler she had danced alone for him. One of her acts was called 'The Blue Flower', which like her film *The Blue Light* was inspired by the vision of the blue flower in Novalis's novel *Heinrich von Ofterdingen*, that established the mood of spiritual yearning as central to the German Romantic tradition. In his flight from earthly restrictions, Novalis's poet searches for the blue flower that he has glimpsed in his dreams. He comes to a pool: 'An irresistible longing to bathe seized him; he undressed and stepped down into the basin. It seemed as if a sunset cloud was enveloping him; a heavenly sensation flowed through his soul; with voluptuous delight countless thoughts seemed to mingle within him. New images never seen before arose and interfused and became visible around him, and every wave of the element clung to him like a tender blossom. The waves appeared to be charming girls dissolved, which momentarily embodied themselves as they touched the youth . . . ' These waves that dissolved into charming girls as he swam foreshadow the poet's reunification with his wife who had earlier drowned in the 'blue' river, a mysterious figure inspired by Novalis's bitter memories of Sophie von Kuhn, a girl whom he first met when she was aged thirteen and who died two days after her fifteenth birthday. The poet's swim was a form of initiation, a vital stage in his miraculous transition into a higher world, as the aqueous woman merges into the Blue Flower to become the incarnation of whatever he desired and eventually found.

This revolt of the swimmer against society's mundane conventions first finds expression in the experience of Goethe, whose early works provided all the subsequent themes of German Romanticism. It took place during a trip to Switzerland in 1773, a quarter of a century before Jahn inspired the exodus to the Baltic shores. He was accompanied on his trip by the aristocratic brothers Stolberg, who were themselves successful poets and translators of Homer's *Iliad*. They were all followers of the 'Sturm und Drang' (Storm and Stress) movement, that centred around Goethe, and enjoyed shocking the bourgeoisie in their enthusiasm to escape the narrowness of their lives in pursuit of personal independence and freedom. The brothers were already used to outraging the locals by diving naked into the lake of Darmstadt, as according to Goethe 'they could not resist doing the things which were not done, having endured the things which were done for so long'. They regarded Switzerland as the very place to realise the freedom of nature, to 'idyllise' the fresh independence of youth inspired by the sketches and poetry of Gessner, that intensified their longing for pastoral scenes:

> In fact bathing in wide waters seems to be one of the best qualifications for expressing such poetic talents. Upon our journey thus far, such natural exercises had not seemed exactly suitable to modern customs, and we had, in some degree, abstained from them.
>
> But in Switzerland, the sight of the cool stream – flowing, running, rushing, then gathering on the plain, and gradually spreading out to a lake – presented a temptation that was not to be resisted. I can not deny that I joined my companions in bathing in the clear lake, but we chose a spot far enough, as we supposed, from all human eyes. But naked bodies shine a good

way, and whoever chanced to see us doubtless took offence.

The good innocent youths who thought it nowise shocking to see themselves half-naked, like poetic shepherds, or entirely naked, like heathen deities, were admonished to leave off all such practices. They were given to understand that they were living not in primaeval nature but in a land where it was esteemed good and salutary to adhere to the old institutions and customs which had been handed down from the Middle Ages. They were not disinclined to acknowledge the propriety of all this, especially as the appeal was made to the Middle Ages, which, to them, seemed venerable as a second nature. Accordingly, they left the more public lake shores, but when in their walks through the mountains they fell in with the clear, rustling, refreshing streams, it seemed to them impossible, in the middle of July, to abstain from the reinvigorating exercise . . . Far from every habitation, and even from all trodden footpaths, they thought there could be no objection here to their throwing off their clothes and boldly meeting the foaming waves. This was not indeed done without a shriek, without a wild shout of joy, excited partly by the chill and partly by the satisfaction by which they thought to consecrate these gloomy, wooded rocks into an idyllic scene.

But, whether persons previously ill-disposed had crept after them, or whether this poetic tumult called forth adversaries even in the solitude, can not be determined. Suffice to say, stone after stone was thrown at them from the motionless bushes above, whether by one or more, whether accidentally or purposely, they could not tell; however, they thought it wisest to renounce the quickening element and look after their clothes.

No one got hit, they sustained no injury but the moral one of surprise and chagrin, and full of young life as they were, they easily shook off the recollection of this awkward affair. But the most disagreeable consequences fell upon Lavater, our host, who was blamed for having given so friendly a welcome to such undisciplined youth, as even to have arranged walks with them, and otherwise shown attention to persons whose wild, unbridled, unchristian, and even heathenish habits, had caused so much scandal to a moral and well-regulated neighbourhood.

In these memories of his youthful swims in the clear waters of Swiss lakes and streams that are disrupted by the stones and insults of the 'well-regulated' locals, Goethe crystallised the opposition between those who longed to return to the old pastoral and pagan world with its delight in the naked body and water, and the common herd who still adhered to the proprieties of the mediaeval morality that had taken its place. Goethe had formed the opinion that Greeks were people who, beyond all others, lived in accordance with nature, free from constraints imposed by a society such as that which Goethe lived in.

It was a theme that was to obsess the Romantic painter Carl Blechen, as he painted five different versions of *Girls Bathing in the Park at Terni* after a visit to Rome in 1828. As the two girls in the painting pause before bathing in the blue pool among the shadows of the mysterious trees, it seems at first glance a perfect idyll. But there is a jarring note in the fierce red of the fabric among their discarded clothes, a suggestion of the shock that Goethe must have felt on hearing the splash of those first stones. And on closer inspection the atmosphere is not idyllic at all, but one of alarm and disapproval as these descendants of the nymphs of antiquity anxiously attempt to avoid the spectators' prurient gaze and conceal their nakedness from public view.

Goethe comes to realise in Switzerland that swimming offered him his only chance of identifying with the spirit of Greek mythology, and satisfying his pleasure and curiosity in the sight of the naked body. After seeing in a private collection a Hellenistic sculpture depicting one of the Danaë, he felt frustrated that in reality he had little experience of the human form. As a result he asked one of his friends to bathe naked in the lake – 'How beautiful he looked, perfect in every respect. My imagination was enriched by this perfect example of the human form. I peopled the woods, meadows and mountains around me with these beautiful figures. I saw them as Adonis chasing the boar or Narcissus who longed for his image in the water.' But he is disappointed by the lack of naked women available, that the beautiful nymph Echo is missing who mourned Narcissus's death – 'So I then decided, no matter what, I would have to see a maiden just as I had seen my friends.' He made an arrangement with a procuress to produce a girl for him, and thus sees, apparently for the first time, a naked woman.

Carl Diem, the scholar who provided Riefenstahl

with much of the classical background for her Olympic film, annotated Goethe's enthusiasm for sport in order to endorse the hysterical athleticism of his time with the stamp of the poet's divine approval. According to Diem, swimming was extremely rare in Germany in the eighteenth century, as everywhere else, but Rousseau's 'return to nature' philosophy created an atmosphere where only a little encouragement was needed – one person to show the way – for swimming to become popular. The impulse was provided by Goethe. As a result of his example thousands took to bathing in freezing water, and doctors began prescribing cold baths in rivers for a variety of ailments 'because the celebrated Goethe had advised it'. Perhaps Goethe had been influenced by his correspondence with his friend Lichtenberg, the aphorist and anglophile, who was so struck when in England by the muscularity and enterprise of English men, the beauty of the women, and in a long letter described his amazement at Margate, England's oldest public bathing resort, a phenomenon then unknown in Germany. No doubt Goethe wished to instil in the young Germans of his time, those 'pale, short-sighted scholars with hollow chests', something of the dash and style displayed by those swimming English aristocrats like Byron who came to pay their respects to him as they travelled through Weimar on their European tours. 'Is it their origin, the soil, or is it due to the free constitution and the sound education?' Goethe remarked to Eckermann when confessing his admiration. 'They are never put out and are as much at their ease as if the whole world belonged to them. It is also this that pleases our womenfolk, and it is why they cause such devastation in the hearts of our young ladies . . . They are dangerous young people, but admittedly it is this very fact that is their great virtue. How different', Goethe continued sadly, 'are the Germans. Everything is concentrated on taming our young, driving out all naturalness, all originality, and all their wild spirits, so that finally nothing remains but the Philistines. Of healthy feelings and sensual enjoyment there is not a trace.'

Goethe taught his foster son to swim, also the sons of his friends. In his *Wilhelm Meister*, which is full of references to the beneficial effects of swimming, a head-master of a boarding-school remarks that as he watched his pupils learning to swim, he was always impressed by their expressions of surprise as the element which seemed to be pulling them down also made them feel weightless, and lifted and supported them at the same time. For Goethe a cold bathe 'transformed bourgeois sensual exhaustion into a fresh and vigorous existence'.

Almost all Goethe's swimming took place in the river that flowed along the bottom of his garden in Weimar. He would swim there throughout the year, even in deepest winter, early in the morning or in the middle of the night, as a form of self-discipline or as a means of self-immersion in the romantic effects of nature. 'I bathed last night', he writes one summer to Charlotte Stein, 'but not near the weir and saw the most glorious moon.' And on 2 July: 'Night time, half past ten. The moon was so divine that I had to run into the water. In the meadow – into the moon.' Then in his diaries: 28 July – 'Bathed early.' 30 July – 'Bathed. Went shooting (birds), fried trout in the evening after bathing in the lake (in the East of town).' 9 August – 'Bathed at one o'clock.' On 6 September he writes to Frau Stein that when he got up, he felt like swimming, an urge which he satisfied straight away, that made him feel wonderful, and not merely superficially.

Still, well into November, he is bathing at night. At the end of the month he writes from Weimar, after recovering from a mood of dejection: 'Last night the town and its surroundings looked at me with such strange eyes. It seemed to me that I should not stay. This is when I went into the water and drowned my overwrought imagination.' His debt to the soothing effects of swimming is again reflected in some lines of verse: 'And when I walk along my favourite old path,/ Along my beloved meadow,/ I immerse myself with the early morning sun,/ Then bathe in the moon, washing away the day's sorrow and troubles . . . ' Goethe owned an engraving after a Michelangelo drawing of soldiers bathing in a river, that he treasured because he felt it revealed swimming as the most sublime form of relaxation, the furthest removed from all those strifes and tensions associated with war. To Goethe it seemed that in this scene of utter lassitude Michelangelo was paying tribute to the swimmer's self-absorption, released from the distractions and demands of a troubled world.

On his return from Switzerland, Goethe had to adapt himself to the formalities of court life at Weimar. Reflecting on his conversion, he compared himself to a 'well-intentioned bird that has plunged into the water and, when it was on the point of drowning, the gods have gradually started to transform its wings into fins. The fishes busying themselves about it do not understand why it does not immediately feel at ease in the element.' The metaphor contained a certain literal truth, as now, instead of swimming naked in the Ilm, he wore a special linen waistcoat and trousers that he mentions in his accounts. They cost him ten silver groschen. One of his friends recalls an incident that occurred after one of his swims near his home, when some ladies were present. Because of some mishap his bathing suit had become disarranged, so that 'something which Goethe had thought carefully covered was bared and showed that he was physically as well endowed as he was mentally'. He became by far the best swimmer in the area, just as he was the 'best dancer, actor, fencer, and best-looking man'. As in the Swiss lakes, it was an aristocratic circle of swimmers that included the Duke of Weimar. They seemed to be out to shock the more respectable citizens. In one incident reminiscent of George Borrow, Goethe refers to swimming late one night, when a farmer returning home from Upper Weimar nearly died of fright on seeing a white shape with long black hair floating and singing strangely. It seemed as if he believed he had seen a mermaid.

Goethe's swimming experiences appear to have made a profound effect on his imagination. Swimming metaphors constantly recur to colour his conversation and letters. After emerging from a fit of depression, he remarked that he was probably 'unlikely to swim in that river again'. When expressing gratitude for someone's help, he would write: 'Without you, I could not swim or wade even.' He compares in a letter the gradual

involvement in a love affair to the sensations of the swimmer: 'In surrendering to passion the individual shudders
momentarily, as if entering an unknown element; but as
soon as he has yielded, he will be embraced and carried
away just like a swimmer by water. He revels in this
and does not want to touch the ground until he loses
his strength or cramp might threaten to drown him.'
A gift from Herder is 'more precious than myrrh, and
just like the feel of a rough towel after a bathe'. After
an absence of some months, he writes to Charlotte Stein
that the first thing he will do on returning will be to
'say "Good Morning" to you, like a diver who has been
invisible underwater for some time'. On being reunited
with the Stolberg brothers some years after their Swiss
experiences, he mentions that it was 'wonderful to be able
to bathe in the sea of my youth through memories'.

When Goethe and the Stolberg brothers revelled
in the Swiss lakes, none of them in fact knew how
to swim. It was just that like Shelley they found
water irresistible. Some months after his return Goethe
designed for himself a life-jacket made of cork in order
to learn. The life-jacket as a means of support became
a significant symbol for him. Referring to some difficulties Mendelssohn was experiencing as a composer,
Goethe wrote that the 'beautiful life-jacket of his talent
will help him through the turmoil of barbarism'. Elsewhere he mentions that 'serious love affairs, and mild
ones too, buoy one up as does a life-jacket those who
are drowning'. To his protégé Kraft, who was being
overwhelmed by various misfortunes, Goethe wrote
some words of encouragement: 'He who has ever fought
against the waves knows the moment of despair, when

he realises that willing hands on the shore have not the strength to help him. There is nothing more terrible than to be unable to help and see the other drown. Take then whatever small thing I can throw to you, such as a floating life-jacket, in order to give us time.'

Throughout his life Goethe was haunted by memories of people drowning. He felt personally responsible when an unhappy woman drowned herself after reading *The Sorrows of Young Werther*. In 1774 four boys drowned as he was watching from the riverside. He tried unsuccessfully to revive one of them with 'desperate arms, sweat, and tears'. The beautiful fisher boy in *Wilhelm Meister*, who could never resist the temptation to bathe, joins a group of children who are wading out into deep water, across the dangerous rocks. They begin to slip, then pull and snatch for support, dragging each other down. In his novels and plays boys fall into rivers during firework displays, desperate lovers are carried away on strong currents, or dive from rocks into the black sea at night. Goethe was to admit that the many happy hours of his life that he had devoted to swimming had enriched him poetically. Much of his verse refers directly to swimming, 'merrily' and 'boldly', 'joyfully screaming' during Walpurgis Night in *Faust*, or slipping silently into the water among the reeds. When one of the ladies of the Weimar court drowns herself after an unhappy love affair, Goethe tries to console the unhappy Eckermann in characteristic fashion: 'If only you knew how the tiny fish feels/ So comfortable on the sea bed,/ You would swim down, the way you are,/ And only then feel well . . . '

When working on *Faust*, Goethe mentioned to Schiller

that his work was not going smoothly that day, 'even though I went swimming'. There is no evidence that the consumptive Schiller ever joined Goethe in the water, but his ballad 'Der Taucher' – The Diver – intensified the notion of the swimmer as someone rather remote and distinct, in touch with experiences and mysteries denied to the common man. It is a poem that is studied by every German schoolboy, of such significance that at a moment of great danger in the depths of the Caribbean Hans Hass repeated it to himself over and over again as if it were some form of talisman.

The ballad retells the fable of how Frederick II, the Emperor of Germany and King of Sicily, threw a golden goblet into the sea, as a challenge to any diver brave enough to swim down and recover it. Frederick had ushered in a new intellectual age, translated Aristotle, and came near, in his feeling for Hellenism, to recapturing a love for the deep seas that had long been forgotten. He chose as the scene of the challenge the black waters of Charybdis off Sicily, because of Homer's description of this whirlpool. Its purpose was to find out from the diver the secrets of the hidden world beneath the waves, undisclosed to man. Like Goethe's Faust he desired absolute knowledge. To acquire it he turned to the swimmer for assistance.

In the original legend the diver who took up the challenge was Nicholas Persée, whose birthday was marked in the Eton calendar, a lone swimmer with fingers and toes webbed like a goose, who lived on raw fish and spent his days swimming among the Lipari islands delivering letters in a watertight bag and diving for pearls. He lived at the time of Frederick II and fascinated him. It seems that Schiller heard about the diver from Goethe, who encouraged him over the ballad and wrote to him on 10 June 1797, after visiting him in Jena: 'Keep well, and let your diver drown as soon as possible.' A few months later Schiller wrote back: 'I have discovered that I have transformed an ordinary diver, the subject of the legend, into someone rather exceptional and divine.' Nicholas Persée ('The Fish') is in fact ignored by Schiller. It is a young squire, more German than Italian, who dives from the cliff top through the vortex of the whirlpool, down the path that seems 'winding in darkness to hell'. Eventually he emerges from the waves, and describes to the king how he was spun around by the currents until he managed to cling to a crag within reach of the goblet. Far below, at the bottom of the cliff that stretched down to the seabed, he had watched through the dark water vast reptiles swarming, salamanders, dragons, snakes, before the current swept him up again and restored him to the surface. The king however is not satisfied. He insists on knowing what lies hidden in the 'innermost' sea. He offers his daughter to the diver as an inducement to return to the depths. The diver once more accepts the challenge and never returns.

Another monarch to suffer from an intense curiosity in water was one a leading figure of late German Romanticism, Ludwig of Bavaria, whose corpse on his demise was discovered floating in the shallows. 'The cold waters of the Alpsee beckon to me,' he once wrote in his diary. The fatal charm of the Lorelei had been conceived by Brentano, then embellished by Heine. Ludwig bathed obsessively in the lakes below his castles. To stage Wagner he created a series of lakes and cascades, fed by a complex system of water-pipes and machines for producing waves, designed by the inventor of the submarine, Wilhelm Bauer. This preoccupation with swimming, with water and the effects of water seems, like the fabrication of his fabulous castles, an outlet for his creative urge, a means of escape from the harshness of the real world which grew ever more distasteful to him.

In the novels of Thomas Mann, a spiritual descendant of Novalis and the German Romantics, there is the same concern with the tragic divide that distinguishes the real from the ideal world, symbolised as so often by the swimmer who resumes his traditional role as a classical figure, like those mythical beings, inspired by the sight of his swimming friend, whose presence was felt by Goethe in the wooded landscape around the Swiss lakes. In Hans Castorp's vision on the upper slopes of *The Magic Mountain*, of a Mediterranean bay – a scene that he had never seen, yet somehow remembered – the 'children of the sun' exulted among the breaking waves, and young folk 'hesitated at the water's edge, with crossed arms clutching either shoulder as they tested the chill waters with their toes'. Meanwhile, further down the mountainside, below this Mediterranean landscape with its white houses that gleamed among cypress groves and palms, its swimmers and piping shepherds, the occupants of the Sanatorium, a microcosm of the sick European society before the Great War, carried on arguing relentlessly.

For Aschenbach on the Venice Lido, Tadzio revived memories of Narcissus and Phaedrus, the young disciple who with Socrates had dipped his toes into the cool waters of the river Ilissus. As he sat in his deck chair during the long mornings on the beach, his heavy gaze would rest, a 'fixed and reckless stare', on the figure of the boy as he emerged on the edge of the sea – 'It conjured up mythologies, it was like a primaeval legend, handed down from the beginning of time, of the birth of form, of the origin of the gods.' After the news of the plague spread round the city and the various Europeans had fled back to their native shores, it seemed to the dying Aschenbach as he lingered among the empty bathing cabins that the 'pale and lovely' swimmer on the sand bar 'smiled at him and beckoned; as though with the hand he lifted from his hip, he pointed outward as he hovered on before into an immensity of richest expectation'.

Thomas Mann's *Tonio Kröger* suffered at school from an infatuation with the fair-haired, blue-eyed Hans, who 'swam to perfection'. The figure of Hans was based on a particular swimming hero of Mann's during his schooldays, who in later life was to take to drink and suffer a melancholy end in Africa. Hans was everything Tonio Kröger was not, popular with the masters and boys, untroubled and athletic. However much he tries, Kröger can make little impression on him. On leaving school Tonio Kröger follows the instincts bred in him by his artistic mother, travels to the South and devotes himself to writing. Though successful, his heart is never in it. A series of empty affairs leaves him cold and dissatisfied. Eventually, to escape his sense of desolation, he returns one summer to the Baltic and the scenes of his youth. In a hotel by the seashore he wakes up early – 'the sun's disk rose in splendour from the crisply glittering sea that seemed to quiver and burn beneath it. So began the day. In a joyous daze Tonio Kröger flung on his clothes, and breakfasting on the veranda before everybody else, swam from the little wooden bathhouse some distance out into the sound . . . ' But this swim far out into the waters of the sound differs from other Romantic bathes in that it was the last, desperate attempt of an artist, not to escape the influence of the common herd, but to join its ranks. The lone, poetic existence advocated by Novalis was insufficient. He had lost all feeling. His bathe expressed his longing to be accepted by the 'healthy and happy, the mediocre and bourgeois', those who had never understood him, 'whose speech was not his speech', that 'blond, fair-haired breed of the steel-blue eyes, which stood to him for the pure, the blithe, the untroubled in life'. When on holiday as a boy he had never entered the water where Hans swam all day, but would 'wander off somewhere and lie down in the sand and stare at the strange and mysterious changes that whisk over the face of the sea'. Whatever his intentions now, however, they come to nothing. When Hans and his blonde wife, with whom Tonio had once been in love, miraculously reappear in his life and come to the hotel that night, their attitude is one of indifference. They behave as though they had never known him. As they laugh and dance, Tonio looks on longingly from the dark veranda, as he had always done in his youth.

For the nervous, desiccated intellectuals of Thomas Mann, the swimmer was a personification of all the health and beauty they had never enjoyed. But while the pale figure on the Venetian shore offered glimpses of a re-mote, romantic, Platonic ideal, in the swagger and disdain of Hans there is every suggestion of the Wagnerian image of Nordic man, the blond and born fighter, the 'fair-haired breed of the steel-blue eyes', the anti-intellectual. The dark, artistic Kröger adored Hans because 'in every way he was his own opposite and foil'. Hans represented the new emerging Germany from which he would be excluded, in which he could never play a part.

In the early years of the century when *Tonio Kröger* was written, the German swimmer was just emerging as a national symbol, an expression of male vigour and fortitude as in Japan before the last war. German divers were now the best in the world, and Germans had taken over the supremacy in the breaststroke with which England's great swimmers had long been associated. One of Captain Webb's rare defeats was at the hands of von Schoening, a wealthy German who climbed down from his private yacht and beat him for the 'Championship of America' in the cold waters off Brooklyn. The breaststroke in Germany was essentially a military stroke and had been taught to their soldiers for years. According to an army manual it was the stroke that 'best utilised the power of the German legs' that spread wide then slammed together with maximum force, like those of that legendary Teutonic warrior who by the grip of his thighs made his war horse groan beneath him.

From mythical times the German hero has been a swimmer. Although Danish, Beowulf was incorporated as part of German folklore. Like other mythic heroes he is noble, strong, brave, civilised, but differs from them in his heroic attributes as a swimmer. In adolescence he made a pact with another young noble 'to venture our lives on the open sea'. For five days they swam, until storms drove them apart. Beowulf was dragged down by sea monsters to the bottom, but kills seven and is carried by the tide to the coast of Lapland. 'For almost a day' he swam down through the dark water to the lair of Grendel's mother at the bottom of the lake, then returns with her severed head to the surface. From a raid on the Frisians he swims home 'solitary and wretched', carrying through the waves the chain mail of thirty of his men. Although they were the feats of a superman, they were neither purely imaginary nor entirely unrelated to the experiences of those who lived at the time the epic evolved.

The fierce German tribes that occupied the borders of the Roman Empire had always been noted for their swimming. The Suebi, the 'largest and most warlike nation among the Germans', according to Caesar 'trained themselves to wear nothing, even in the coldest localities, except for skins . . . and they bathe in the rivers'. Among the Germani 'both men and women bathe in the river, and they wear skins or small cloaks of reindeer hide, leaving a great part of their body bare'. When defeated on the west bank of the Rhine, most of the Germani were killed, but a few 'trusting to their strength, set themselves to swim the river and so won safety'. These brave German swimmers were employed as auxiliaries by the Roman army, swimming across the Menai Strait to conquer Anglesey, to the astonishment of the Britons, and through the cold currents of the Danube for Hadrian.

It was from this ancient barbarian tradition that Nazi Germany claimed to draw her strength. It was not to them, though, but to the Ancient Greeks that

Hitler looked back when his attention was arrested once by the photograph of a beautiful female German swimmer: 'What splendid bodies you can see today. It is only in our century that young people have once again approached Hellenistic ideals through sports.' He laughed at a photograph of Mussolini in a bathing costume. Perhaps it was to please Hitler that Eva Braun bathed in the Bavarian lakes, and as recorded in a famous piece of film followed the precepts of Jahn in exercising elastically on a towel laid out on the shingle to the sound of the lapping waves. Perhaps too those diving figures that brought to a close Riefenstahl's Olympic film were less expressions of mystical aspiration, more a premonition of those German eagles and Condor legions that were soon to sweep down and devastate Guernica and Poland. Hitler had descended on the city from out of the clouds in Riefenstahl's film on the Nuremberg rally, the outline of his plane as it flew casting a shadow over the countryside.

In *Afrikanische Spiele* – African Diversions – that was published in 1936, the same year as the Olympische Spiele took place in Berlin, Ernst Jünger expressed an attitude to war that was typically German in its blend of the romantic and Homeric. In the book Jünger looks back to his early years, when he was confined as an adolescent in a sleepy little town on the Weser. In a mood of abject frustration he sets his heart on joining the Foreign Legion, lured by the attractions of the dark and unknown, the adventure and the danger: 'for the whine of bullets was like the music of the spheres to me . . . I was ready to swear in under any colours, if only they would take me to the equator like Faust's magic cloak.' But as he trembled on the brink, the prospect of crossing the frontier, of translating his dreams into reality and taking the first step from an 'ordered life into the disorders of the world' proved almost too formidable – 'If you stand on a high diving-board and are unused to diving you can clearly distinguish between two persons – one who wants to jump and another who keeps drawing back. If the attempt to throw yourself in, as it were, fails, there is another solution. It consists in tricking yourself by making your body sway to and fro on the extreme edge of the board until you are suddenly forced to jump. I quite realised that nothing was more of an obstacle to my efforts to take the first plunge into the world of adventure than my own fear.'

And so in the image of the diver and swimmer the Germans have expressed the spirit of war and adventure, their yearning for Faustian depths of knowledge, for spiritual and physical perfection. Through swimming they were able to recover contact with the mythical past, both Greek and their own. With all these classical and romantic associations, swimming seems to have appealed to something fundamental in the German soul. So it is no surprise perhaps that the legendary swimmers of the world – Weissmuller, Ederle, Bauer, Laufer, Keiffer, Meyer, Schollander, von Saltza, Spitz, Gross – have been of Germanic extraction.

VII

The American Dream

He had swum too long, been immersed too
long . . .

'The politicians of the ancient world were always
talking of morals and virtue; ours speak of noth-
ing but commerce and money.'
J.-J. Rousseau

ON THE THIRD FLOOR of the exclusive New York
Athletic Club overlooking Central Park lies a Roman pool.
The Club conforms to the classical formula adopted by all
Athletic Clubs throughout America. Swimmers were
naked until the recent admission of women, while
the pool is surrounded by steam baths, pump rooms,
frigidaria, a running track, a library, and instead of statues
in colonnades dedicated to their athletic heroes there are
photographs along the walls of the corridors. Among them
is the smiling Charles Daniels. A sophisticated financier
and the local squash and bridge champion, he refined the

crude strokes of the Australian style popular at the time into the harmonious rhythms of the American crawl. When he won the freestyle events in the 1904 Olympic Games in St Louis, it marked the end of an era. Four years before, in Paris, the English had won everything. The fastest swimmers from now on were almost all to come from America. An extraordinary glamour would surround them, and they would swim in the most lavish and fanciful pools in the world. These sapphire pools, liquid emanations of the American Dream, sought-after status symbols, emblems of material success, became for some a means of escape from the contamination of a corrupt society.

Like those ancient German tribes that swam beside the frontiers of the Roman Empire, the indigenous Indians provided American swimming with a historical perspective, an image of the noble savage fated somehow to be at odds with the world, and in their decline imbued the 'swimmer' with an elegiac quality that it has never really lost. Nothing reveals their religious sense of nature, their feeling that they were linked somehow to the rivers, lakes and waterfalls around them, more vividly than this swimming scene described by George Catlin, who painted the Indian way of life in its last years of existence, before it finally disappeared from the plains: 'At a distance of half a mile or so above the village, is the customary place where the women and girls resort every morning in the summer months, to bathe in the river. To this spot they repair by hundreds, every morning at sunrise, where, on a beautiful beach, they can be seen running and glistening in the sun, whilst they are playing their innocent gambols and leaping into the stream. They all learn to swim well and the poorest swimmer among them will dash fearlessly into the boiling and eddying current of the Missouri, and cross it with perfect ease . . . Around this bathing place are stationed sentinels, with their bows and arrows in hand, to guard and protect this sacred ground from the approach of boys or men in any directions. Perhaps no people on earth have taken more pains to learn swimming, nor any to turn it to better account.'

References abound to the Indian love of swimming. Longfellow's Hiawatha plunged 'beneath the bubbling surface' and 'through the whirlpool chased the beaver', while Pocahontas was renowned for her swimming and diving skills. The name 'Wichita' derives from the Indian for 'waist-deep', as the squaws were pushed forward into the rivers to test their depth and if convenient for crossing, would cry out 'Wichita' to those on the bank. It was from the ranks of these Indians that two challengers were chosen, Flying Gull and Tobacco, to represent America against the English champion Kenworthy in 1845, and amazed Londoners with their overarm windmill stroke. Their flailing style was to be the inspiration for the greatest of American swimmers, Johnny Weissmuller, whose coach based his action on theirs, the whirling rotation of his arms and the powerful propulsion of his legs that drove his torso far above the surface of the water. When towards the end of his life Trelawny emerged from the waves on to the beach at Sompting, Americans passing by presumed him to be an Indian. Rupert Brooke, when watching Indians swimming in the Northern Lakes, found them 'more in touch with permanent things than the America that had succeeded them', and far superior to the 'weedy, furtive, acquisitive youth that may figure our age and type'.

The heroic attitudes of Catlin's Indian swimmers, the mythic atmosphere that surrounds them, are reproduced in the two great swimming scenes of American painting, by John Singleton Copley and Thomas Eakins. The figures in both paintings are derived from classical statuary. Copley's painting, commissioned by the victim, Brook Watson, depicts a dreadful episode in the life of the future Lord Mayor of London when at the age of fourteen, while swimming in Havana harbour in 1749, he had been attacked by a monstrous shark. It had already torn off the flesh from his calf and snapped off his foot, and was now circling round for the final assault. There is though no hint of blood or carnage in the swimming figure that floats on the surface like some Ancient Greek statue retrieved from the depths, a rope encircling his extended arm like the serpent round the son of Laocoön, the limbs half submerged and the fair hair cascading down into the green water. The dark skinned rescuers in the boat stretch out their hands towards the naked marble figure, as if in longing for some long lost classical ideal. The swimmer was modelled on a gladiator in the Villa Borghese, and painted in the first flush of excitement over the rediscovery of the classical past in the 1760s.

In Thomas Eakins' *The Swimming Hole* three men lounge or stand on a stone jetty, one clings to the side, another dives into calm water that ripples at the edge and reveals the varying depths and rocks below the surface. In the right hand corner Eakins himself floats and surveys the scene, while his setter Harry swims towards the submerged hand of the red-haired boy who reaches down into the water. The pyramidical composition of the bodies suggests the frieze of a classical pediment. The reclining and twisting figures on the left are based on classical models. One seems to be warding off a blow with his shield, like the Borghese warrior that inspired the attitude of Brook Watson. In this almost visionary scene, where the dark woods and sunlit fields slope down to the edge of the water, on whose serene surface the young men look down or penetrate it tentatively with their hands, the artist seems to be evoking the America that 'flowered once for Dutch sailors' eyes', when 'for a transitory enchanted moment man must have held his breath in the presence of this continent'. The 'waterhole' was to become an evocative symbol for Americans, the subject of numerous popular songs that expressed a longing to return to the innocence of youth. The painting was the last of an Arcadian interlude in Eakins' career, when he painted a series of Giorgionesque landscapes where naked boys play pipes by the edge of pools and young girls listen. These paintings were his only departure from a severely realistic style, and express his unconventional attitudes, his dissatisfaction with contemporary life and nostalgia for the freedom and unashamed nakedness of the pagan world. His experiences in the classical studios of Couture in Paris had left their mark. Eakins admired the Romans because 'they never became civilised'. He was always encouraging his pupils to swim naked, as so many of his photographs reveal.

The Swimming Hole expressed above all Eakins' own passion for bathing. He was apparently a strong swimmer and inventive diver. As a boy he rowed and swam in the Delaware river near Philadelphia. There on hot days in the deep places of the creek the men, dogs, and horses would go to bathe. Max Schmitt, the famous oarsman whom he painted sculling, wrote to persuade Eakins to swim with him in the local Schuylkill river – 'Then shall we again have belly smashers, back bumbers, side switches etc. Then shall we see [sketches of a youth diving and swimming], and divers other beautiful performances by the immortal T. E. [Eakins]. Guess I'll never beat you in swimming – have given that up!'

Eakins' Arcadian scenes were painted in Avondale, where his sister and her husband had bought a large farm with a stream where they all swam naked. When his niece committed suicide there, Eakins was blamed for contaminating her with his 'beastly ideas' and banished for ever from Arcadia. He was expelled from teaching in Pennsylvania Academy because he insisted on nude male models for women. Women would be pestered to pose naked for him, and one of his infatuated students, in a vain effort to attract his attention, was arrested by the police in a Philadelphia street wearing only a bathing suit. To Elizabeth Burton, an artist whose portrait he painted, he wrote at the height of one summer that she might now be going in to swim 'without much of a bathing suit'. In the country Eakins often swam in the private pool of some friends. After the others had retired, he would return, remove his bathing suit and enjoy the pool alone, naked. When on a walk he and his wife came across some boys swimming with nothing on, he offered to stand guard and give them warning if any policeman should appear. His devotion to nudity and the masculine beauty of swimmers and prizefighters derived from his detestation of the growing influence of a middle-class

America, whose domesticity and sense of decorum he always found hard to bear.

The spirit of Eakins' *Swimming Hole* has often been compared to that of Walt Whitman's young men bathing in 'Song of Myself', those 'Twenty-eight young men' who 'bathe by the shore'. As they 'float on their backs and their white bellies bulge to the sun', they are watched by a lonely woman 'handsome and richly drest' from behind the window-blinds of her house on the shore. The unseen intruder longs to run down the beach and join them in the sea. When she eventually slips into the water, they continue splashing and remain unaffected by her disturbing presence. It is to the 'homeliest' looking of them that she is attracted, that seems 'most beautiful' to her.

Whitman was painted by Eakins when he lived not far away across the Delaware, where he had retired in order to recover from a stroke. In an effort to regain his health he would sunbathe in secluded valleys, and swim in the streams of clear water. Whitman avoided conventional medicine, and influenced by Fowler and Wells' *The Science of Swimming* would seek his salvation through water. He would hoard clippings on swimming, and attributed to it mysterious powers of restoration. In 'Faith' he describes a man who to refresh himself swims round a ship that is becalmed at sea – 'a deaf and dumb boy, his younger brother, is looking over, and the swimmer floating easily on his back smiles and beckons with his head. Without waiting a moment, the young child laughing and clucking springs into the sea and as he rises to the surface feels no fear but laughs and though he sink and drown he feels it not for the man is with him there.'

In cities Whitman plunged daily into the local baths, and in his passion for health declared himself a 'swimmer in the river or bay or by the seashore'.

It was by the seashore that Moncure Conway found him, when he travelled from England to write an article on Whitman. He tracked him down on a beach on Staten Island, lying indolently 'like Bacchus', face to the glaring sun, apparently his favourite posture for writing poetry. The rolling lines of his verse, he once claimed, had been inspired by the 'soothing rustle' of the surf on the beaches of Long Island. According to Conway they passed the day 'roaming or loafing. Whilst we bathed, I was impressed by a certain grandeur about the man. His body was a ruddy blond, pure and noble, his form being at the same time remarkable for fine curves and well-knit bones. The first glow of any kind that I saw about him was when he entered the water, which he fairly hugged with a lover's enthusiasm.' After the day's swimming Conway remained sleepless all night – 'he had so magnetised, so charged me'.

On reading the article Swinburne wrote in a high state of excitement to congratulate Conway: 'One passage above all delights me – that in which you speak of his amorous embrace of the sea in bathing, for at the time the article appeared, I was fighting the tides as a swimmer on the west coast of Wales. I knew that the man who has spoken as he has of the sea must be a fellow seabird with me; and I would give something to have a dip in the rough water with him . . . ' No doubt Swinburne relished the appeals in Whitman's verse to the seductive charms of his 'lover' the sea – 'Cushion me soft, rock me in billowy drowse,/ Dash me with amorous wet'

– the solitude of the swimmer – 'When I wandered alone over the beach, and undressing, bathed,/ Laughing with the waters' – the narcissism – 'While they discuss I am silent, and go bathe and admire myself' – and sense of spiritual adventure – 'Long enough have you dreamed contemptible dreams,/ Long have you timidly waded holding a plank by the shore,/ Now I will you to be a bold swimmer.'

But while the excitable Swinburne loved to plunge through rough seas, Whitman classed himself merely a 'first rate aquatic loafer – I possessed almost unlimited capacity for floating on my back'. He associated himself with his swimmer in 'I sing the Body Electric', swimming naked through the 'transparent green-slime', or lying face-up and rolling 'silently to and fro in the heave of the water'. Swinburne though, with his taste for 'sea-foam and the frothing of blood', would have been struck by his image in 'The Sleepers' of a 'beautiful gigantic swimmer swimming naked through the eddies of the sea', who from some mysterious impulse strikes out courageously from the shore, though battered by the rocks and waves that are stained with his blood. Swinburne had experienced the same irresistible impulse when he swam miles from the beach at Etretat on the outgoing tide, and Whitman too had once felt himself 'carried along, as it were, like some expert swimmer, who has tired himself, and to rest his limbs, allows them to float drowsily and unresistingly on the bosom of the sunny river. Real things lost their reality. A dusky mist spread itself before my eyes.'

Another to succumb to this compulsion to swim out on the outgoing tide was Jack London, who, at the age of seventeen, when drunk and dejected one night, fell overboard from his yacht into San Francisco bay. He was rapidly carried out on the terrific current that sweeps through the Straits, but made no attempt to attract attention. Passing Solano Wharf which was full of lights and people, he purposely kept silent so as to avoid being rescued. On drifting out into the open sea, he lay on his back and sang death chants to the stars. The water was 'delicious'. The prospect of release from years of factory work, the brutal waterfront life and general disillusionment excited him. But as daylight broke and the cold water sobered him up, he determined to make an effort to survive. By then it was almost too late. He was caught between two conflicting currents, and the wind from the shore was washing the waves into his mouth. He managed to carry on swimming mechanically until, almost unconscious, a couple of Greek fishermen hauled him over the side of their boat.

For London it was a delirious experience as well as a drunken attempt at suicide. His autobiographical hero Martin Eden does finally commit suicide by squeezing through a porthole and plunging into the sea, after being seduced by the melodious siren song of some verses of Swinburne that he was reading in his cabin – 'he let himself go and sank without movement, a white statue, into the sea'. In a letter London describes Martin Eden's predicament as 'exactly parallel with that of a beautiful young man, with the body of an Adonis, who can not swim, who is thrown into deep water, and who drowns'. Unlike Melville's Whitejacket, his exhilarating descent into the sea disassociates him from humanity. For him drowning was the self-sacrifice of an individualist. His literary success and fame had made him part of the bourgeois world, 'with all the psychological cramp and intellectual futility of their kind'.

Jack London was an American George Borrow in his hatred of the bourgeoisie, his love of 'the Road', his cult of the physique and passion for boxers and swimmers. It was from some boys swimming in the Sacramento river, 'road kids', that he first heard about the excitements of the road, who revealed to him prospects of a more vital and exhilarating world beyond the confines of San Francisco – 'Far better to be a people of the wilderness and desert, than to be a people of the machine and the Abyss.' In London's novel *The Valley of the Moon* a prizefighter and his wife decide to abandon their servile existence in San Francisco and travel in search of a farm in a valley where they can live the life of their dreams. Taking the road across the hills from Monterey, they descend gradually to the bay of Carmel. They walk through the pines and across the rolling sandhills, when suddenly the girl catches her breath, then screams with delight at the sight of an 'amazing peacock-blue of a breaker, shot through with golden sunlight, overfalling in a mile-long sweep and thundering into white ruin of foam on a crescent beach of sand'. A man emerges from the dark pines, runs across the sand, dives into the waves and disappears. They watch tensely as the 'mighty mass of water fell in thunder on the beach, but beyond appeared a yellow head, one arm out-reaching, and a portion of a shoulder. Only a few strokes was he able to make before he was compelled to dive through another breaker. This was the battle – to win seaward against the sweep of the shoreward-hastening sea. Each time he dived and was lost to view, Saxon caught her breath and clenched her hands. Sometimes, after the passage of a breaker, they could not find him, and when they did he would be scores of feet away, flung there like a chip by a smoke-bearded breaker.'

This passage, more than any other in London's novels, sums up his philosophy of the lone man against the elements, strong and self-reliant, pitting his courage and endurance against great odds. Here, naked among the waves, he has no protection at all. The sight of the swimmer struggling towards the horizon restores the prizefighter's faith in the 'old stock' and makes him feel deficient. He had only swum in tanks and bays. Now he is determined to become an ocean swimmer – 'If I could do that, I'd be so proud you couldn't come within forty feet of me.' They join the Carmel set of artists and writers who live simply by the shore, in this 'region of Greek mystery', and hunt for abalone, as Jack London himself had done with the poet George Sterling, the 'perfect Greek' whom J. C. Powys had once admired swimming in the fountains of San Francisco. Whenever the artists swim far out to sea and play among the sea lions, the prizefighter would follow them with his eyes, 'yearning after them'. Gradually he learns to swim out through the breakers, and becomes accepted by the community. After some months the couple move on, and find their cherished farm with a spring that crossed the valley in little brooks, and on the boundary a creek with a deep pool where they could swim and high dive.

This was the farm that London himself acquired in Sonoma among the hills of Northern California. The river had been dammed to create a seven million gallon reservoir, where he could spend every afternoon after writing his daily one thousand words. He would swim for two hours, then sit naked in the sun. Just as Byron confessed himself to be more proud of having swum the Hellespont than any other of his achievements, London once claimed that he would rather win a race in a swimming pool than write the great American novel. He was always inviting his friends to Sonoma to swim, and once tried to tempt Bob Fitzsimmons to stay, who had knocked out Jim Corbett for the heavyweight championship of the world, with the offer of a 'dandy' pool. His letters would often be brought to a close with the words 'Going swimming.' 'The best of the swimming crowd is almost gone,' he notes sadly one autumn. His wife knew he was dying when she noticed he no longer swam, but just watched others in the pool.

With the help of an architect he designed a baronial mansion on a knoll overlooking the valley, Wolf House, that was burnt to the ground by an arsonist the night before he was due to move in. Its wings enclosed a 40 x 15ft swimming pool, fed by a mountain stream and overlooked by covered balconies. This pool became central to the action of the last novel published in his lifetime, written to salvage his dreams, *The Little Lady of the Big House*. Those who live there swim in the pool at five every morning, play strip poker around it, and the wife enters the story by riding her giant stallion into it in her bathing suit. Her husband, a thinly disguised self-portrait, looks on helplessly as she falls for the heroic attributes of a visitor to the ranch who once with his Marquesan lover had swum through a hurricane in the Pacific, then become a local legend by diving from a rock far above the sea. Like the suitors of Atalanta, he accepts a challenge to chase and catch the wife within ten minutes in the confines of the pool. She begins by launching herself into space with a beautiful swallow (in America 'swan') dive, and her startling dives, the product of her instinctive genius, a matter of timing and abandon, form a recurrent motif in the story.

In the act of diving, as in swimming, London projected his heroic attitude to life: 'The achievement of a difficult feat is successful adjustment to a sternly exacting environment. Thus it is with the man who leaps forward from the springboard, out over the swimming pool, and with a backward half-revolution of the body, enters the water head first. Once he leaves the springboard his environment becomes immediately savage, and savage the penalty it will exact should he fail and strike the water flat. Of course, the man does not have to run the risk of the penalty. He could remain on the bank in a sweet and placid environment of summer air, sunshine, and stability. Only he is not made that way. In that swift mid-air movement he lives as he could never live on the bank.'

By the reservoir local boys would clamour round London to be taught to dive off the high board, from where he would often somersault before retiring stiff and sore. In the final year of his life he was to write to his daughter about the approach to diving – 'diving is first of all a psychological matter, after that it becomes physical' – adding instructions on how to swim the crawl, his favourite stroke: 'When I tell you that the present champion of the world, a Kanaka from Hawaii, without using his hands at all in the crawl stroke, has broken the world's swimming record for women for fifty yards by the propulsion of his feet, you may get some idea of what a wonderful thing the crawl stroke is.'

The Kanaka from Hawaii was the first streamlined exponent of the crawl, Duke Kahanamoku. London had watched him racing in Honolulu Harbour. It was in the Pacific islands that London, like Brooke, enjoyed his most romantic bathing, often by moonlight, among the rollers, in pools below waterfalls or the rock basins of ravines, once in the mouth of a river while the sailors of his yacht stood on guard in the bush to protect them from possible headhunters. His article 'A Royal Sport' helped to revive the declining art of surfing among the Hawaiians, and inspired the formation of a swimming club, with a steel diving stage erected far out at sea.

In the transparent waters of the tropics, London, like Melville before him, became aware of the ghostly presence of the shark. He tried to interest his publishers in a 'dandy' article on them, that would combine first-hand eye-witness accounts with his own scientific knowledge and experiences. But the shark and the threat of the submarine world played little part in London's imagination. Like Byron he was a surface swimmer. Waves fascinated him. He would analyse their various qualities and it was their power that provided the challenge for his swimmers. In contrast Melville's cabin boy from *Moby Dick* goes mad when he falls by accident into the wondrous depths of the Pacific and sees, like Schiller's diver, 'strange shapes of the unwarped primal world gliding to and fro before his passive eyes'.

Jack London was obsessed by a fantasy of swimming far out to sea beyond the breaking waves with a woman he loved. It originated one quiet afternoon as he lay in a depressed mood face down in the sand on a Californian beach, and heard from far away, above the murmur of the surf, the voices of a man and a woman. He couldn't make out where the voices came from, as no one was around on the beach, until looking out to sea he caught sight of the heads of two figures leisurely approaching the shore, laughing and talking as happily and easily in the deep water as if they were sitting comfortably in deck chairs on the sand: 'Something inside me suddenly yearned after them – they were so blest, those two together. And I wondered, lying there sadly enough, if there was a woman in the world for me – the little woman who would be the right woman – with whom I could go out to sea, without boat or life-preserver, hours in the water holding long comradely talks on everything under the sun, with no more awareness of the means of locomotion than if walking.'

His first wife Bessie hardly fulfilled the role, though he was clearly proud of a photograph of their swimming together that he sent to various friends from Santa Cruz. But in his second, the emancipated and courageous Charmian, he felt he had found his 'Wolf-Mate'. She served as the model for Saxon, the prizefighter's wife in *The Valley of the Moon*, whose body was admired by the women in Carmel as she swam in the river – 'they called her Venus, and made her crouch and assume different poses' – while her husband thought she had Annette Kellermann, then a successful swimming film star, 'beat a mile'. For weeks London coached Charmian to dive through the waves of the Pacific. Their swims became longer from day to day – 'still inside the barrier reef, through the breakers we would work', Charmian relates, 'emerging with back-flung hair on their climbing backs while they roared shoreward – until one stormy afternoon, when not even the canoeists would venture out on the ocean, he took me out beyond the diving stage and through the waves into the open sea, and on our return we came in strong with our best strokes to the beach'. Charmian had never seen him more elated – 'and now we look forward to days when together we shall swim for hours beyond the breakers at Waikiki, and anywhere in the world'.

Although older than London and well into her forties, Charmian still cut the best figure on the beach. 'I love you for your beautiful body,' London once wrote, and dedicated four enthusiastic pages of notes to it, while his own was slowly deteriorating. Once it too had been beautiful, and he was 'as proud as the devil of it', but various maladies contracted on his voyages had left him overweight and feeble. Their roles gradually reversed. He became jealous of her for the first time, and once in deep water, when he was seized with cramp, she had to nurse him carefully back to shore. He translated his predicament into the short story 'The Kanaka Surf', which again dealt with the theme of a husband's supine jealousy that haunted London in his final years. It opens with two majestic swimmers, a husband and wife, walking down the beach to a mixture of gasps of admiration and sneers of resentment from the shapeless tourists lying on the sand around them. They run the last few yards and leap into the shallows. A ship's captain watches them through binoculars in disbelief as they swim out far beyond the diving platform and disappear into the distance. He alerts his crew for a possible rescue, then is astonished to see them returning through the waves, fearless and laughing. This swim forms an important daily ritual in their lives, but their happiness is threatened when the wife becomes attracted to a wealthy Hawaiian. In order to salvage their marriage and test her love, the husband feigns cramp while swimming in deep water and pretends to drown. The prospect of losing him brings the wife to her senses, and she supports him in her arms back to the shore.

London devotes several pages to the resentment felt by the emasculated tourists towards this dazzling pair of swimmers, as if they were heroic anachronisms, relics of mediaeval saga and romance and out of place in a world where 'the giants are long since past. In the mud of their complacently perpetuated barnyard pond, they assert that no bright-browed, bright-apparelled shining figures can exist outside of fairy books, old histories, and ancient superstitions.'

And so the 'swimmer' has come gradually to represent characters with a heightened sensitivity to the promises of life, who are spiritually dissatisfied with worldly ambitions and find it hard to compromise. For the 'swimmer' the ordered forms of everyday life seem inadequate and therefore intolerable. The Loman brothers in *Death of a Salesman* liked to disappear from the office and swim in the middle of the day as a gesture of defiance to the humdrum world they loathed, 'the measly manner of existence. To get on that subway on the hot mornings in summer. To devote your whole life to keeping stock, or making phone calls, or selling or buying. To suffer fifty weeks of the year for the sake of a two-week vacation; when all you really desire is to be outdoors, with your shirt off . . . ' A recent television interview with Arthur Miller began with him diving into the lake in his garden and swimming across, a ritual he goes through every day.

The attitude to the 'swimmer' is sometimes ambivalent. John Cheever's short story 'The Swimmer' traces a swimmer's decline from self-delusion to disillusion, as he decides suddenly one Sunday afternoon to swim the eight miles back to his home across the pools of his neighbours, that 'quasi-subterranean stream that curves across the country'. He appears at first the archetypal American hero. As he swims and runs across the grass that separates the pools, he feels like a 'pilgrim, an explorer, a man with a destiny'. Though far from young, he has retained the slim figure of a youth and could be compared to a 'summer's day, particularly the last hours of one'. He longs to swim naked, in order to experience fully his return to man's natural condition. He is convinced that he is 'swimming home'. Like London's swimmers he feels himself a legendary figure, distinct from the crowd for whom he expresses contempt – the Crosscups, Lerys, Welshers, Sachses, Biswangers, who discuss commerce and money over their poolside cocktails and never hurl themselves into the water. He imagines his swim as a romantic voyage into unknown waters, a form of knightly quest. Moving from pool to pool, his influence is that of some mythical figure, as he awakens in the women a sense of something missing, that there is more to life than brick barbecues, the best filters money can buy.

Gradually, however, one's faith in the swimmer is undermined. There are whispered suggestions of business failures, financial losses. As he crosses the main road, half-naked, people in cars jeer and laugh at him, a pitiful image of the swimmer bewildered by the forces of modern life. He is tempted to return, but his self-delusion has taken him too far along the way. Among the shrill, harsh sounds of a public pool he is confronted by the regimentation of the real world, the pressure to conform. ALL SWIMMERS, a notice-board declares in large letters, MUST TAKE A SHOWER BEFORE USING THE POOL. ALL SWIMMERS MUST USE THE FOOTBATH. ALL SWIMMERS MUST WEAR THEIR IDENTIFICATION DISCS. After the sapphire waters of the private pools these stink of chlorine. Scowling with distaste, he has to inch his way along the surface among the jostling crowds with his head held high to avoid contamination. He is kicked and splashed, until his ordeal ends when a lifeguard shouts to him from the side – 'Hey you without a disc, get outa the water.' He is ejected too from the pool of his mistress who has taken on a younger man. By now it is dark. He is tired, cold, and confused – 'he had swum too long, been immersed too long'. Rather than dive he climbs down steps for the first time in his life, and his once proud crawl is reduced to a 'hobbled sidestroke'. Finally he arrives home to find it locked. He pounds on the door in the rain, then looks through windows and realises the house is empty. His family had gone.

For the solitary, brooding Cheever swimming formed the 'apex of the day, its heart.' 'We were the last swimmers in the Caspian,' he records in his journal during an autumn visit to Russia, and he always made sure he was the 'last swimmer' of the year in his own Connecticut pool. The film that was made from the short story required Burt Lancaster to undergo three months of swimming lessons to help him overcome mild hydrophobia. It opens with him walking through a wood bare-foot and in bathing trunks among rabbits and deer, the sunlight through the trees glancing off his youthful, muscular body. Suddenly he bursts out of the wood on to a typically suburban scene – a well-tended lawn and some figures lying limply sipping drinks. They blink as he disturbs their inertia with a cry of greeting, then runs to the edge and in one long unbroken movement leaps exultantly into the pool. In slow motion he swims its lengths, leaving a trail of bubbles that sparkle in his wake. On emerging he greets the wife with a line from the Song of Solomon – 'How beautiful are thy feet in sandals, O Prince's daughter,' at which the husband grimaces and grunts through an alcoholic haze – 'We drank too much last night.' An old friend appears – the swimmer's age but, unlike the swimmer, shows it. The swimmer grabs his lapel – 'Do you know how long it's been since we had a swim together?' 'Don't remind me,' he mutters. 'Remember,' the swimmer insists, 'how we used to take off our suits and swim for miles up that river? We just never got tired. The water up there, remember? That transparent, light green water! It – it felt different.' The memory of it shows in his eyes. 'What a beautiful feeling. We could have swum around the world in those days.'

The 'swimmer' has often been identified with the 'Southern' tragic sense of life, the mood of regret for vanished ideals and civilised values, the belief that 'life is essentially a cheat and its conditions those of defeat'. In 'The Swimmers' Allen Tait remembers as a boy 'fleeing to water under the dry Kentucky sun', and the small-time hoodlum played by Sterling Hayden in Huston's film *The Asphalt Jungle* dreams of returning some day to the farm in Kentucky where he was brought up. He decides to make one more killing, then head for home – 'the first thing I'll do is take a bathe in some creek, and get this city dirt off me'. Disenchanted with his experience of the outside world, Chance Wayne in Tennessee Williams' *Sweet Bird of Youth* returns to the scenes of his youthful promise, his hometown and the beach where he once dazzled spectators with diving exhibitions from the high tower. He is now a little off form, but can still just about get away with a double back somersault, though someone comments: 'He's been away too long.' The narrator of Penn Warren's *All the King's Men* is in love with a girl who becomes the mistress of the corrupt governor, and everything he feels for the lost innocence of the South is embodied in his description of her dive: 'Anne was crazy about diving that summer. She would go up high, and stand up there in the sunlight poised at the very verge. Then, when she lifted her arms, I would feel that something was about to snap in me. Then down she would fly, a beautiful swan dive, with her arms flung wide to emphasise her trim breasts and her narrow back arched and her long legs close and sweet together. She would come flying down in the sunlight, and as I watched her it would be as though nobody else was there. I would hold my breath till whatever was going to snap inside me snapped. Then she would knife into the water, and her twin heels would draw through the wreath of ripple and the flicker of spray, and be gone.'

The image of the diver was used by Edgar Allan Poe to express the uncontrollable urge for self-destruction that he believed inherent in everyone: 'There is no passion in nature so demonically impatient as that of him who, shuddering upon the edge of a precipice, thus meditates a plunge.' It was in those lone seven-mile river swims of this 'poet of water', this 'displaced aristocrat', that the Southern affinity with swimming originated. It continued through Mark Twain and his description of Tom Sawyer and his friends naked and 'tumbling over each other in the shallow limpid water. They felt no longing for the little village sleeping in the distance. A vagrant current had carried off their raft, but this only gratified them, since its going was something like burning the bridge between them and civilisation.'

Gradually swimming became established in the Southern imagination as a symbol of evasion, a means of refuge and withdrawal from all they loathed and found distasteful in so-called 'civilisation'. Those who are attracted to water tend to be dreamers, outcasts, the 'fugitive kind' who by temperament, character, or birth are fated to be anachronisms trapped in a world 'lit by lightning'. Sebastian of Tennessee Williams' *Suddenly Last Summer* 'couldn't stay out of the water', while the narcissistic hero of Herlihy's *All Fall Down*, who is adored by a nymph called Echo, is described as 'nuts about water. Every place he goes, it's got water.' *The Moviegoer* of Walker Percy is a lonely romantic whose only experience of reality is through films. He is obliged at some stage of the novel to wrench himself away from his home in the Elysian Fields, New Orleans, in order to take a brief trip north to Chicago. He feels lost and desolate among the monumental buildings of the 'windy' city, until by chance he comes across the pool in which 'Tarzan-Johnny Weissmuller used to swim – an echoing underground place where a cold grey light filtered down from a three-storey skylight and muscular men wearing metal discs swam and shouted, their voices ringing against the wet tile walls'. In the poem 'Coming Back to America' the Southerner James Dickey describes his return from Europe to the basement of a New York hotel. After a restless night in an airless room, with 'forty floors of home weighed on us', he rises early and follows the 'signs that said SWIMMING POOL'. The lift carries him up:

> Through ceiling after ceiling of sleeping salesmen
>   and whores, and
> came out
> On the roof. The pool water trembled with the
>   few in their rooms
> Still making love. This was air.

Here, in the early light, he sits and talks with a skinny girl lifeguard who was working at her nails. Suddenly:

> She leapt and was in the fragile green pool as though
> I were still sleeping it off eleven floors under her:
>   she turned in a water
> Ballet by herself   graceful   unredeemable   her
>   tough face exactly
> As beautiful and integral as the sun come out of
>   the city.

Scott Fitzgerald's Dick Diver was a Southerner in temperament and background, devoted to the ideals of honour, courtesy and courage, the manners and moral code that Fitzgerald always associated with the pre-Civil War South. Like Gatsby, he was a romantic hero with a mythic conception of life, who was able to dispense 'starlight to hungry moths', opening up whole new worlds of magnificent possibilities for others. Gatsby, disillusioned that he could not revive the past with a Southern girl, died in his marble swimming pool, while Diver from a pile of pebbles created a 'bright tan prayer rug of a beach' on the Mediterranean shore, a momentary haven for a group of talented and vulnerable friends, dark-skinned and stylish swimmers as opposed to the pale figures further along who merely 'batted the sea with a stiff-armed crawl'. To an outsider their life on the beach seemed to express the perfection of their existence, their days 'spaced like the days of the older civilisations to yield the utmost from the materials at hand'. Up north, meanwhile, the 'true world thundered by', the material world embodied by Nicole, who began to hate the beach as she resented all the places where she was forced to play 'planet to Dick's sun'. The mystique of the beach depended entirely on Dick's 'Southern' qualities of charm and consideration. In his decline it became 'perverted to the taste of the tasteless', full of dull and fashionable people who never swam 'save for a short hangover dip at noon', a decline noted by Nicole when she became aware that Dick Diver for the first time was avoiding the high boards and no longer living up to his name. Like Conrad's *Nostromo*, by which it was heavily influenced, *Tender is the Night* traces the moral disintegration of an 'incomparable swimmer'. It was after reading Fitzgerald's novel that the girl mysteriously disappeared while swimming from the yacht among the Lipari islands, at the start of Antonioni's *L'Avventura*.

Many of the themes contained in *Tender is the Night* had been worked out already by Fitzgerald in the short

story 'The Swimmers', that makes the most explicit identification of the swimmer with the South, and vindicates
all he stands for. Its hero, Henry Clay Marston, is a
Virginian businessman working in Paris, who had left
America because he had been unable to come to terms
with the moral confusion of an 'ever-new, ever-changing'
country. Not that he finds the atmosphere any more congenial in France. The story opens in his office, surrounded by the noise of cars and fumes of gasoline
exhaust. A mood of black depression suddenly descends.
He retires to the washroom, and stands trembling just inside the door. Looking out of the window he is dazzled by
a garish advertisement for shirts, which in *The Great
Gatsby* symbolise a taste for vulgar and ostentatious
wealth. His trembling slowly subsides, and he resumes
work in a shaken state. Then when he returns home
unexpectedly and finds his French wife with another
man, his nervous condition declines into one of chaos
and despair.

   In order to recover he travels to the coast with his
family. There on the beach he sees a swimmer whom he
feels to be the 'perfect type of American – her arms,
like flying fish, clipped the water in a crawl', then 'her
body spread in a shallow dive or doubled in a jack knife
from the springboard'. Momentarily she is in trouble,
and he struggles out to help her, although he can't
swim. She offers to teach him. He makes a pathetic start,
but in time becomes a swimmer and so brings about his
recovery. He asks the American girl what she intends to
do now – 'My brother and I are going to Antibes; there's
swimming there all through October. Then Florida.'
'And swim?' he asked with some amusement. 'Why, yes.

We'll swim.' 'Why do you swim?' 'To get clean,' she answered, and this reply of hers takes on for him a greater national significance – 'I mean we've got too fastidious even to clean up our messes,' he comments sadly. Inspired by this vision Marston returns to America, where his wife begins another affair with his wealthy backer, Charles Wiese, the type of American he detests. He himself comes from a different background: 'Henry Clay Marston was a Virginian of the kind who are prouder of being Virginians than of being Americans. That mighty word printed across a continent was less to him than the memory of his grandfather, who freed his slaves in '58, fought from Manassas to Appomattox, knew Huxley and Spencer as light reading, and believed in caste when it expressed the best of race.'

Now, as a swimmer, Marston finds release from the perplexities of his life among the waves: 'When difficulties became insurmountable, inevitable, Henry sought surcease in exercise. For three years, swimming had been a sort of refuge, and he turned to it as one man to music or another to drink. There was a point when he would resolutely stop thinking and go to the Virginian coast for a week to wash his mind in the water. Far out past the breakers he could survey the green-and-brown line of the Old Dominion with the pleasant informality of a porpoise. The burden of his wretched marriage fell away with the buoyant tumble of his body among the swells, and he would begin to move in a child's dream of space. Sometimes remembered playmates of his youth swam with him; sometimes, with his two sons beside him, he seemed to be setting off along the bright pathway to the moon. Americans, he liked to say, should be born with fins . . . ' One afternoon, when swimming back to shore with a 'slow trudgeon', he rests by a raft and glances up to find the 'perfect American girl' who had taught him to swim four years before in France. He is overjoyed. He recognises her as a fellow Virginian – he should have presumed it in France, from her 'laziness, the apparent casualness that masked an unfailing courtesy and attention'. They talk and laugh as before, and once again she coaches his swimming, by demonstrating a 'sitting-down, standing-up dive from the high springboard, and he emulated her inexpertly – and that was fun'.

Fortified by this chance reunion with the swimmer, he decides on a confrontation with his wife and her lover. He wants to retain custody of his two boys. One warm summer evening the three of them sail out into the bay in Wiese's motorboat. Wiese is at the controls, and feels in command of the situation. Although one of the richest men in Virginia, he is not originally from there, his voice being 'too deliberately Southern, a cross between a carpet-bagger and a poor white'. Far out in the bay he switches off the engine and turning to Marston, demands his submission. 'Money is power,' he declares proudly, 'money made this country, built its great and glorious cities, created its industries, covered it with an iron network of railroads. It's money that harnesses the forces of Nature, creates the machine and makes it go when money says go, and stop when money says stop.' But in these distant waters the power of money is of no account. It is unharnessed nature that is in control. As Wiese is talking, the engine cuts out, and the boat 'meandered in a placid little circle'. Wiese tries desperately to restart the motor, but fails. 'Without will or direction' the boats drifts out to sea. Now, in the grip of the outgoing tide, their survival depends on Marston. He alone is in tune with Nature, as only he can swim. After forcing them to submit to his terms, he swims to shore to get help, knowing all the while, as they didn't, that a cross-current would soon have washed them back to safety. Marston, the Southern, 'natural' man, had triumphed over the forces of money.

Once again Marston returns to Europe. His attitude to America has changed. He has resolved the 'moral confusion', and what had once appeared 'ever-new, ever-changing' now seems to him firmly established on the old Southern concepts and traditions, the power of an earlier American culture that in him still survived. From the deck of the *Majestic* he looks back at the city and shoreline as they fade away in the distance, the shoreline that had 'once pandered in whispers to the last and greatest of human dreams' – 'He had a sense of overwhelming gratitude and of gladness that America was there, that under the ugly debris of industry, the rich land still pushed up, incorrigibly lavish and fertile, and that in the heart of the leaderless people the old generosities and devotions fought on, breaking out sometimes in fanaticism and excess, but indomitable and undefeated. There was a lost generation in the saddle at the moment, but it seemed to him that the men coming on, the men of the war, were better; and all his old feeling that America was a bizarre accident, a sort of historical sport, had gone forever. The best of America was the best of the world . . . France was a land, England was a people, but America, having about it still that quality of the idea, was harder to utter – it was the graves of

Shiloh, and the tired, drawn, nervous faces of its great men, and the country boys dying in the Argonne for a phrase that was empty before their bodies withered. It was a willingness of the heart.'

As Marston goes down the steps to the purser's office, he meets again his swimming coach, the 'perfect American girl'. 'Oh hello!' she cries, 'I'm glad you're going! I was just asking when the pool opened. The great thing about this ship is that you can always get a swim.' 'Why do you like to swim?' 'You always ask me that,' she replies, laughing. 'Perhaps you'd tell me if we had dinner together tonight.'

This Southern swimmer, the 'perfect American girl', was no doubt modelled on Fitzgerald's wife, Zelda. As a child in Montgomery, Alabama, Zelda had been famous for her swimming and fearless diving – 'I liked to jump from high places, I loved to dive.' When older she admitted to caring for only two things in life – boys and swimming. One of these boys commented that she 'wasn't afraid of anything. There was this board rigged up at the swimming pool and, well, almost nobody ever dived from the top. But Zelda did, and I was hard put to match her. I really didn't want to. She swam and dived as well as any of the boys and better than most of us.' She wore a one-piece flesh-coloured silk jersey swimming suit, and made no effort to deny rumours that she swam naked. Once with a group of girls she drove out to a pool with a high diving-board. In a moment she was climbing the ladder and preparing herself for a swallow dive. She found though that in extending her arms sideways they became entangled in the straps of her costume, so she undid them, discarded her suit, 'stood poised for an instant like a water nymph, rose upon her toes, and leaped from the board'. Everyone around the pool was held spellbound by her impudence and beauty.

On honeymoon in New York she dived naked into the fountain of Union Square, fully clothed into the Pulitzer fountain. When she swam when pregnant in the public pool of Montgomery, she was asked to leave. Scott soon came to realise that swimming was compulsive for her. Whenever they rented a house, he thought that as long as they found a place close to water, she would be happy. Years later he would rent houses with pools in Hollywood to please Sheilah Graham, and would sit watching her swimming from the side. Zelda's frenzied desire to plunge into water may have been partly caused by her nervous eczema, though she blamed her suffering on nobody ever having taught her to play tennis - 'When I'm most miserable, there's always your game to think of.' No doubt in diving she experienced the same 'exaltation' as she claimed to derive from dancing, the 'feeling for the flights of the human soul divorced from the person'. In the South of France, where the Murphys had created the beach at La Garoupe that was the inspiration for *Tender is the Night*, Sara Murphy once warned the Fitzgeralds to avoid their reckless diving from the rocks high above the sea: 'One had to be a superb diver in order to make it. There were notches cut in the rock at five, ten, up to thirty feet. Now, that's a high dive, a dangerous dive at any time, but especially at night, one had to have a perfect sense of timing or one would have been smashed on the rocks below. Zelda would strip to her slip and very quietly ask Scott if he cared for a swim. I remember one evening when I was with them that he was absolutely trembling when she challenged him, but he followed her. It was breathtaking. They took each dive, returning from the sea all shivering and white, until the last, the one at thirty feet. Scott hesitated and watched Zelda until she surfaced; I didn't think he could go through with it, but he did. When I remonstrated with them, Zelda said very sweetly in her low, husky voice: "But Saayra – didn't you know, we don't believe in conservation." And that was that!'

From her mental asylum Zelda wrote an anguished note to Scott in 1935, wishing 'we could spend July by the sea, browning ourselves and feeling water-weighted hair flow behind us from a dive'. Shortly before he died, in a final letter to his wife and daughter after he had seen them both for the last time, Scott wrote that 'all he wanted to think of was the two of them together, swimming, diving from great heights, and being very trim and graceful in the water'. Although in 'The Crackup' Fitzgerald describes 'all good writing' as 'swimming underwater and holding your breath', he tended to avoid swimming as he was ashamed of his feet. Nor did he like the sun, and on the beaches of southern France would race down to the sea, plunge into the shallows, and immediately get out. But like Zelda and his daughter who dived for Vassar, he was fond of showing off his diving. Dick Diver's symbolic decline when he avoided the high boards, and his final collapse when attempting to lift a man on his water skis off a crowded beach, can be attributed to an incident in Fitzgerald's own life when he went swimming with a nurse he had hired in a fit of depression while writing *Tender is the Night*. She happened to be young and pretty, and in trying to impress her with a swallow dive, he fractured his shoulder.

Many of these Southern writers were passionate swimmers themselves, none more than Tennessee Williams. He was always proud of his 'good swimmer's physique', and learnt to swim among the mountain streams of the Appalachians, in a pool of 'fabulously cool, clear water formed by the dam, which offered a sparkling waterfall over bone-white rocks'. His aunt would try and support him in the water. When he told her that he would rather depend on himself, she replied: 'Oh Tom, dear Tom, when you depend on yourself, you're depending on a broken reed.' He always kept on his desk a photograph of Glenway Westcott in the bloom of youth bathing naked in a mountain lake, and often swam off Nantucket with Carson McCullers. Beaches and YMCA pools were for Williams places of seduction, where he could entice young men with his charm and didn't have to rely, like Sebastian of *Suddenly Last Summer*, on a sister extended as bait in a transparent costume. Tomatoes he once described as firm to the touch 'like a young swimmer's pectoral muscles'.

When bored in America he would long to fly to Italy and 'rent a farm, employ a gardener chauffeur, and swim, swim and swim in that still, fresh, cool, water'. On the Venice Lido he used to stay at the hotel where Aschenbach became mesmerised by the young Tadzio, the Excelsior, with a balcony over the Adriatic, though he was disappointed by having to wade out so far into water 'not translucent'. His selection of hotels tended to be based on the quality of the pool they offered. He particularly favoured the Hollywood Roosevelt, an oasis among palms on the edge of the strident boulevard, with circles painted on the bottom by Hockney that seem to writhe and sparkle on its surface in the sunshine. 'I want to spend the spring in London', he would write to an English friend, 'PROVIDED you can get me a flat with a pool to swim in, CAN YOU?' The ritual of morning swims was so ingrained that if omitted would cause Williams to disappear during lunch without a word, and reappear half an hour later apologetically with soaking hair. He chose to live in Key West because swimming 'was prac- tically a way of life with me, and since Key West was the southernmost point in America, I figured I would be able to swim there'. When in New Orleans he would go to the Athletic Club on North Rampart Street, where the pool was fed by a spring of artesian water and it was 'cool from the underground – and it would pick me up'.

It was Tennessee Williams's dying request that his remains be dropped in the ocean as near as possible to where Hart Crane disappeared off the stern of the *Orizaba* into the Bay of Mexico, because 'I've always admired the gentleman and I never had the opportunity to meet him'. For the same reason a certain sympathy with Tennessee Williams has made me want to swim wherever he bathed, in the Hollywood Roosevelt, off Santa Monica, in the shallow waters of the Venice Lido, from the beach at Barcelona, with Alan Ross stretched out on the shore from where Sebastian's sister/Elizabeth Taylor lured the young men, in water that forced the fastidious Williams to go out a mile in a boat to find 'sea fit to swim in'. It has made me climb over the rickety fence of his deserted house on Duncan Street, Key West, to swim through the green slime of his pool among a jungle of tropical plants, and plunge alone and naked into the spring waters of the marble baths of the New Orleans Athletic Club. After which it seemed only proper to submit my body to the hands of the Black Masseur who mangled the poor clerk in the Williams short story and still haunts its recesses. As my limbs were wrenched and stretched on the stone slab, I felt for the demented clerk who died so happily in his arms.

James Dickey made a film of Penn Warren swimming alone across a lake. Throughout his life he was an assiduous and inveterate swimmer, and in his youth loved to swallow dive from great heights into waterholes, like the girl in his novel who flew down in the sunlight, 'her arms flung wide to emphasise her trim breasts and her narrow back arched and her long legs close and sweet together'. Diving was a preoccupation of the years between the wars. The best divers in the world were now all American, ever since one of the Swedish divers Ernst Bransten had defected to America in 1920 and betrayed the secrets of the art. There was just one exception, an emotional Egyptian Farid ('Fred') Simaika, who at the 1928 Olympics was declared the winner of the high-diving competition, then halfway through the Egyptian national anthem demoted to second place because of a miscount. His head was later found suspended by strings threaded through each ear, after he had landed among headhunters when shot down over the Pacific during the last war. The Americans were the stars of the diving scenes in Riefenstahl's Olympic film. I have telephoned them all, and managed to contact two. Marjorie Gestring, whose smile of girlish delight at winning the springboard title when only thirteen was captured by Riefenstahl, was gratified to be still remembered, while Dick Degener from somewhere in Philadelphia growled it was all ancient history, he had never heard of Riefenstahl, and besides, his dinner was on the table.

The swallow/swan dive that so appealed to Leni Riefenstahl and the London crowds who watched the diving Swedes, Jack London and Robert Penn Warren, Scott and Zelda Fitzgerald, had been brought to perfection by the diminutive American Desjardins at the end of the Twenties. It was the blond Marshall Wayne's prolonged backward swallow from the springboard that transformed the whole mood and tempo of Riefenstahl's sequence, raising it from the level of a documentary into a work of art. His name and graceful diving became the inspiration for Tennessee Williams' Chance Wayne, who charmed spectators with his dives from the high platform in *Sweet Bird of Youth*. At the 1924 Olympics Caroline Smith had been far behind the leaders until her final dive, a perfect swallow that came down 'like a soaring bird, and landed with barely a splash' before ten thousand spectators. It won her the gold medal and a standing ovation from the grudging Parisians. She then disappeared into show business.

The swallow was the dive of the times, and seemed in some ways to express them. Musicals were full of girls swallow diving from the tops of waterfalls. Jane swallow dived from out of the trees into the arms of Tarzan. Weissmuller himself was an immaculate swallow diver, as photographs show, but he preferred to take part in competitions where the result was not dependent on the whims of judges. In the 1914 film *A Daughter of the Gods*

Annette Kellermann set a world high-dive record when, with a beautiful swallow dive from one hundred feet, she escaped from a prison tower by plunging into the sea. This record was broken four years later by Alick Wickham's startling dive, another swallow, from 205 ft. 9 in. into the Yarra River in Australia, a record that not surprisingly still stands. A newspaper report describes how this simple Solomon islander was duped into accepting an offer of £100 if he dived from a platform a hundred feet high on the banks of the river Yarra at Melbourne. On his arrival, he found that the platform was positioned on top of a 105 ft. 9 in. cliff. A crowd of 60,000 had already gathered. Women screamed and fainted as Wickham several times looked down from the board, hesitated, and moved back. He confessed afterwards that the height did not worry him as much as the fear he might hit the opposite bank, which looked so close from 205 ft. 9 in. The crowd gasped when he jumped off and hovered motionless above the river, his arms outstretched like the spread wings of a bird, then swooped down towards the water. He survived, but the three costumes he wore as protection for the dive were ripped off by the impact. For a week he lay in a coma, and if anyone talked to him he would cry out with pain.

For the deprived and down-trodden, the film public of the depression years, the swallow dive became a distant vision of perfection, of physical grace and freedom. In Aldous Huxley's *After Many a Summer*, published in 1939, the families of poor transients from Kansas are working in the orange groves of California, below Hearst's San Simeon, in silence, when suddenly the youngest of the children lets out a shrill cry: "'Look there!" She pointed. In front of them was the castle. From the summit of its highest tower rose a spidery metal structure, carrying a succession of platforms to a height of twenty or thirty feet above the parapet. On the highest of these platforms, black against the shining sky, stood a tiny human figure. As they looked, the figure spread its arms and plunged foremost out of sight behind the battlements.'

In his long elegy to the heroic age of bullfighting, Hemingway compares the slow, stately motion of the bullfighter to a diver who 'could control his speed in the air and prolong the vision of a swallow dive'. Hart Crane, some say, executed an exquisite version of the dive when he plunged to his death into the Bay of Mexico from the steamship *Orizaba* in 1932. Mentioned in Alvarez's disquisition on suicide is the case of a gifted and graceful American climber of the time, who in a mood of depression caused by the breakup of a love affair drove out to some cliffs on the East coast, which are vertical and between two and three hundred feet high, and jumped off. 'Physical perfectionist to the last, he performed as he fell an immaculate swallow dive.'

These were the last years of pure diving, symbolised by the prolonged symmetry of the swallow dive, before it became a series of flickering twists and turns, a gymnastic exercise too intricate for the naked eye to follow. The demise of the swallow dive, like that performed by Christopher Hampton's father in Alexandria in 1936 illustrated on the programme cover of his play that traces the graceful decay of British power in the Middle East, marked the passing of an era. Now in its decline it went the way of those breathtaking strokes of the past,

Gandar Dower and Cochet's half-volley, Ranji's leg-glance and those slashing off-side strokes that were the hallmark of these carefree amateur cricketers at the turn of the century, above all the loose-wristed cover drive whose loss brought home to John Gale his divorce from all the natural 'timing and innocence' of youth: 'I was twelve or thirteen, and in the cricket nets at school: the mathematics master, a man with false teeth and a good heart, bowled me a half-volley outside the off-stump: I struck the ball into the covers, a lovely blow, and it went like butter. After I had played the stroke I sensed that it was the last for me that would be natural, easy, and perfectly-timed: I had leant into the ball and stroked it away without thinking, a movement of almost pagan simplicity. But from that moment on, my batting became stiff, fierce, and premeditated: I hooked, cut, pulled and slashed, self-consciously, but never again could I stroke a ball through the covers without a thought. I never did again, even when I was a man. From that day on, something had gone from me: I have never rediscovered it: I have searched for it ever since.'

At a time when the majority of champion swimmers are concentrated in Eastern Europe, pale figures who have used up their youth on innumerable lengths of sunless pools, it is tempting to look back to the golden age of swimming between the wars, when it seemed to express the *joie de vivre* of Pacific coast life and the Hollywood film industry. Great swimmers often turned to films at the end of their careers, a tradition that began with Duke Kahanamoku, whom Jack London had watched swimming and surfing in Honolulu. Perhaps the most graceful swimmer of the period, Alberto Zorilla, appeared in a few musicals after winning an Olympic gold medal in Amsterdam and the world ballroom dancing championship one year in Biarritz. Weissmuller followed the Hawaiian as world champion, and never lost a race in his five years as an amateur before retiring to take on the role of Tarzan, whose mistrust of civilisation and sympathy with primitive life seem to epitomise the various romantic notions that have accumulated around the swimmer. After a series of unsuccessful marriages that included Lupe Velez, notable for her dramatic suicide, he died penniless in Mexico, befriended by a millionaire. His successor as Tarzan, Buster Crabbe, secured the part with an extraordinary finish in the 1932 Los Angeles Games, when he made up yards on the final length to win by a touch from the Frenchman Jean Taris who, like Carpentier when knocked out by Dempsey eleven years before, was already a legendary figure in Europe.

Taris himself was the subject of one of only four films that were made by Jean Vigo. It follows the swimmer as he swims lengths of a Parisian pool. Most of the film was shot underwater, using special lenses and lamps that illuminated the bottom, as Taris twists and turns through shafts of sunlight, among patterns of bubbles, like a plunging dolphin in an aquarium. Vigo created an isolated fantasy world where time seems suspended and space unconfined, rather like the dream sequence of his *L'Atalante*, when the young man dives into the river from the barge, turns two somersaults, and watches his missing bride float towards him, smiling, in her wedding dress. Vigo refers to Jean Taris in *Zéro de Conduite* when the drawing of a swimmer by the young and sympathetic master is transformed before the eyes of the disappointed schoolboys into that of Napoleon in full military uniform. At the end of *Jean Taris* the swimmer resumes his felt hat and pin-stripe suit, but in his dreamlike escape into the realms of the imagination, his transitory release from the discipline and confinement of the mundane, Vigo expressed in ten minutes all that was central to his work and feeling.

It is strange how in films of the time brief underwater scenes are so memorable, like those clear gravelly streams in early Italian paintings, where the water is suggested by a ripple around the ankle, a slight discolouring of the skin: the gold coins sinking to the riverbed in *The Nibelungenlied*; the divers of Riefenstahl returning to the surface; an officer from the *Potemkin* discarded on the ocean floor; the fugitive from the chain gang submerged in the shallows and breathing through a reed to evade his pursuers. Scenes such as these reveal not so much mere pride in novel camera techniques, as a sudden, excited curiosity in a newly discovered world, a fresh, mysterious, magical element whose attractions were now being experienced for the first time on a wide scale.

Women had only just been released from the bloused, skirted, stockinged pantaloons to which they had been subjected for so many years. As recently as 1919 the blonde Olympic swimmer Etheldra Bleibtrey had been jailed for swimming nude on Manhattan Beach because she had removed her stockings. This new sense of liberation owed much to the example of the Australian Annette Kellermann, who herself was arrested on Revere Beach soon after arriving in Boston, then went on to star in Vaudeville and five early silent films that were very popular and fascinated among others Jack London.

Now in their races women no longer had to drag yards of heavy, sodden clothing along with them, and they exulted in their newly acquired freedom of movement. For a brief period between the wars they were perhaps the only group of female athletes who have ever been able to combine a certain delicate sophistication with genuine athletic achievement.

These swimmers were allowed to compete in the Olympic Games eight years before other female athletes. Like Weissmuller, the majority of them dived as stylishly as they swam. Many were beautiful. No swimmer apparently was more graceful than Sybil Bauer, who died at her zenith at twenty-two from cancer, yet she could swim the backstroke faster than any man of her time. Jane Fauntz, an elegant swimmer and diver, starred on the covers of magazines, modelled furs at Saks in Chicago, and endorsed Camel cigarettes. The style of Martha Norelius, who became the centre of the social set at the Breakers hotel, was described by a Parisian as 'poetry in motion', and her coach L. de B. Handley, a great influence on women's swimming at the time, never tired of watching her. When in 1926 Gertrude Ederle became the first woman to swim the Channel, swimming crawl all the way to beat the existing men's record by two hours, sirens greeted her on her return to New York, flowers showered down from planes, and the enthusiasm of her ticker-tape welcome equalled that of Lindberg the following year. Unfortunately she lost millions in sponsorship when she delayed her return some months in order to visit a grandmother in Germany, and the Channel in the meantime was swum by a mother. Ederle's hearing had been permanently affected by the waves, and throughout the rest of her life she suffered from nervous breakdowns, although with various other swimmers she appeared in films like *Swim, Girl, Swim* and Rose's Aquacades.

Champion divers would be invited by Randolph Hearst to give exhibitions at his Grecian and Roman pools in San Simeon. Doris O'Mara recalls an exhibition they gave for the Vanderbilts and their friends, at the Vanderbilt estate in North Carolina: 'When we entered the pool, there were lackeys standing in a line with their hands out. We had on our bathing suits and caps and a towel wrapped around us, and as each one of us came by we just dropped our towels.' The diving girl on the side of the Jantzen costume became one of the symbols of the age. A sticker was also designed for car windshields. Millions were sold, though some states like Massachusetts refused to grant a licence to drivers displaying anything so risqué. Pages were devoted to swimwear in fashion magazines, with models tucking their hair into bathing caps, posing beside classical statues by garden pools. Man Ray photographed the alluringly scarred surrealist painter Meret Oppenheim in bathing suit and cap, while the beautiful backstroker Eleanor Holm was depicted in a series of murals by Salvador Dali as a mermaid in a grotto. Picasso was so struck by the stylish way Sara Murphy wore a pearl necklace above her bathing costume on the beach at La Garoupe, that in his neo-classical paintings of the period his monumental women wear only pearl necklaces.

Newspapers began to rely for their circulation on photographs of young girls in revealing costumes poised on the edge of pools and boards, or arching their bodies in full flight. At a time of strong censorship, the fact that they were athletic made them legitimate. Cavalcades of women stars were tempted south by the real estate promoters of the great Florida boom, where they were photographed competing in the pools of new developments: Coral Gables, Roney Plaza, Miami-Biltmore, or Palm Beach. Ziegfeld showgirls would be invited down by the lonely and anaemic industrialist James Deering, to enjoy the exquisite marble pool on his Vizcaya estate near Miami, where they could swim out among the brilliant blue tiles into the sunshine through fountains and arches, from a dark grotto whose walls were encrusted with shells and fish, their surface obscured by a continuous veil of dripping water.

I once spent a week swimming through these Florida pools, including Vizcaya. Some of them, like so much else, were destroyed in the euphoria of the Sixties, but the two most romantic still survive in Coral Gables. This suburb was designed in the early Twenties as a Mediterranean haven to counteract the urban sprawl of Miami. A quarry pit was transformed by Phineas Paist in 1924 into a public pool, called the 'Venetian', that is shaped irregularly like a lagoon, fed by an artesian spring, and bordered by waterfalls, caves, fountains and porticoes crammed with bougainvillaea. Instead of diving-boards there are high rocks and hump-backed Venetian bridges. On the day I was there they were cleaning the pool and it was empty, so I walked along the bottom and tried to imagine it in its heyday, when the swimming and film stars all swam there, and couples danced among the palms at night to Paul Whiteman and his Orchestra, who would abandon their tuxedos and play from the

shallows in their bathing suits. When they constructed
the Biltmore hotel, the crater that was formed from
quarrying the rock for the building was filled with
water to create a vast L-shaped pool. A colonnade
was added, and a pink campanile as a diving platform
from where the Olympic stars would exhibit fancy dives
before the war. I swam there alone one night and lay in
the black water, looking up through the darkness to the
illuminated bedrooms where couples were changing for
dinner. It was almost Christmas, and in some distant
room a choir was rehearsing carols, while nearer the
pool in the central tower silhouettes of dancers lurched
to the jerky rhythm of 'Louie, Louie'.

On the other side of Miami, on the fifteenth floor
of an apartment block high above a blue pool, lives
the backstroker once painted by Dali and described
by *Time* magazine as the most beautiful athlete in the
world, though all that remains of her boyish beauty is her
long, eager mouth. Eleanor Holm never swims now, not
even after her strenuous games of tennis, but in 1932
she won the backstroke at the Los Angeles Games, and
caused a sensation when four years later, as a certainty
for another gold, she was banned by Avery Brundage
from competing at Berlin when he caught her drinking
champagne late at night in the first-class cabin of some
newspapermen. Unlike other swimmers, she was used
to late nights as she was married to the band leader
Art Jarrett with whom she sang duets. Before races
she would smoke in the changing room to show off her
insouciance. Her suspension turned her into a celebrity
overnight. In Berlin she was consoled by Hitler, while
Riefenstahl, who was rarely fascinated by women, con-

stantly followed her around and filmed her swimming in the Olympic pool. On her return to America she played Jane to the Tarzan of Glenn Morris who had won the decathlon in Berlin, but she left the film when the wire snapped that held back an alligator and she was forced to swim for her life.

She then married another musician, Billy Rose, the entrepreneur and lyricist of various popular songs like 'Barney Google' and 'It's only a Paper Moon'. The Renoirs he left her after their acrimonious divorce still decorate her drawing room – 'some of his pupils painted most of what's there, but that's his authenticated signature' she was assured. Rose made her the star of the great Aquacades he began to promote in 1937. Annette Kellermann had already popularised mermaid spectaculars in theatres and films, but Rose's first Aquacade was staged in the lake off Cleveland. Eleanor Holm would march at night on to the stage in silver high-heeled slippers and cape, which she would remove dramatically before diving into the black water in a silver leotard, where she performed a prolonged water ballet with Weissmuller, while the orchestra played 'The Blue Danube' or occasionally Bing Crosby crooned. 'Eleanor was darn near Nijinsky in a bathing cap,' Rose enthused. They would be followed by comedian divers like Stubby Kruger and some spectacular floodlit dives by Desjardins and Marshall Wayne from seventy-five feet.

The show moved on to New York, but by the time it reached San Francisco Esther Williams had taken over her role. When these sensational Aquacades were transformed into Hollywood spectaculars a few years later, it was Esther Williams who became their star. She had won the hundred metres final in the National Swimming Championships shortly before the war, and no American woman was to swim the distance faster for another seven years. The film *Neptune's Daughter* in fact begins with her competing in a hundred metre race, watched by her future agent who describes his impressions of her as she swims: 'I'd like to tell you a story about a guy, a girl, and a bathing suit. I saw her at every swimming meet the city ever had, just like this one. She was always lined up with a group of other girls, but she stood out like a swan in a bunch of mud hens. I saw the starter take his place and call "swimmers up". She hit the water and cut through it like a million-dollar yacht. At the turn it was neck and neck. She soon pulled away, away out in front. And that's where she belonged, out in front. She walked to the dressing room on air, and I went right after her . . . ' The agent persuades her to turn professional and model a range of bathing suits, those various one-piece costumes with their siren names – 'Double Entendre', 'Side Issue', 'Honey Child', 'Diamond Lil' – whose charms were soon to be superseded by the bikini that Esther Williams always refused to wear. At the end of the film, clad in the 'Streamliner', she swan dives from a rock into an indoor pool. She was the last and most successful of the many beautiful swimming stars tempted to seek success in Hollywood, who could dive as elegantly as they swam, those 'swans in a bunch of mud hens' who 'belonged away out in front'.

Before the expansion of the film industry, the pools of California were concentrated in the North. The great Sutro Baths of San Francisco were founded in 1896 by an engineer who had made his fortune from devising a tunnel to drain the flooded shafts of the silver mines in Nevada. Sutro then turned his aquatic genius to designing the most remarkable pool ever built. The railway company ran two lines directly to its entrance, from where stairs descended to what was the largest glass-roofed building in existence, situated high above the Pacific, full of palm trees that stretched up to its ceiling, stuffed anacondas, a Tropic beach, restaurants, and in the main amphitheatre, seven separate swimming pools overlooking the ocean. Their temperature varied from ice-cold to warm. They held two million gallons of sea water, and could accommodate ten thousand bathers at a time, who could vary their swimming with swinging from the rings and trapezes, or diving off the nine springboards and several high platforms. In its largest pool, the longest indoors in the world, the Hawaiian Duke Kahanamoku made his first appearance on the mainland and immediately broke the world sprint record. The baths were dismantled in 1966. On the other side of the Bay was the largest open-air pool in the world, the Fleishhacker, that resembled a lake with an Italian Renaissance changing room stretching almost its entire length. But the water was never warm, and divers were put off by the perpetual mist that hovered over its surface, though Roy Woods trained here for months before his tragic dive of almost 200 feet from the Bay bridge, that broke his back and left him permanently paralysed from the waist down. Both these pools were vast public places, scenes of boisterous and daredevil activity, where families picnicked and spent the day.

No one swims across the Los Angeles pools. Strict lanes are imposed for devotees of 'serious' swimming.

In the wake of Hollywood, swimming has become symptomatic of the search for physical perfection, the desperate effort to remain forever young. In the Twenties a network of sapphire pools began to blossom among the Hollywood hills and spread across the valleys. Their tropical profusion charmed Hockney as his plane flew low over the city before he landed in Los Angeles for the first time. Immediately he arrived he visited the Hollywood-Greek swimming pool in the studios of the magazine *Physique Pictorial* whose photographs of muscled beach boys had been his inspiration for going there. In the cold, rainy atmosphere of northern England pools had been a luxury, but here they seemed to be everywhere and available to everyone. He first began to paint them after being mesmerised by the sight of the blue-and-yellow speckled tiles that decorate the pool designed by Frank Lloyd Wright at the Biltmore hotel in Phoenix, Arizona. His enthusiasm for the brilliance of their colour made me drive for sixteen hours across the desert for an evening swim among these Aztec tiles, as the sun disappeared behind the ziggurat diving platform. I wanted besides to experience a pool conceived by an architect to whom water obviously meant so much, who was one of the first to integrate swimming pools with buildings, and designed houses in the form of waves, that overhung waterfalls and streams where the families loved to bathe.

In Hollywood, Hockney became fascinated by the effect of sunlight on water. In England the rivers and sea had appeared opaque, their colour dependent on that of the sky, but in these transparent waters the Californian sun transformed a still surface into a pattern of dancing lines enlivened by the various colours of the spectrum. And so a series of paintings evolved, of blue pools against a background of tropical trees and rectangular curtained windows, that became icons of the Californian way of life and the scenario of so many of the blue films produced there. In the paintings vague, dematerialised figures splash or immerse themselves in the water, among the reflections and the shadows cast on the surface by diving-boards and palms, the sinuous patterns of light that irradiate from the depths. In *Portrait of an Artist* a figure gazes down on his submerged self, a projection of the isolation and self-absorption of the artist in general. This same pool was used by Hockney in his design for the set of a ballet inspired by an epitaph on a Roman gravestone in the museum of Antibes, that commemorated a boy 'Septentrion' in the local theatre who once 'saltavit et placuit' – danced and gave pleasure. Hockney turned him into a swimmer who emerges from this Californian pool and charms a group of bored and fashionable bystanders with a narcissistic display of dancing, then seduces each one of them in turn. His effect though is only momentary. Rather than respond to his offer of a world of enchantment, they reject him and return to their state of inertia. The dancing swimmer kills himself, and in his death Hockney felt he had depicted the fate of the true artist who refuses to compromise.

Secluded behind high walls, these Hollywood pools offer a retreat, a suspended world that induces a mood of fantasy and self-delusion in those that use them. In Sirk's film *There's always Tomorrow*, Fred MacMurray lies by the side of a pool with a woman he once loved, and dreams of breaking away from his unhappy marriage.

The sounds of laughing, splashing swimmers remind him of all he has missed as a married man – 'You don't do the things you used to do, you get afraid of life,' he murmurs sadly, before finally returning to his wife. In the pool of the Beverly Hills Hotel young starlets would swim around day after day in a desperate bid to attract attention, while on its artificial beach of imported white sand lounged the minor agents, bribing waiters to relay fictitious messages on the loudspeaker that they were required urgently by Mr Darryl Zanuck or Mr David Selznick. It was the artifice of these pools that attracted Hockney, the fact that their shape, colour, size and surroundings were entirely adaptable to the taste and fancies of the owner. Among the adobe bungalows of the Garden of Allah occupied by writers such as Scott Fitzgerald was a central oasis surrounded by palms, an eccentrically shaped pool designed by the actress Alla Nazimova in the form of the Black sea, to remind her of her childhood in Yalta. Nazimova's nephew, the imaginative Val Lewton, conjured up a macabre pool scene for his film *Cat People*, in which a blonde descends into the dark recesses of a deserted hotel pool, whose waters become a refuge where she revolves in terror as the atmosphere around her is transformed into that of a jungle, an atavistic region of growls and roars and wriggling, dancing lines reflected on the ceiling off the surface of the pool. From out of the midst of this fantasy emerges the feral shape of the Cat Woman.

The condition of these pools serves as a form of gauge that registers the varying fortunes of Hollywood stars and characters. As John Gilbert began to lose his popularity, his decline was symbolised by his 'sad, leaf-filled pool'. At the beginning of *Citizen Kane*, before the light in the tower snaps off, one of the images is of Kane's great swimming pool, now empty, a newspaper blowing across the cracked floor of the tank. Wilder's *Sunset Boulevard* is based on a circular narrative that revolves around a swimming pool. The opening shot is William Holden's body floating on its surface, filmed from below. 'The poor dope,' comments a detective, 'he always wanted a pool, but in the end the price turned out a little too high.' The film describes how he came to be there. On the run from the police, Holden becomes trapped in the opulent home of a reclusive fading star played by Gloria Swanson. He looks out of his bedroom window at night and sees the 'ghost' of a tennis court, an empty pool crawling with rats and refuse. When eventually Swanson contrives to seduce him, Holden emerges the next morning from a bathe in the swimming pool, now miraculously brimful of water, as if to confirm that he has become her lover. Feeling suddenly in control of his life and confident that he owns Swanson and her pool, he mentions casually to the girl he loves – 'When you get back, if you ever feel like taking a swim, well, here's the pool.' The enraged Swanson finally shoots him in a fit of jealousy and Holden falls into the illuminated pool. The scene fades to the present, and the commentary wraps up the story: 'Well, here we are where we started, at the pool again, the one he always wanted . . . '

These little strips of blue water became images of purity in a cynical world, quasi-inviolate shrines like those still pools that shimmer beside the Islamic mosques of India and Isfahan. Looking down at them spread out below from the hills of Los Angeles, I have never seen one actually being used. Fans have been known to commit suicide in the pools of their chosen stars, in the manner of those English officers who shot themselves by the Taj Mahal because they wanted to die in the 'loveliest place on earth'. To illustrate how deeply the Japanese were wounded before the war by Western social and diplomatic discrimination, a Japanese-American described how the Californian public pool he and others of his race were allowed to swim in on Fridays, was drained and cleaned before being used by whites on Saturdays. What elsewhere is generally left unsaid is writ large and to the point on notice-boards above Californian pools: PERSONS WITH INFLAMED EYES, NASAL OR EAR DISCHARGES, BOILS OR OTHER EVIDENT SKIN OR BODILY INFECTIONS SHALL BE EXCLUDED FROM THIS POOL or URINATING, DISCHARGE OF FECAL MATTER, EXPECTORATING OR BLOWING THE NOSE IN SWIMMING POOL IS PROHIBITED. Signs of urine in his pool shocked Orson Welles. In an attempt to embarrass the culprits, he found a chemist who had developed a clear, colourless liquid which on insertion in the water could immediately detect those who had abused their privileges: 'We put this stuff in and we invited our friends out, naturally, at the weekend, and they were swimming around in raspberry-coloured clouds. They were all doing it, you see. We discovered during our scientific investigation that it was overwhelmingly the men who did it, and women of advanced years.' The 'awful revelation' that so many of his sophisticated friends habitually misused the pool in this way greatly dismayed him.

'I have always wanted a swimming pool', writes

Joan Didion in *Holy Water*, 'and never had one . . . A swimming pool requires, once it has been filled and the filter has begun its process of cleaning and recirculating the water, virtually no water, but the symbolic content of swimming pools has always been interesting: a pool is misapprehended as a trapping of affluence, real or pretended, and of a kind of hedonistic attention to the body. Actually a pool is, for many of us in the West, a symbol not of affluence but of order, of control over the uncontrollable. A pool is water, made available and useful, and is, as such, infinitely soothing to the Western eye.' By 'Western' she was referring to those living in the arid landscape of Western America, beyond the point where the average annual rainfall is below twenty inches. As soon as he arrived there, Hockney became fascinated by the 'symbolic content' of its water. His first paintings were of young men showering by the beach, caressing the water against their naked bodies as it rebounded and cascaded over them, the spiralling jets of lawn sprinklers, *Different kinds of water pouring into a swimming pool, Santa Monica*.

Nowadays Southern California appears a paradise of water. The myriads of pools and fountains, gushing pumps, irrigation channels and green sprinkled lawns create a deceptive atmosphere. 'God never intended Southern California to be anything but desert. Man has made it what it is,' a visitor once remarked. There are no natural rivers or lakes. Water is transported hundreds of miles across mountains and deserts, from remote regions in the North, the Owens valley and the Colorado river, after a gradual and sinister process of acquisition recorded in Polanski's film *Chinatown*. The wonderful liquid sounds in that film, as water gushes from showers, sprinkles lawns, and pours into ponds reveal the reverence for water felt in an area that is haunted by the fear that its resources will someday dry up and the land return to its semi-arid condition. When touring California, J. B. Priestley was struck by its peculiar air of transience, the fact that it was all 'as impermanent and brittle as a reel of film'. This sense of desperation has created the wealth of water brokers, and caused the rise of water development companies who attempt by every means to divert water away from farms into cities. Here water runs 'not downhill, but towards money'. Jack London fought hard for his water in the Sonoma valley, and castigated the farmers around him who were prepared to accept offers for their 'riparian rights'. The commodity is so precious that there are now water bars, providing fifteen varieties of 'designer water' and nothing else, where a glass of Evian or Perrier is served in a watery blue light, to the taped sound of waves and videos of clouds and waterfalls.

Frequently heard on the car radios of Los Angeles is the advertisement:'When Caesar Augustus sipped his first drop of Perrier, he is said to have exclaimed "Templa deis aquae construite" – "Build temples to the gods of water."' The dignified tones of classicism sanctify so much out there. When the first settlers, many of them Southern after the Civil War, arrived in California, their Virgil packed in their bean bags, they dreamed of creating a new classical world on the shores of the Pacific. Here they could establish a fresh civilisation animated by a full play of sense and spirit, distinguished from all the grasp and greed they had left behind in the East, where a new breed of strong and heroic people could live in simple harmony with the landscape, and enjoy that synthesis of rural life and the sea that is the charm of the idylls of Theocritus and the paintings of Claude. Once more, like Rome, the cities would flow with water. Every piazza would have its fountain, every garden its pool. Although great pools were to be built in the country estates of the East on classical lines, revivals of the 'impluvia' of the Roman villa – the Whitneys' at Greentree contained elements of the Baths of Titus, Caracalla, and Pompeii – nothing there was to rival the style and magnificence of Hearst's 'natatoria' at San Simeon.

The construction of these pools conforms to the prologue of *Citizen Kane*, that describes the fragments of diverse cultures, figments of an American Dream, jammed by a fretful imagination into a strange and opulent coherence. The architect's original intention was to build one modest clover-shaped pool surrounded by palms among the guest cottages, no larger than various private pools already existing in some luxurious California gardens. But when Hearst acquired in New York some pediments and columns that could be put together to form the façade of a classical temple, the pool was enlarged to over one hundred feet to become by far the longest outdoor heated pool in the world. The temperature was maintained at a constant eighty degrees. New semi-circular colonnades were constructed, and a staircase leading up to an Italianate terrace. Beneath its foundations were located seventeen dressing rooms, each with its bath and full-length mirrors. The staircase was bordered by cypresses and illuminated by globes mounted on duplicates of old Roman boundary markers, which continued around the periphery of the pool. For the alcove where the staircase divided at its base Hearst commissioned a fountain from Cassou in Paris, of Neptune driving his horses through the waves, modelled on the Fontana di Trevi in Rome.

Stars of the day – Weissmuller, Crabbe, Ederle, Esther Williams – would be invited up to submerge in 34,500 gallons of spring water, that sparkled in the California sun above the marble slabs patterned with antique green mosaics. Hearst would emerge to answer telephones hidden in plant boxes, behind trees and beneath rocks. Here it was possible, as at Pliny's pool near Rome, to swim and watch the sea at the same time. 'Floating on the translucent water', writes Huxley of San Simeon in *After Many a Summer*, 'one had only to turn one's head to see, between the battlements, successive vistas of plain and mountain, of green and tawny and violet and faint blue. One floated, one looked, and one thought, that is, if one were Jeremy Pordage, of that tower in "Epipsychidion", that tower with its chambers "Looking towards the golden Eastern air/ And level with the living winds". Not so, if one were Virginia Maunciple. Virginia neither floated, nor looked, nor thought of "Epipsychidion", but took another sip of whisky and soda, climbed to the highest platform of the diving tower, spread her arms, plunged, and glided under water . . . '

During the construction of the exterior Neptune pool, Hearst began to form ideas of another indoors, with salt water, on the further side of the castle. He wrote to his architect with some proposals for a 'hothouse for palms, orchids, and ferns, to surround an indoor pool, glass dome and lattice windows – a loggia to serve tea or poi and a turtle – a "South Sea Island" on the hill with sharks' [24 April 1927]. She replied that she liked his 'combination orchid-greenhouse and indoor pool – with plate glass partition for sharks!' The sharks never materialised, but within a week the top of the hill had been removed and excavations begun on the project. Five years later it was completed, at a cost of millions of dollars. Lapis lazuli and gold-leafed tiles from Murano encrusted the whole interior. Crews of artisans were brought over from Italy to lay them in intricate patterns on the walls, floor, and central arched diving platform that divided the main pool from a domed alcove containing shallower water, whose shape and design had been inspired by the Galla Placidia in Ravenna. The brilliant dark blue tiles studded with gold stars create the illusion of vast and mysterious depths and transform the interior at night into an underwater grotto. It was then that Hearst preferred to swim, lap after lap alone in this majestic 'Roman' pool, among the shadows of statues cast on its surface by the dim light of alabaster lamps that quivered in the indigo water pumped from the sea seven miles away.

Hearst shared a passion for pools with his architect Julia Morgan. A tiny, punctilious spinster who had specialised in classical architecture in Paris, she seemed to derive compensation for the austerity of her life in designing for others these temples of hedonism. Although she scarcely swam herself, she expressed the inherent sensuousness of her nature in a series of beautiful pools she created along the California shoreline, few of which still exist. She liberated the demure tradition of women's clubs by designing for them in the Twenties turquoise-tiled pools in the middle of balconied courtyards, and others indoors that stretched along the entire wing of the building, in which women could swim rather than merely bathe. Her association with the Hearsts began when she created an interior heated pool for Hearst's mother. On Mrs Hearst's death William Randolph Hearst commissioned Morgan to design a 'gymnasium' for women at Berkeley in her memory, whose principal features were three pools, the longest marble-lined and surrounded by Roman friezes and sarcophagi. As well as the San Simeon pools, she designed one for Wyntoon, Hearst's estate in Northern California, of blue-green marble with an artificial beach of sand. Now a ruin, it was described in its time by *Fortune* magazine as a 'sylvan jewel which dazzles you as you come on it unexpectedly while strolling through the woods. An instructor attends at all hours, and outfits the guests with costumes. Men receive trunks and coloured towels ten feet square. The No. 1 Bathhouse is labelled W. R. H.'

On acquiring St Donats Castle in Wales, Hearst sent Morgan a telegram, asking her to send full details of the Wyntoon pool to his architect in England, 'including tile samples'. The pool there was positioned at the end of a series of terraces descending gradually to the sea. Unlike San Simeon, here there were no telephones concealed beneath rocks, so on receipt of a call from America the butler would make his way down the terraces to the pool and announce, 'New York is on the telephone, Mr Hearst.' Although now an International College, the pool has been filled in, as has that of Hearst's mistress, Marion Davies, beside the ocean on Santa Monica. Once the size of a small lake and spanned by a marble Venetian bridge, it was demolished in 1960 to make way for a car-park.

If you care to enter the 'atrium' of Caesar's Palace, Las Vegas, flanked by Praetorian guards and vestal virgins, and make your way through the 'Appian way' of shops and the glittering phalanx of slot machines, the corridors bordered, like the streets of Pompeii, by streams and fountains, by statues of 'Venus Anadyomene' after 'Diodaisus *circa* 250 BC' and reliefs of the Sabine women; if you can resist the temptations of the Bacchanal restaurant with its 'sumptuous feast fit for the gods of Ancient Rome, 7 courses and 3 wines, prix fixe', you will emerge eventually by a blue pool, rectangular and bisected by a bulge. In conception it owes much to San Simeon's Neptune pool overlooking the Pacific, but here the diving-boards and ladders are plated with gold, and the surrounding rotundas made of concrete rather than the ancient fragments assembled by Hearst. A gold notice-board announces the latest gambling odds. Jets of water gush into a jacuzzi from the nipples of the Medici Venus. Few swim. Mostly they lie on floats drinking or recovering from hangovers, or arguing over the finer percentages of deals, to the blare of rock music that is regularly interrupted by a request from the reception for 'Mr Sultan Shah . . . Mr Prestige Johnson . . . Mr Mike Ruggiero . . . Mr Aldo Bladder . . . Mr Joe Swag . . . '

On the plains below San Simeon stands the Madonna Inn, established in 1958 by Alex Madonna and described somewhere as an exotic offshoot of the Roman grotto. Though a lone traveller, I was offered the 'Caveman Suite' favoured by honeymooners, a sparsely decorated cavity of black rock that seemed to have been chiselled out of the side of a mountain. The branches of a tree hung low over a vast bed covered with zebra skins. At its foot, from out of the ceiling, a waterfall plunged into a scalloped basin. Was this, I wondered, a continuation of that tumultuous waterfall that served as a lavatory down the corridor, into which men urinated heartily as it cascaded over their shoes.

VIII

The Japanese Decade

The Way of the Warrior

ONLY JAPAN, AMONG Asiatic and African nations, has ever won an Olympic swimming medal. In fact, in the decade leading up to the last war, Japan produced the greatest team of male swimmers the world had seen. In the Los Angeles Games of 1932, intended as a showpiece for American swimming, the Japanese emerged from nowhere to win five out of the six possible events. Their overall superiority was demonstrated in the 1500 metres when Taris and Crabbe who had fought out the most memorable of finals at the shorter distance, were favoured to do the same in the longest event. By a third of the way

Taris was leading the rest of the field by half a length, but at the halfway mark two Japanese had taken the lead and the race was eventually won by Kitamura. He had nonchalantly returned to the dressing room by the time the first non-Japanese had finished. Kitamura, aged only fourteen, a little over five feet in height and weighing less than eight stone, was typical of the Japanese swimmers of the period. Though only boys and dwarfed by the lunging Americans, they swept all before them. Of the eighteen medals awarded in the men's events, eleven went to the Japanese. Americans won only four. In Berlin four years later the Japanese were almost as successful, winning ten medals to America's five.

How had the Japanese come to assume this remarkable ascendancy they held throughout the Thirties? They have always been masters at copying Western skills, then surpassing them. At the 1928 Amsterdam Games, where Tsurata won their first and only gold medal in breaking the German hold on the breaststroke, Japanese officials made extensive notes on every aspect of Weissmuller's crawl. They returned home with numerous diagrams and photographs, and proceeded to adapt Weissmuller's style to their own physical requirements. Compared to the long and lithe Americans, the Japanese physique tended to be squat and square. Their legs and arms were shorter, their hands smaller than those of the long-fingered Americans who in photographs of the time seem to caress the water as they break the surface. On the other hand the outline of their bodies was more rounded and streamlined, and to make up for what they lacked physically they employed a longer, deeper stroke underwater, a faster recovery rate, and more flexible leg and ankle movement. They appeared to skim across the surface in a series of glides, pausing with one arm poised above the water until the recovery of the other arm was almost completed.

Their youthful swimmers all lived together on Lake Hamana, where their training was subject to a strict military discipline. For centuries this lake had been a centre for swimming, where whole families would swim naked together, often far out to the islands six miles away, with their picnic lunches attached to their heads. Swimming was pursued with an almost religious devotion. The National Championships were held annually at the Meiji shrine pool, and afterwards the competitors would walk in solemn procession behind their coach to pay their respects to the shrine. The tradition of competitive swimming began in Japan many centuries before anywhere else in the world. Great competitions took place there in 36 BC during the reign of the emperor Sugiu, in the same century as the art of sumo wrestling originated. The first races in Europe took place in 1837 in England. Long before the English they organised swimming on a national level. An Imperial Edict of 1603 made swimming an integral part of the school curriculum, at about the same period as sumo wrestling became professional. Inter-school matches were promoted. In 1810, at a time when Europeans were learning to swim again, a great competition took place in the presence of the Shogun, when the twenty-five best swimmers of each clan raced against each other for three days.

Swimming was by no means an exclusively masculine pursuit. For 2,000 years the Ama, the highly revered women of the sea, have dived for shellfish and edible seaweed. Confined mostly to the Eastern and Western shores of Honshu Island, the largest in the Japanese archipelago, they start diving at the age of ten and have been known to continue till eighty, submerging for up to three minutes to depths of sixty feet. The younger divers, the 'kachido' or 'walking people', fish from just off the shore, but the older and more experienced, the 'funado' or 'ship people', dive far down into the sea from anchored boats. Men are excluded because they could not stand the cold. Instead they tend to the boats. The funado can spend up to four hours a day beneath the surface, wearing a waistband filled with stones to offset their natural buoyancy. Attached to their waist is a rope up which they rise again to the surface, and tied to the top of the rope is a floating bucket. Conditions are dangerous. Over the years many have been killed by sharks. In an effort to keep them at bay, they wear the white costume round their middle that gives them their name 'ama'. Visitors to the islands are discouraged. They have preserved their own primitive culture and customs. They rarely marry outside the tribe, and in consequence have become a race apart. Their numbers have gradually declined. Now only about a thousand are active. People prefer cheaper, cultured pearls that began to be manufactured in the Twenties and can be adapted to any size or colour.

The primitive mystery of these diving girls, their nudity and daring, became a constant source of fascination for Japanese artists. Like St Sebastian in the Renaissance, they provided artists with an excuse for depicting the naked human form, examples of which are rare in Japanese art despite the numerous erotic prints.

Utamaro illustrated the fantasy of a diving girl as she crouches on an island and looks down into the sea, which here and elsewhere symbolises the unconscious mind. Under the water she sees herself seized and outraged by two male demons, kappa-devils or river goblins that lurked in the sea in the neighbourhood of river mouths. Shunsho depicted numerous others entwined and raped underwater by humans and beasts, a concept that was to take its most exotic form in the brilliant *shunga* design executed by his pupil Hokusai, of a *Diving Girl and Octopuses*. When towards the end of the century Europeans became aware of this erotic fantasy of a diving girl, they reacted with a mixture of shock and excitement. Edmund de Goncourt wrote of 'this terrifying plate . . . the nude form of a woman swooning with pleasure . . . ' while J-K. Huysmans, in recognising the design as the pictorial embodiment of Valéry's 'fornication avec l'onde', described it as most beautiful and also 'truly frightening: it is of a Japanese woman mounted by an octopus; with its tentacles, the horrible beast sucks the tips of her breasts and rummages in her mouth, while its head drinks from her lower parts. The almost superhuman expression of agony and sorrow – which convulses this long, graceful female figure with aquiline nose – and the hysterical joy – which emanates at the same time from her forehead, from those eyes closed as in death – are admirable.'

Surrounded by the sea and living on islands inundated with rivers, lakes and swamps, the Japanese over the years formulated different styles of swimming suitable for the varying conditions, the vagaries of the depths and currents of their waters. Swimming was incorporated into the Samurai code and became primarily a military art. Twelve distinct styles of swimming evolved, adapted for different uses and regions. Each form of swimming had its own name, like the various holds in sumo wrestling. A form of breaststroke was used for swimming long distances in the open sea, a circular movement of the legs for firing arrows from swift flowing rivers. Other strokes were invented for going up river, for carrying weapons, for moving underwater and for swimming silently. Young Samurai were made to develop their legs, to enable them to jump from the water 'like grey mullet' into enemy boats, or free their bodies when entangled in seaweed or drawn into whirlpools. They dived from cliffs sixty feet high into three feet of water. But above all for the Samurai, swimming was a ceremonial exercise, a form of art like firing arrows, or calligraphy, and in pageants performed in the presence of warlords they displayed their self-command in their slow and stately strokes across the surface of lakes. Swimming became a form of ritual, more highly refined than the Spartan morning swims in the Eurotas. In winter the Samurai would break the ice over streams to bathe. The Spartans offered sacrifices to frontier rivers, and a Samurai army, resting on its march, would send a deputation to the nearest spring where the water was known to be pure, and priests accompanied them to bless it.

It was this antique Samurai style that had to be brought up to date to compete with Western advances. When they entered the Olympics for the first time in 1920 and failed, a competitor on his return remarked that swimming in Japan was merely a means of crossing the sea or river, and could never be adapted to the calm waters of a pool. Officials attempted to revolutionise their methods, and met at first with fierce resistance. A Classical Swimming Federation was formed, to preserve the Samurai style from any modern encroachments on its traditions. Gradually, however, their resistance gave way and the Samurai spirit fused with their adaptation of the latest Western techniques to give them that edge which resulted in their decade of pre-eminence.

Those youths who swam in the historic waters of Lake Hamana were, like the sumo wrestlers, inheritors of an ancient tradition with military and religious associations. They were trained from childhood in a vigorous litany of exercise, subjected to a severe physical and spiritual discipline, and treated as an élite, privileged caste, divinely favoured. Before the breaststroke final in Berlin, in what for many was a 'poetic memory' of those Games, a swarm of butterflies, blown over by some kamikaze or divine wind, collected low over the pool, then split into three groups to follow the three Japanese competitors all the way as they came in first, third, and fifth. The Japanese attitude was openly nationalistic, and on their success seemed to depend in some ways the morale of the Japanese people. 'Our swimmers are imbued with the national spirit,' commented their coach after their triumphs in Los Angeles, 'and what superiority we have can be attributed to this.' In one of Yukio Mishima's last novels the young Samurai conspirators in revolt against Western capitalist influences find it easy to recruit swimmers to their cause, as 'at that very time, at the Olympic Games in Los Angeles, the Japanese swimming team was gaining glory for the homeland'. When, after the war, the remarkable

Furuhashi broke almost all the world freestyle records, Kitamura, the hero of Los Angeles, spoke of his effect: 'After the surrender following World War II, Japan was in a state of shock, but Furuhashi's accomplishments in swimming lifted the morale and spirit of the Japanese people, and few swimmers of the past can have equalled his feat under the most unfavourable circumstances.'

After the war, when the old military traditions faded away and the swords of the Samurai were symbolically broken, there vanished from Japanese swimming this remarkable collective surge and spirit. Their cause had gone. But two extraordinary individual swimmers were to make their mark. Japan in 1948 was banned from the London Olympics, but Furuhashi, swimming the same month in Tokyo with a unique ungainly crawl stroke that relied heavily on overdeveloped arms, swam far better times than those that won the events in London and smashed all the world records over the longer distances. At the Olympics eight years later, Furukawa produced an equally idiosyncratic performance in the breaststroke. He swam almost the whole way underwater. He was glimpsed at the start, then when he turned at the end of the pool, and finally when he emerged to win. He was awarded the gold medal, but caused the rules to be changed. The authorities felt it was unfair to other competitors, and dull for the spectators. Furukawa was never the same force again.

The sense of spiritual dislocation suffered by the Japanese is examined in the novel *Kokoro* – The Heart of Things – written by Natsume Soseki in 1914 two years before he died, soon after the end of the Meiji era during which Japan emerged as a modern nation. It scrutinises the loneliness of a man whose ideals clash with reality, who had turned his back on a world now devoted to 'Money'. His attitude is that of a 'wild beast captured in the mountains that stares angrily from its cage at the world outside'. Described as a Samurai in his unbending regard for principles and honour, he leads a hopeless and frustrated life. Finally, when the news comes through of the suicide of General Nogi, he decides to cut his wrists. Nogi's death caused a sensation at the time. As a young officer in the Satsuma rebellion, he had lost his banner to the enemy. Thirty-five years later, immediately after the death of Emperor Meiji, this hero of the Russo-Japanese war killed himself. He had delayed the moment when he would redeem his honour until he was of no further use to his Emperor. The character in the novel feels himself part of that world – 'I was overcome with the feeling that I and others, who had been brought up in that era, were now left behind to live as anachronisms.' On the night of the Imperial funeral he sits alone in his study and 'listened to the booming of the cannon. To me, it sounded like the last lament of the passing of an age.'

The character's sense of distinction and divorce from the world around him is established in the opening pages, as he swims ritually in the sea every day, far out beyond the crowded beaches. The sympathetic narrator, a self-confessed 'swimmer', watches him from the shore: 'Sensei had just taken his clothes off and was about to go for a swim when I first laid eyes on him in the teahouse. As I watched, he and a companion strode determinedly into the water and, making their way through the noisy crowd, finally reached a quieter and deeper part of the sea. Then they began to swim out, and did not stop until their heads had almost disappeared from sight. They turned around and swam straight back to the beach.' The narrator becomes fascinated by the spectacle. The next day at exactly the same hour he returns to the shore in the hope of seeing Sensei: 'after tying his hand towel round his head, he once more walked quickly down to the beach. And when I saw him wading through the same noisy crowd, and then swim out all alone, I was suddenly overcome with the desire to follow him. I splashed through the shallow water until I was far enough out, and then began to swim towards Sensei. Contrary to my expectations, however, he made his way back to the beach in a sort of arc, rather than in a straight line.' Every day the narrator returns to the beach to watch enthralled as at the usual hour 'he would arrive punctually, and depart as punctually after his swim. He was always aloof, and no matter how gay the crowd around him might be he seemed totally indifferent to his surroundings. Sensei was always alone.'

It is strange how significant a role swimming has played in the lives of those two artists who seem to have felt most keenly the loss of Samurai values in modern Japanese society, the writer Yukio Mishima and the film director Akira Kurosawa. The remnants of Kurosawa's *Seven Samurai* walk finally down a lonely road to an unknown fate, forgotten and discarded, without a place in a society they had helped to restore. Kurosawa himself was the son of a soldier who took pride in his Samurai ancestry. As an instructor at a gymnastics school, he had tried to revive the traditional martial arts. He built there, according to his son, Japan's first swimming pool, where Kurosawa learnt to combine the old Samurai strokes with mastery of the 'newly imported' Australian crawl. Under his father's tutelage he learnt to love swimming.

Two heroic experiences in water as a boy seem to haunt Kurosawa's memory, as they are described with such intensity in his autobiography. With some friends he used to enjoy in the summer months a 'kind of mountain Samurai's existence'. One day they came upon a waterfall that 'emerged from what seemed to be a rock tunnel cut through the mountain wall, and plunged some thirty feet into a pool'. For the Japanese waterfalls are of great sacred and even sexual significance. At critical moments in their lives they stand for hours beneath their fall. Kurosawa felt compelled to penetrate its mystery and reveal to the others what lay at the other end of the tunnel. Despite their protestations he climbed the cliff and entered the cavity from which the waterfall emerged. Grasping the sides of the slippery walls with his hands, he walked through the darkness to the faint light in the far distance, while the water roared and swirled about his feet. On reaching the other end he momentarily relaxed his grip and was swept into the stream: 'I don't know how I came back through the tunnel, but before I could gather my wits I was astride the top of the waterfall and plunging headlong over it into the pool below. I seem to have come through unharmed, because I surfaced and swam to the edge of the pool, where the terrified children all stared at me in amazement.'

Their village lay near a river, whose currents formed a whirlpool as it rounded a bend. It was a place that all swimmers avoided. Once again Kurosawa offered to satisfy their curiosity, and prepared to swim down to the bottom of the whirlpool in order to reveal the secrets of its depths. His friends turned pale and tried to dissuade him. Finally they relented on condition that he made a rope of all their sashes, to enable them to pull him out if he should get into difficulty. To swim down into the vortex he used one of the traditional strokes of Samurai swimming: 'I had taken lessons in the Kankairyu swimming style from the time I entered middle school. I had been made to swim under a huge cargo junk as part of these lessons. At that time exactly what the teacher had told me would happen occurred. When I reached the midpoint under the belly of the ship, I was suddenly sucked against its bottom boards. But, exactly as the teacher had told me, I did not panic. Instead, I turned over. My back had been pinned to the junk but now I pushed off with all four limbs and swam on. Since I had had this experience with a junk, a mere whirlpool seemed like nothing to me. But no sooner did I dive into the whirlpool than I was pinned to the bottom of the river. Recalling the junk, I repeated over and over to myself, "Don't panic", and I tried to crawl along the river bottom, away from the whirlpool. But the boys on the bank were pulling on the sash rope tied around my waist with all their might, so I couldn't move at all. I did panic. But I still couldn't move. I had no choice but to try crawling in the direction from which I was being pulled by the waist, against the current. After what seemed like hours of extreme pain and abject terror, I began to float towards the surface. I kicked my feet and shot out of the water.' Once more as he emerged his fearful friends stared at him in amazement. In these extraordinary memories of 'rebirth' through the miraculous effects of water, the whirlpool and waterfall, mythic regions of dream and the unconscious that have always held for the Japanese such symbolic significance, Kurosawa expressed his kinship with the traditional virtues of the Samurai spirit, a preoccupation with the mysteries of nature and reckless bravery on behalf of others.

Unlike Kurosawa, Yukio Mishima did not learn to swim as a boy. His family spent the summer holidays on the coast, but he was never to lose his fear of the sea. It would always be a malignant force, 'like someone pulling'. It was only after visiting Greece alone in 1952, at the age of twenty-seven, that he determined to learn to swim. He only stayed there one week, but in that time experienced all that he longed for. When standing outside a bookshop in Tokyo two years before and gazing at those who used it, he had experienced a sudden revulsion for the ugliness of intellectuals. He was to modify his attitude later – 'I was probably mistaken. My antipathy for intellectuals was a reaction against my own enormous sensitivity. That is why I wanted to become a classicist.' In the classical sense of proportion, the harmony of body and mind, in the abundant evidence of their physical pride and splendour untouched as yet by 'spirituality', Mishima found an antidote in Greece to the morbid sensitivity and introspection from which he had suffered for so long. Wandering through the 'copious virulent light' of the Delphi museum, he felt his senses reawaken as he gazed at the statues of Greek youths, Hadrian's Antinous 'the last unbaptised flower of Greece', the young charioteer 'bashful with victory'. The effect of Greece was 'intoxicating'. It cured him of his 'self-hatred and loneliness', and awoke in him a 'will to health in the Nietzschean sense'. From now on he would 'learn the language of the flesh, much as one would learn a foreign language'. Words had tended to 'corrode his being – as if ants were eating into his person'. Now, after a lifetime of devotion to sunsets, he would gaze 'lovestruck' at the sun.

Unlike other Japanese writers, Mishima had for years been fascinated by Greek literature. One of his short stories had been based on the *Medea* of Euripides, and he had read in translation Homer and the great Tragedians. At an early age he had been seduced by the image of the Roman martyr St Sebastian, and revelled in the blood and butchery of the gladiatorial scenes of the film *Quo Vadis*. Since childhood he had felt an instinctive, romantic sympathy with the nobility and cruelty of the classical world, 'l'antiquité Héliogabelesque'. In his last novel before he left for Greece, *Forbidden Colours*, an ageing novelist uses a beautiful homosexual, modelled on Mishima's vision of Greek statuary, to avenge himself on womankind for having wrecked his life. The novelist first sets eyes on him swimming far out at sea – 'A delicate, white splashing like an advancing wave developed. The ripple advanced rapidly in the direction of this part of the shore. As it reached the shallows and seemed about to break, suddenly in the middle of the wave a swimmer stood out. Quickly his body seemed to erase the wave. Then he stood up. His sturdy legs kicked the ocean shallows as he walked forward. It was an amazingly beautiful young man. His body surpassed the sculptures of Ancient Greece. It was like the Apollo moulded in bronze by an artist of the Peloponnesus school.'

The statues of the Greek divinities had always formed his ideals of beauty, and reproductions of antique sculpture such as the Borghese Warrior decorated his drawing room and garden in Japan. Greece had seemed a country where the sun and sea combined to produce beautiful gods. In its atmosphere Mishima began to despise 'mere cool intelligence'. What he wanted now was to match intelligence with pure physical existence, 'like a statue. And for this I need the sun. I need to leave my dark, cave-like study.' He returned from Greece an ardent classicist, and immediately enrolled in a Greek course. He felt that one part of his life was over. He was now embarking on a new phase of his career, consecrated to the sun and the cultivation of his body.

As soon as he got back to Japan, the first form of exercise adopted by Mishima was swimming. He still could not swim, nor had he tried to since the emotional shock of his early experiences in the sea. Learning to swim was never easy for him. Badly coordinated, he would in the manner of Shelley jump in and sink to the bottom like a stone. But he never gave up, and his determination made him succeed. Once mastered, he became fiercely proud of his swimming. Bathing with the novelist Morio Kita in a Tokyo hotel pool in the late Fifties, Mishima began swimming a length with his favourite breaststroke. Kita plunged in, speedily overtook him using the crawl, and waited for Mishima to join him at the far end of the pool: 'I expected him to say at least "you're faster than you look". But he didn't say a word, he didn't even smile. He got out of the pool without looking at me and went into the bar.' In the final summer before his dramatic suicide by hara-kiri, as if to prepare his body for this last 'beautiful' Samurai ritual, he went swimming every day for a month at Shimoda, in the pool in the morning and the sea in the afternoon, wearing a brief black cotton costume with large brass buckles on the thighs. It was his belief that a romantic death requires a 'strictly classical body as its vehicle'.

In his first book published on his return to Japan, *The Sound of Waves*, Mishima expressed his newly discovered love of swimming and Greece in transposing the Hellenistic idyll of 'Daphnis and Chloe' to the island of Kamijima off the coast of Ise. It was written at a time when he was 'seeing Greece everywhere he looked', and reflected his realisation in the Greek sunlight that the darker side of human nature, that had absorbed his writing until now, was not the entire truth. The hero, a fisher boy fashioned like 'some piece of heroic sculpture' and powerful enough to swim the circumference of the island five times without stopping, falls in love with a young pearl diver. She wins the contest for collecting the highest number of abalone in an hour, while he gains her as a wife with the effect of a brave swim through stormy seas to save his boat.

In Mishima's final quartet of novels, a succession of doomed, refined, heroic figures, remarkable for their physical beauty and symbols of all that Japan had lost, reveal themselves in a series of sacred waters, rivers, waterfalls and the sea, watched by the recurring figure of Honda. Depressed by the spiritual vacuum of Japan, the gradual corruption of its ancient traditions, Honda realises more clearly than ever the 'simplicity and purity of things Japanese, like transparent stream water through which one could glimpse pebbles below'. After the war he noted that 'now the river was stagnant, and barges and garbage floated slowly downstream – this muddied, polluted water was the very symbol of prosperity'. As a refuge, he creates in his garden a swimming pool of pure water which becomes something of a shrine. The old nobility attend its formal opening, served by waiters in white uniforms. No one before had built a private pool – 'old time Japanese, on reaching Honda's age, would have thought of building a treasury storage-house celebrating longevity. Honda was building, of all things, a swimming pool! It was a cruel attempt to float his sagging decrepit flesh in an abundance of blue water.'

On the point of dying, a day before his appointment at the Cancer Research Institute, Honda glances at the television. On the screen was a shot of a swimming pool, and the sight of the young swimmers and the sounds of their splashing and jumping made him ponder. He would end his life 'without having known the feelings of the owner of beautiful flesh. If for a single month he could live in it! He should have had a try. What must it be like, to wear such a beautiful covering? To see people fall down before it. When admiration passed the gentle and docile and became lunatic worship, it would become torment for the possessor. In the delirium and the torment were true holiness. What Honda had missed had been the dark, narrow path through the flesh to holiness. To travel it was of course the privilege of few.' Mishima himself had had a try. In his opinion he was perhaps the possessor of beautiful flesh, and one of the privileged few. In almost the last page he wrote Mishima sought to justify his philosophy of the swimmer.

With Byron, his hero, and André Gide, a favourite author, Mishima had various affinities, shared certain characteristics – an upper-class background, a mother's smothering love in childhood, a strong streak of narcissism and susceptibility to the attractions of his own sex, a romantic yearning for the classical past that expressed itself through a love of water and a passion for swimming. In the classical waters of Sicily and Southern Italy, Gide's 'Immoralist' underwent a conversion, a transfiguration similar to that experienced by Mishima in Greece. He arrives there from Africa in a state of convalescence from a nervous illness, and views with distaste his thin arms and stooping shoulders, the whiteness of his skin. In Sicily he dips his hand into the fountain of Arethusa in Syracuse and visits the shores of Cyane 'still flowing among the papyri as on the day when it wept for Proserpine'. At Ravello near Paestum, 'by the beautiful temple in which Greece still breathes', he is tempted to undress slowly and expose his body to the sun – 'soon a delicious burning enveloped me; my whole being surged up into my skin'.

On one of his last mornings there Gide grew bolder still: 'In a hollow of the rock there flowed a spring of transparent water. At this very place it fell in a little cascade – not a very abundant one to be sure, but the fall had hollowed out a deeper basin at its foot in which the water lingered, exquisitely pure and clear. Three times already I had been there, leaned over it, stretched myself along its bank, thirsty and longing; I had gazed at the bottom of polished rock, where not a stain, not a weed was to be seen, and where the sun shot its dancing and iridescent rays. On this fourth day, I came to the spot with my mind already made up. The water looked as bright and as clear as ever, and without pausing to think, I plunged straight in. It struck an instant chill through me and I jumped out again quickly and flung myself down on the grass in the sun. There was some wild thyme growing nearby; I picked some of the sweet-smelling leaves, crushed them in my hands, and rubbed my wet and burning body with them. I looked at myself for a long while – with no more shame now, with joy. Although not yet robust, I felt myself capable of becoming so – harmonious, sensuous, almost beautiful.' He begins to loathe his previous existence as an archaeologist, a bookworm, and feels now reborn, as though he had taken off a mask, and free to cultivate a 'new self' liberated from the oppression of books and erudition.

Gide was particularly responsive to the subtle and varied sensations of water, the spas at Lamalou-les-Bains whose baths gave him 'cooked skin and frozen bones'; the green, sulphurous springs at Vaucluse where the skin becomes 'so exquisitely soft that it feels more delicious than ever to the touch'. He liked to lose and dissolve himself in water, surrender to its obscure forces. Throughout his life he was haunted by a homosexual reverie, that he was watching children 'bathing in the river, their frail torsos and suntanned limbs immersed in the enveloping coolness. I was overcome by a mad frenzy at not being one of them . . . I should have liked to swim around near them and, with my hands, feel the softness of their brown skin. But I was all alone; then I suddenly began to shudder, and I wept for the elusive passing of the dream.'

As a boy Gide had worshipped his cousin, Albert, who excelled in all sports, especially swimming, then later in life became devoted to painting, music, and poetry. To Gide he came to personify 'art, courage, and freedom'. 'Every time', he advised Gide, 'you see a piece of water in which you can swim, do so without hesitation.' And so he did. He was to write lyrically to Paul Valéry in 1894, that he was 'happy tonight, for this afternoon I bathed completely naked in a green mountain torrent; afterward, to dry myself off, I rolled about in the warm grass'. After returning once from North Africa, he wrote rapturously of his bathes there: 'O you foaming torrents! You waterfalls and icy lakes. Shady streams, limpid springs, translucent halls of the sea, how your coolness tempts me! And then how sweet to rest on the yellow sand beside the backward curl of the waves! For it was not the bathe alone that I loved but afterwards the expectant, the mythological waiting for the god's naked and enfolding flame . . . I brought back with me, on my return to France, the secret of a man newly risen from the grave . . . Nothing that had occupied me before seemed now to have any importance. I was no longer the same . . . '

At an early age Gide had discovered the Greeks, who were to exert such a decisive influence on his mind. The mere name of Agamemnon was enough to open some 'secret floodgate' in his heart. With his friends he was to pursue an ideal of 'equilibrium, plenitude, and health – my first aspiration to what is known as classicism'. When in 1893 Gide embarked for Algiers, 'it was not so much for a new land that my impulse sped me, as towards that – towards that Golden Fleece, fired by the same enthusiasm as that which thrilled the gallant youth of Greece, setting sail on the Argo'. At twenty-one an intimacy with Virgil began that lasted until his death. It was in North Africa that he felt most deeply the influence of his 'languorous and liquid' verses, among the shepherds and flocks, the oleander and pools and running channels. Here, reclining among the oases and palms, murmuring Virgil or immersed in Homer, Gide would re-experience the Golden Age.

At one time, under Roman rule, it had been possible to walk from one side of North Africa to the other in the shade. Roman olive groves had drawn their life from a judiciously managed water supply. Fragments of masonry still cling to cliff sides, all that remain of Roman dams which then blocked the valleys. Streams, if they exist, have lost their vivacious grace and trickle pathetically through the sands, to finally expire among the desert wastes. Arabs, with their wandering, pastoral mode of life, have gradually converted fertile, arable land into pasture and eventual aridity. The waterfalls and oases of Gabes, the most beautiful Gide had known, have now almost dried up, though one Roman spring survives, a sleepy pool of green water choked with weeds and frogs. Near Tunis, Gide admired the plain marked out at long intervals by the huge ruined arches of the Roman aqueduct – 'I imagined it was the very same that in ancient days had brought the limpid waters of the Nymphaeum to Carthage. We left Zaghoun without having seen the Nymphaeum, so I am able to imagine it as one of the most beautiful places in the world.' In Carthage these limpid waters from the springs of Zaghoun poured into one of the longest and most sumptuous baths of the Empire, established like so many by the aquaphile Hadrian. The huge chunks of masonry that supported its foundations still lie along the shore or submerged in the shallows. Throughout the desert are scattered the ruins of Roman villas, each with their private pool and fountains, their interiors, preserved in the museums of Sousse and Sfax, remarkable for their marine mosaics, of Venus or Neptune erupting from the sea among swarms of rays, dolphins, cuttle fish. Far to the South in Douz, Arabs still soap themselves in the Roman pools.

'Erat inter ingentes solitudines oppidum magnum' – There was amid the desert wastes a great town – begins Sallust's description of Gafsa on the edge of the Sahara, in his account of Marius's campaign against the glamorous Numidian king, Jugurtha. 'It had but one flowing spring', he continues, 'which was within the walls, but otherwise it depended upon rainwater.' After capturing the town the Romans built two pools surrounding the spring, and three centuries later these pools were almost all that remained of the town. They are still there now, at the far end of the bazaar, marked by signposts to the 'Piscine Romaine', though the Arabs still refer to them by the old Greek word 'termid'. Aleister Crowley had once bathed here, with his companion the Earl of Tankerville, before they disappeared to tramp across the desert for a week. When standing by the deep basin of Sicilian Cyane, Gide was reminded of these swimming pools of Gafsa, 'those pools of warm water where huge blind fish, supposedly left by the great Tanit, brush against the swimmers and one can see blue snakes wriggling over the tiles on the bottom'.

The blue snakes, the blind fish and tiles have disappeared. So too have the turtles that Norman Douglas
found there, in the miserable winter months he spent
in Gafsa at the beginning of the century. But the
boys still hang around who, at the offer of a sou
from Douglas, would jump down from the parapet
and 'wallow among the muddy ooze at the bottom'. He
found the water 'though transparent, not colourless, but
rather of the blue-green tint of the aquamarine crystal;
it flows rapidly, and all impurities are carried away'.
The two pools, one rectangular and the other square,
lie side by side below the arches of an Arab colonnade,
encased in massive blocks of Roman masonry. At the
end of the rectangular pool is an empty niche, which
once held a statue dedicated to the divinity of the pool.
Dry terracotta channels are all that remain of streams
of water that flowed around its base. Above the alcove,
on the pitted stone, a few Roman words are inscribed.
Only 'aquae' is still decipherable. Steps lead down
to below the surface, which reached halfway up the
pools in Douglas's time. Now the depth varies from
two to five feet, and bottles and cans litter the uneven
bottom where once blue snakes wriggled along the tiles.
A low, dark corridor connects the two pools. Bats cling
to its ceiling, and when I swam through, one dropped
into the water and flapped its wings energetically across
the surface.

Soon afterwards an Arab slithered out from a hole
beneath the water. He led me round those parts of the
pools where the springs emerged and I swam down with
him to touch the spots where the tiny clouds of loose sand
trembled and hovered above the openings. He acted as if

he were the guardian of the pool, some priest of Nemi determined to protect his sacred grove against any foreign challenge. Sleek and serpentine, he proposed a race, then embarked on a series of dives from various stages of the parapet that I was supposed to follow. I did, until he pointed to the tops of the palms that swayed high above the water. He swallow dived down with the grace of the tragic Egyptian who lost his head in the Solomons, and all I could do was watch from below. I had often dived, when marooned in the Middle East, from the top of a cliff into a circular, transparent, bottomless pool, as a romantic reaction to the aridity of life in the desert, devoid now of the Bathshebas and Susannas that once lay exposed in the green waters of their marble baths. But here in Gafsa he was diving into three feet of water, and I lacked the nerve to follow.

He did though take me down below the surface to the narrow archway from where he had emerged into the pool. We squeezed through and crawled down a tunnel above a sluice of ancient brickwork beautifully laid tongue-and-groove, which opened out into a labyrinth of subterranean chambers filled with the running streams of the spring, medicinal baths built by the Romans, where obscure figures lay and groaned in the darkness. But the medicinal properties of the place had been diminished by the odours of some lavatories installed in the far corners. The French had tried to eradicate them, but when the Arabs objected they gave way. And so, in the space of a few yards, the sacred springs of Gafsa, those laughing, chattering, amorous waters of the Romans that well up here in a river of warmth and purity, had been reduced to those of a Cloaca Maxima.

Acknowledgments

I am indebted to various references to the subject in books by J. P. V. D. Balsdon; Miriam Benkovitz; Dea Birkitt; Sara Boutelle; Susan Chitty; Katharine Chorley; Rupert Christiansen; Timothy d'Arch Smith; Catharine Dinn; Philippe Diolé; Lloyd Goodrich; R. P. Graves; H. A. Harris; Alethea Hayter; Anthony Hern; Richard Holmes; Juliette Huxley; Peter Levi (Edition of Pausanias); Leslie Marchand; Robert Bernard Martin; Jeffrey Meyers; Nancy Milford; John Nathan; Jeffrey Richards; Henry Scott Stokes; Andrew Sinclair; Robert Sklar; Kevin Starr; Donald Thomas; David Wainright; Peter Webb; Tim Webb. Particularly relevant was Nicholas Orme's excellent *Early British Swimming 55 BC–AD 1719*, (University of Exeter Press, 1983).

I would also like to thank Hans Christian Adam; Don Bachardy; Paul Cartledge; Adrian Dannatt; Mike Dibb; Dennis Enright; Jeffrey Farrell; Christopher Hawtree; James Henry; David Hockney; the *Independent* and *The Times* newspapers; Doris Littlefield; Christopher McKane; Michael Meredith; Iris Murdoch; Frances Partridge; Robert Pavlik; Michael Phelps; Paul Quarrie; Donald Ritchie; Audrey Salkeld; Al Schoenfield; Irv and Margie Seiler; the Amateur Swimming Association; the International Swimming Hall of Fame, Fort Lauderdale;

Sonya Zorilla; Ian Whitcomb, for various ideas and numerous California swims; Jeremy Lewis, the Sussex breaststroker and swimmer of Nemi; Alan Ross, for publishing the original article in the *London Magazine*; and finally David Godwin and Nicholas Pearson of Jonathan Cape for their sympathetic encouragement.

For permission to reproduce illustrations, the author and publishers are grateful to the following: Hans Christian Adam – pls. 5, 7, 14; Lucien Aigner – pl. 4; Amon Carter Museum, Fort Worth – pl. 16; The Architectural Association, London (photo: Andrew Holmes) – pl. 15; Collection of Ross J. Bastiaan, O.A.M. (from *Images of Gallipoli: Photographs from the Collection of Ross J. Bastiaan*, O.U.P. 1988) – pl. 8; John Gutmann – pl. 10; Harvard Theater Collection (Frederick R. Koch Collection) – pl. 11; The Kobal Collection – pls. 2, 12, 13; Association des Amis de Jacques Henri Lartigue – pl. 21; Prints and Photographs Division, Library of Congress, Washington – pls. 19, 20; Gerhard Pulverer Collection (Photo: Fachlabor Fachor) – pl. 18; Georg Schäfer Collection, Schweinfurt – pl. 6; Staley-Wise Gallery, New York – pl. 3; The Sutcliffe Gallery, Whitby – pl. 9; National Gallery, Washington, Ferdinand Lammot Belin Fund – pl. 17.